OXFORD LATIN COURSE

PART III
SECOND EDITION

MAURICE BALME & JAMES MORWOOD

OXFORD
UNIVERSITY PRESS

OXFORD
UNIVERSITY PRESS

198 Madison Avenue, New York 10016

Oxford University Press is a department of the University of Oxford.
It furthers the University's objective of excellence in research,
scholarship, and education by publishing worldwide in

Oxford   New York

Auckland   Cape Town   Dar es Salaam   Hong Kong   Karachi
Kuala Lumpur   Madrid   Melbourne   Mexico City   Nairobi
New Delhi   Shanghai   Taipei   Toronto

With offices in

Argentina   Austria   Brazil   Chile   Czech Republic   France   Greece
Guatemala   Hungary   Italy   Japan   Poland   Portugal   Singapore
South Korea   Switzerland   Thailand   Turkey   Ukraine   Vietnam

Oxford is a registered trade mark of Oxford University Press
in the UK and in certain other countries

British Library Cataloguing in Publication Data

Data available

Paperback edition:
ISBN-13: 978-0-19-521207-5

Hardback edition:
ISBN-13: 978-0-19-521552-6

30 29 28 27 26 25 24 23 22 21

Printed in India

Contents

Acknowledgements

The publisher and authors would like to thank the many consultants
in the United Kingdom and the United States for comments and
suggestions that have contributed towards this second edition. In
particular: (UK) Julian Morgan, Deborah Bennett, David Cartwright,
Alison Doubleday, John Powell, Philip Powell, Jeremy Rider,
Tim Reader, F. R. Thorn, Andrew Wilson; (US) John Gruber-Miller,
Carlos Fandal, Dennis Herer, James Lowe, Diana Stone and Jeffrey Wills.

*The publishers would like to thank the following for permission to
reproduce photographs;*

©AKG p.10 (Erich Lessing), p.14 (Erich Lessing), p.94 top (Vatican Museums,
Rome), p.100 (Erich Lessing & Musée du Louvre, Paris), p.114 (British
Museum, London); Archivi Alinari p.62 (bottom), p.88, p.125; Ancient Art &
Architecture Collection p.33 (bottom); Art Gallery of Ontario, Toronto p.84
(Poussin, Nicolas French 1595-1665 'Venus, Mother of Aeneas presenting him
with arms forged by Vulcan' c.1635 oil on canvas 107.9 x 134.6 cm Gift of the
Reuben Wells Leonard Estate 1936 acc no 48/5 photo by Carlo Catenazzi, AGO;
Ashmolean Museum Oxford p.82 (bottom); D. Coles/Ashmolean Museum ©The
Egyptian Exploration Society, p.57; The Barber Institute of Fine Arts, the
University of Birmingham p.52; Biblioteca Vaticana p.51 (bottom); ©British
Museum p.119; J. Allan Cash Photolibrary p.103; ©Donald Cooper, Photostage
p.89; Roger Dalladay p.17 (bottom), p.23 (bottom), p.25, p.26, p.51 (top), p.60,
p.62 (top), p.73 (top), p.96, p.99, p.107, p.126; Deutsches Archäologisches
Institut, Istanbul p.183; C.M. Dixon p.33 (top), p.69 (bottom); Eric Dugdale
p.80; Sonia Halliday Photographs p.68 (F.H.C. Birch); Robert Harding Picture
Library p.11 (top) (Tony Gervis), p.27 (Tony Gervis), p.36 (top) (Tony Gervis);
©Michael Holford p.13, p.44, p.118; Images Colour Library p.66; Kostas
Kontos p.85, p.105; Kunsthistorisches Museum, Vienna p.98; James Morwood
p.11 (bottom), p.36 (bottom), p.53, p.67, p.69 (top), p.79, p.82 (top), p.86
(bottom), p.91, p.93, p.108, p.112, p.117, p.124; Scala, Florence cover; title
page, p.8, p.20, p.34, p.40, p.42, p.43, p.46, p.50, p.56, p.58, p.63, p.72, p.73
(bottom), p.75, p.86 (top), p.94 (bottom), p.102, p.111, p.113, p.123; Spectrum
Colour Library p.31; Franca Speranza s r l p.38 (Foto Mairani)

Cover photo by Scala

The cartoons are by Cathy Balme, and the illustrations on p.17 and p.23
are by Peter Connolly

Introduction

Part I of the course told the story of the childhood of the poet Horace (full name: Quintus Horatius Flaccus) in Venusia, a town in the remote south of Italy. Born in 65 BC, he was a very clever child, and at the beginning of Part II his father, Flaccus, took him to Rome so that he might have the best education available at the school of Orbilius. He spent seven years in Rome where he became friends with Marcus Cicero, the son of the great orator and statesman. After leaving Orbilius' school he went on to a rhetorical school. While he was there, Julius Caesar was murdered (15 March 44 BC); in the ensuing chaos, when civil war threatened, Flaccus decided to send Quintus to Athens to study philosophy and himself returned to Venusia to look after his family.

In Athens, where Quintus studied under Theomnestus, the head of the Academy, he again met Marcus Cicero, who was studying at the other university of Athens, the Lyceum. In September 44 BC Brutus, the leader of the conspirators who had murdered Julius Caesar, arrived in Athens; he attended lectures on philosophy and made friends with many of the students, whom he persuaded to accompany him to Macedonia (north Greece) where he was assembling an army to resist Antony and Octavian, the adopted son of Julius Caesar. Amongst others who followed him to Macedonia was Marcus Cicero.

Meanwhile Antony and Octavian had seized power in Rome and were murdering their enemies, amongst them Cicero, Marcus' father, who had led the resistance of the senate against Antony. When Quintus heard this news, he decided that he too must join the army of Brutus. But before doing so, he visited Apollo's famous shrine at Delphi. This is where the story of Part III begins.

Parts I and II contain a good deal of fiction, but in Part III the story is closely based on historical fact; we know much more about Horace's life from the time he joined the army of Brutus, largely from what he says about himself in his poetry, and he is playing a part in well-known historical events. We give below a chronological chart which provides the framework of the story.

BC

44	Brutus arrives in Athens (September)
42	Horace joins his army in Asia: he is made *tribūnus mīlitum*; the two battles of Philippi (October, November) in which Horace commands a legion: Brutus and Cassius are defeated and commit suicide
41?	Horace returns to Italy to find that the family farm has been confiscated and his family have disappeared; he goes to Rome; he is appointed clerk in the Treasury; he begins to write poetry; he becomes friends with Virgil
40?	Virgil introduces Horace to Maecenas, who admits him to the circle of his friends
35	Horace publishes his first book of *Satires*
33?	Maecenas gives Horace a farm in the Sabine hills
31	Battle of Actium: Octavian defeats Antony and Cleopatra
30	Octavian defeats Antony at Alexandria: Antony and Cleopatra commit suicide; Horace publishes the *Epodes*

This was the last battle of the civil wars, which left Octavian master of the Roman world. He became known as Caesar Augustus, the first Roman emperor, and established a dynasty which was to last a hundred years. Horace meanwhile became one of the leading poets of the time and the friend not only of Maecenas and other important people but of the emperor himself. He died in 8 BC and could proudly claim:

exēgī monumentum aere perennius . . .
                              ex humilī potēns
('I have raised a monument more lasting than bronze . . . achieving power despite my humble beginnings')

Quīntus Pompēiusque Delphōs vīsērunt ut
Apollinis fānum (*shrine*) vidērent.

Quīntus 'age, Pompēī,' inquit, 'festīnēmus nē
(*lest*) sērō adveniāmus.'

viam sacram ascendērunt ut ad templum
advenīrent.

multī supplicēs (*suppliants*) prō templō
expectābant ut deī ōrācula acciperent.

Vocabulary 34

verbs		adjectives	
dubitō, dubitāre	I doubt, hesitate	**quot?** (indecl.)	how many?
occidō, occidere, occidī, occāsum	I fall, die; I set (of sun)	**situs, -a, -um**	placed, sited
dēspiciō, dēspicere, dēspexī, dēspectum	I look down on	adverb	
		anteā	before
prōspiciō, prōspicere, prōspexī, prōspectum	I look out at	conjunctions	
sciō, scīre, scīvī, scītum	I know	**antequam**	before
age, agite	come on!	**nē** + subjunctive	lest, in order not to
nouns		**ut** + subjunctive	in order to, to
ōrāculum, -ī, n.	oracle		
latus, lateris, n.	side		
sacerdōs, sacerdōtis, m.	priest		
necesse est (+ inf.)	it is necessary to		

Quīntus Delphōs vīsit

Quīntus, ubi dē morte Cicerōnis audīvit, valdē commōtus est. in
Macedoniam festīnāre volēbat ut cum Brūtō mīlitāret mortemque
patris amīcī suī vindicāret. sed antequam Athēnīs discessit,   **vindicāret** avenge
Delphōs vīsere cōnstituit, ut Apollinis nōtissimum fānum vidēret,   **fānum** shrine
5 quō hominēs ex omnibus partibus orbis terrārum veniēbant ut deī
ōrācula peterent.

itaque amīcum quendam nōmine Pompēium petīvit et 'Pompēī,'
inquit, 'vīsne mēcum venīre ut Delphōs vīsāmus?' ille 'certē' inquit
'tēcum veniam. Delphōs enim vīsere iamdūdum cupiō. iter quam   **iamdūdum** for a long time now
10 celerrimē incipiāmus.' Quīntus 'ad Theomnēstum' inquit 'statim
eāmus eumque valēre iubeāmus. crās iter incipiēmus.'
Theomnēstum in tablīnō invēnērunt librum legentem. ille
prōpositum eōrum laudāvit eōsque monuit ut omnia dīligenter   **prōpositum** intention, plan
spectārent.

15 itaque posterō diē Athēnīs discessērunt. prīmum contendēbant
viīs plānīs rēctīsque, sed quārtō diē iter difficilius fīēbat; collēs   **plānīs** flat
ascendēbant et mox in montēs iniērunt; nēminī occurrēbant nisi
pāstōribus quī gregēs dē montibus agēbant paucīsque viātōribus   **pāstōribus** shepherds; **gregēs** flocks
quī Delphīs redībant.

20 subitō Delphōs prōspexērunt, in latere montis sitōs inter duās
rūpēs ingentēs, quae in lūmine sōlis occidentis fulgēbant. paulīsper   **rūpēs** rocks; **fulgēbant** were shining
stābant tacitī, maiestāte locī commōtī. ā sinistrā ad campum
dēspexērunt procul iacentem, ā dexterā montēs abruptī ad caelum   **abruptī** sheer
surgēbant; in mediō fānum Apollinis ad latera montis adhaerēbat.   **adhaerēbat** clung to

25 tandem Quīntus 'age,' inquit, 'festīnēmus, nē nox nōbīs incidat
antequam advēnerimus.' sōl occiderat cum Delphōs advēnērunt;
cēnāvērunt in parvā caupōnā continuōque dormīvērunt.

posterō diē Pompēius Quīntō excitātō 'age, Quīnte,' inquit,

'collem ascendāmus ut templum Apollinis videāmus.' viam sacram
30   lentē ascendērunt. iānuae templī apertae erant. ā fronte hominēs
nōnnūllī sedēbant Pythiam exspectantēs. mox Pythia ipsa ā
sacerdōte adducta est, veste pūrā indūta rāmumque laurūs manū
gerēns. in adytum dēscendit. deinde murmura audīta sunt ex adytō
sonantia; Pythia, ā deō commōta, ōrāculum dīvīnum ēdēbat.
35   murmura dēsiērunt. Pythia ex adytō ascendit oculīsque ad terram
dēmissīs ē templō tacita exiit. sacerdōs ōrāculum in tabulā
scrīptum supplicī trādidit. ille tabulam summā reverentiā acceptam
perlēgit deōque grātiās ēgit.

Quīntus, hanc caerimōniam tam veterem spectāns, penitus
40   commōtus est. ad statuam Apollinis, quae in ultimā parte templī
stābat, sē vertit; manūs ad caelum sustulit deumque ōrāvit ut
propitius sibi esset. eō ipsō tempore hoc scīvit: poēta futūrus erat
vātēsque Apollinis. ē templō tacitus exiit collemque cum Pompēiō
dēscendit. prope viam erat fōns Castalius, Apollinī Mūsīsque sacer.
45   Quīntus cōnstitit aquamque bibit.

ā fronte in front
Pythiam the priestess of Apollo
indūta dressed in, wearing
rāmum laurūs a branch of laurel
adytum the inner shrine
sonantia sounding, echoing
ēdēbat was uttering
dēsiērunt ceased; **dēmissīs** lowered
supplicī to the suppliant
caerimōniam ceremomy
penitus deeply

propitius favorable, propitious
futūrus erat was going to be
vātēs prophet

The Shining Rocks

The Castalian spring

Respondē Latīnē

1 cūr volēbat Quīntus Delphōs vīsere?
2 ubi Quīntus Pompēiusque ad templum Apollinis advēnērunt, quid vīdērunt?
3 ubi Quīntus fontem Castalium vīdit, quid fēcit? cūr hoc fēcit?

Quīntus Pompēiusque ad Brūtum īre parant

Translate the first paragraph and answer the questions on the rest

Quīntus, ubi Athēnās rediit, nōn diūtius dubitāvit. ad Acadēmīam festīnāvit ut Theomnēstō dīceret ea quae in animō habēbat. Theomnēstō occurrit theātrum ineuntī cōnsiliumque eī exposuit. ille nōn temptāvit eum ā prōpositō āvertere. 'rēctē facis, Quīnte,'
5 inquit. 'dēbēs officium tuum perficere. heu! quot iuvenēs iam ad bellum discessērunt!'

Quīntus ab Acadēmīā in urbem festīnāvit ut Pompēium quaereret; ille enim cōnstituerat cum Quīntō ad Brūtum īre. Quīntus eum invēnit rēs suās compōnentem. 'paene parātus es,
10 Pompēī?' inquit; 'hodiē Athēnīs maneāmus. crās māne ad Acadēmīam eāmus ut amīcōs valēre iubeāmus. deinde ad Pīraeum festīnēmus ut nāvem inveniāmus quae nōs ad Brūtum feret.'

postrīdiē igitur Quīntus Pompēiusque prīmum ad Acadēmīam festīnāvērunt ut amīcōs valēre iubērent; deinde ad Pīraeum
15 contendērunt ut nāvem quaererent quae ad Asiam itūra erat; illīc enim Brūtus cum exercitū iam mīlitābat. ubi ad portum advēnērunt, nāvis magistrō in tabernā bibentī occurrērunt quī illō ipsō diē ad Asiam nāvigātūrus erat. ille eōs libenter accēpit nec viāticum rogāvit, quod Brūtī causam adiuvāre volēbat.

itūra about to go

nāvigātūrus about to sail
viāticum a fare

1 Why did Quintus hurry into the city? [2]
2 What did he propose to Pompeius? [5]
3 Why did they have to find a ship going to Asia? [2]
4 What stroke of luck did they have in the harbor? [3]
5 Why did the captain not demand a fare? [2]
6 What do the following words mean: **maneāmus,**
  eāmus, valēre iubeāmus? [1 + 1 + 2]

DELPHI

The Greek god Apollo was powerful in many ways. He was the god of the sun, and was associated with harmony and calm. He was the god of music and poetry, of archery, and of medicine and disease. Above all, he was the god of prophecy.

His most famous shrine was at Delphi, a sanctuary set in a spectacular location on the southern slopes of snow-capped Mount Parnassus, 2,000 feet above the Gulf of Corinth, a 'beautiful place where he was destined to live honored by many men'. Two great cliffs 1,000 feet high, which Quintus sees gleaming in the sunset, tower behind the site. They are called the Shining Rocks.

The myth says that when Apollo first came to Delphi, he killed Python, the monstrous dragon who kept guard there. Hence he was called 'Pythian' Apollo, and his Delphic prophetess was called the Pythia. According to a poem of the sixth century BC, Apollo declared about Delphi:

> Here I intend to build a very beautiful temple to give oracles to men who will always bring sacrifices to this place; and all who dwell in the fertile Peloponnese and all who dwell in Europe and throughout the sea-girt islands will consult it. I wish to give to all of them unerring advice, making prophecies inside the rich temple.

The temple of Apollo

According to legend, Zeus had sent two eagles from opposite ends of the sky and they had met at Delphi. Thus the ancient Greeks regarded it as the centre of the world. Apollo's wish was fulfilled. This holy spot was held in special reverence throughout the Mediterranean countries and the oracle was questioned on many religious matters, both important and unimportant. Apollo told his original priests that they would know the will of the immortals. The oracle could not alter the future, but it did reveal what the gods were going to bring about.

Apollo's priestess would give replies, apparently inspired by the god. It is true that some of her responses were ambiguous or misleading. There is the famous story of how Croesus, the king of Lydia, consulted the oracle about whether he should invade Persia. 'If Croesus crosses the river Halys,' came the reply, 'he will destroy a mighty empire.' Croesus did indeed cross the Halys, only to suffer a calamitous defeat. It was his own empire that was destroyed.

More often, however, the oracle gave matter-of-fact answers to matter-of-fact questions. One old man who wanted children received the response:

> You are late looking for your family:
> but fit a new hook to an old plow-tree.

The old man was encouraged by this down-to-earth piece of advice, and married a young wife who later bore him two sons. Even oracles which were apparently riddles could make perfect sense. When the Persian hordes were descending on Athens in 480 BC, the Athenian general Themistocles interpreted the oracle's

Delphi

promise 'that the wooden wall only shall not fail' as meaning that her wooden ships would save Athens. Sure enough, she won a great naval victory at Salamis.

The site of ancient Delphi remains one of the most impressive and atmospheric in Greece. The sanctuary was a kind of Greek United Nations and the various states competed with each other in putting up splendid buildings to add to their own prestige. The treasury of the Athenians, for example, is a superb architectural miniature. The site is dominated, however, by three buildings: the massive temple of Apollo; the fine stadium, where the Pythian games were held every four years; and the theatre. From the theatre there is a breathtaking view over the temple to the gorge beneath with its vast olive groves and the mountains beyond.

You can still see the Castalian spring where all who came to consult the oracle purified themselves. The Roman poets believed that its waters gave poetic inspiration.

The treasury of the Athenians

You, your family or your school have a problem. You go to Delphi to consult the oracle. Describe what happens.

magister 'sedēte, puerī,' inquit, 'et tacēte.'
(magister puerīs imperat ut sedeant et taceant.)

magister 'Quīnte,' inquit, 'fer mihi tuam tabulam.'
(magister Quīntum rogat ut tabulam sibi ferat.)

magister 'Decime,' inquit, 'nōlī Iūliam vexāre.'
(magister Decimō imperāvit nē Iūliam vexāret.)

Quīntus 'magister,' inquit, 'vīsne mē dīmittere?'
(Quīntus magistrō persuāsit ut sē dīmitteret.)

Vocabulary 35

verbs

cessō, cessāre   I idle, linger

postulō, postulāre   I demand

vetō, vetāre, vetuī, vetitum   ✗   I forbid, order not to

pūniō, pūnīre, pūnīvī, pūnītum   I punish

nouns

disciplīna, -ae, f.   learning, discipline, training

lēgātus legiōnis   legionary commander

tribūnus mīlitum   tribune of the soldiers

tēlum, -ī, n.   missile, javelin

tergum, -ī, n.   back

scūtum, -ī, n.   shield

opus, operis, n.   work; military work, fortification

adjectives

perītus, -a, -um + gen.   skilled in

saevus, -a, -um   savage

secundus, -a, -um   second, following; favorable

mīlitāris, -e   of soldiers, military

adverbs

forte   by chance

omnīnō   altogether, completely

rūrsus   again

preposition

sub + acc.   up to; (of time) towards

conjunction

dōnec   until

Quīntus mīlitat

merīdiē nautae nāvem solvērunt. ventus secundus erat, et sub noctem Dēlum advēnērunt, īnsulam parvam, ubi nātus erat deus Apollō. Quīntus monumenta vīsere volēbat magistrumque rogāvit nē nāvem solveret dōnec rediisset. cum in terram exiisset,

nātus erat was born

The stone lions of Delos

13

The Harbor Street, Ephesus

5 festīnāvit cum Pompēiō ut locum sacrum spectāret ubi Apollō nātus
erat. cum omnia spectāvissent, sōl occiderat; cōnstituērunt igitur in
terrā pernoctāre. postrīdiē cum prīmum in nāvem rediissent,
magister nautīs imperāvit ut nāvem solverent.

    reliquum iter sine cāsū cōnfectum est. tertiō diē lītus Asiae
10 cōnspexērunt merīdiēque ad portum Ephesī advēnērunt. Quīntus
Pompēiusque in urbem festīnāvērunt et, cum in forō sedērent, mīlitī
cuidam occurrērunt quī cum Brūtō mīlitābat. eī persuāsērunt ut sē
ad exercitum dūceret. sine morā iter iniērunt et sub vesperem ad
castra advēnērunt. cum castra intrāvissent, mīles eōs ad centuriōnem
15 dūxit et 'hī iuvenēs' inquit 'Athēnīs vēnērunt ut cum Brūtō mīlitent.'

    ille eīs imperāvit ut sēcum in prīncipia legiōnis venīrent. cum
centuriō eōs in prīncipia dūxisset, tribūnum mīlitum cōnspexērunt
nōmine Rūfum, quī forte eīs nōtus erat. ille eōs hilariter salūtāvit;
'ergō vōs quoque' inquit 'vēnistis ut nōbīscum mīlitētis? vōs dūcam
20 ad lēgātum legiōnis.' lēgātus eōs cōmiter excēpit; 'Rūfus' inquit 'vōs
cūrābit; crās vōs ad imperātōrem dūcam.'

    postrīdiē Rūfus eīs ante lūcem excitātīs imperāvit ut ad lēgātum
festīnārent; ille eōs ad Brūtum dūxit, quī multa eōs rogāvit. tandem
'iuvenēs prūdentēs' inquit 'vidēminī et strēnuī. vōs in exercitum
25 meum accipiam.' ad lēgātum sē vertit: 'mitte hōs iuvenēs' inquit 'ad
lēgātum decimae legiōnis. imperā eī ut eōs cūret disciplīnamque
mīlitārem doceat.' haec dīxit eōsque dīmīsit.

    lēgātus decimae legiōnis eōs trīstis īnspexit. 'ergō' inquit
'Athēnīs vēnistis? in Acadēmīā philosophiae studēbātis? nunc
30 mīlitāre vultis? dī immortālēs! mox nōn exercitum habēbimus sed
scholam philosophōrum. Rūfe, dūc hōs iuvenēs ad Lūcīlium;
imperā eī ut aliquid disciplīnae eōs doceat.'

pernoctāre to spend the night

prīncipia (n. pl.) headquarters

excēpit received

vidēminī you seem; **strēnuī** energetic

aliquid disciplīnae some(thing of) discipline

Respondē Latīnē

1 cum Quīntus Pompēiusque Ephesum advēnissent, quōmodo exercitum Brūtī invēnērunt?

2 cum centuriō eōs in prīncipia legiōnis dūxisset, quem cōnspexērunt?

3 cūr Brūtus eōs in exercitum suum accēpit?

4 quōmodo eōs accēpit lēgātus decimae legiōnis?

Lūcīlius Quīntum ad disciplīnam mīlitārem īnstituit

īnstituit introduces to

Translate the first paragraph and answer the questions on the rest

Rūfus Quīntum Pompēiumque ad Lūcīlium dūxit. ille centuriō erat, vir fortis, disciplīnae mīlitāris diū perītus. mīlitēs pigrōs saevē puniēbat; ab eīs appellātus est 'cēdō alteram'; nam cum vītem in tergō mīlitis frēgerat, alteram postulābat et rūrsus aliam. Quīntus
5 Pompēiusque ad disciplīnam mīlitārem ab eō celeriter īnstitūtī sunt. tēla iacere didicērunt, gladiō ferīre, opera cōnstruere. longa itinera faciēbant arma sarcinamque ferentēs. Lūcīlius numquam eōs quiēscere sīvit; semper eīs imperābat nē cessārent. illī numquam tam fessī fuerant.
10 vīcēsimō diē Lūcīlius, cuius mōs erat reprehendere, eōs laudāvit: 'iuvenēs,' inquit, 'nōn omnīnō inūtilēs estis. aliquid disciplīnae mīlitāris didicistis. itaque ad lēgātum eāmus. vōs eī commendābō.'
cum Lūcīlius eōs ad lēgātum dūxisset, ille eōs trīstis īnspexit:
'ergō' inquit 'disciplīnam mīlitārem
15 iam didicistis? vīgintī diēbus mīlitēs factī estis? vidēbimus. intereā Brūtus mihi imperāvit ut vōs in meam legiōnem accipiam. Lūcīlius vōbīs dīcet quid facere
20 dēbeātis. īte nunc et officia dīligenter perficite.' deinde eōs benignius aspiciēns, 'sine dubiō' inquit 'fortēs vōs praebēbitis et dīligentēs, et mox mīlitēs fīētis
25 decimā legiōne dignī.' cum haec dīxisset, eōs dīmīsit.

pigrōs lazy
'cēdō alteram' 'give me another'
cum whenever; **vītem** vine staff

sarcinam pack

vīcēsimō twentieth
reprehendere to criticize
inūtilēs useless

cedo alteram

1 How did Lucilius' behaviour towards Quintus and Pompeius change on the twentieth day? [2]

2 What did he say to them? [4]

3 When Lucilius took them to the legionary commander, how did the latter react at first? Did he think they were now fully trained? [2 + 2]

4 How did he encourage them? [3]

5 Write short character sketches of Lucilius and the legionary commander. [4 + 3]

THE ROMAN ARMY – I

By the beginning of the first century BC the Roman army had become a professional body, open to any citizen who was willing to serve for payment. Soldiers would undertake to join for sixteen (later for twenty) years. They swore an oath of allegiance to their general, who for his part promised to give them land when they retired, and so there was a great danger that the soldiers would put loyalty to an individual before their duty to the state.

The largest unit of the army was the legion. This would number 6,200 at full strength but normally the total would be anything between 3,000 and 6,000. The legion was divided into ten cohorts, which were made up of six centuries of eighty to one hundred men each.

The army commanders were usually ex-praetors or ex-consuls. These senior magistrates held *imperium*, i.e. the right to command an army. Their tent, the *praetōrium*, would be placed in the middle of the camp. Each legion was commanded by a *lēgātus* who would be aided by six *tribūnī*, usually young men of aristocratic birth. The legate and the tribunes were the higher-ranking officers.

The backbone of the army was provided by the centurions. They were the equivalent of the sergeants in a modern army. Unlike the tribunes, they were long-term professional soldiers. There were sixty of these, with six of them commanding each of the ten cohorts. They were carefully graded in authority and every centurion's ambition was to become *prīmus pīlus*, the senior centurion of the first cohort and therefore of the whole legion. The centurions were key figures, responsible for discipline among the common soldiers. They had the right to flog their men, a right mercilessly enforced by Lucilius in our story, and carried a rod to symbolize this. Other officers were the *optiō*, the centurion's second-in-command, and the *tesserārius*, who was responsible for the watchword.

The legionary soldier wore a linen vest and over that a woollen tunic which reached almost to his knees. He placed on top of this a leather doublet, with plates of metal, if he could afford them, loosely fitted to it with thongs. He had a brown cloak which could be used as a blanket when necessary. He wore heavy hobnailed sandals, had his hair cut extremely short and was always clean-shaven since a beard would offer a handhold to the enemy.

On the battlefield he wore a crested helmet (made of leather and later of metal) and a curving shield (*scūtum*) made of wood and covered with leather. This was four feet long and two and a half feet wide, strengthened by a rim of metal and a bronze or iron boss in the middle. The shield left the right leg uncovered, and so the soldier would protect it with a metal greave.

He fought with a sword, two javelins and sometimes a dagger. The sword was short and wide, about two feet long, two-edged and

A legion charges

well adapted to hand-to-hand fighting. The javelins were about seven feet in length. Made of wood with a two-foot head of iron, they would be thrown at a range of about thirty yards. The metal head was often joined to the shaft with a wooden pin which snapped on impact and made the weapon useless, to prevent the enemy picking up the javelins and throwing them back at the Romans.

The soldier on the march carried in his pack and on his back not only his personal gear and clothing but also tools for pitching camp and stakes for forming a palisade, cooking utensils and food for several days. His wheat ration counted as part of his pay and he had to grind it himself. His drink was more like vinegar than wine.

It was a tough life but it produced a superbly disciplined and effective army.

From Trajan's column

Imagine that you are a Roman soldier drawn up with the enemy advancing on you. Describe what happens.

Discounting changes in equipment and technology, what similarities can you find between the Roman legionary soldier and the modern infantryman?

What is going on here?

Scintilla in casā sedēbat cum tabellārius
ingressus est epistolamque eī trādidit.

Scintilla nōn **morāta est** sed epistolam statim
perlēgit.

Flaccus iam ad agrum **profectus erat**, sed cum
clāmōrēs uxōris audīvisset, celeriter **regressus est**.

Flaccus uxōrem **cōnsōlārī cōnābātur**. dē Quīntī
epistolā diū **loquēbantur**.

NB The verbs in bold are *deponent*: see vocabulary.

Vocabulary 36

deponent verbs

these are passive in form but active in meaning; learn the following common deponent verbs:

	present	*infinitive*	*perfect*	
1st (like **paror**)	**cōnor**	**cōnārī**	**cōnātus sum**	I try
	cōnsōlor	**cōnsōlārī**	**cōnsōlātus sum**	I comfort
	moror	**morārī**	**morātus sum**	I delay
2nd (like **moneor**)	**vereor**	**verērī**	**veritus sum**	I fear
	videor	**vidērī**	**vīsus sum**	I seem
3rd (like **regor**)	**lābor**	**lābī**	**lāpsus sum**	I slip, fall
	loquor	**loquī**	**locūtus sum**	I speak, say
	proficīscor	**proficīscī**	**profectus sum**	I set out
	sequor	**sequī**	**secūtus sum**	I follow
4th (like **audior**)	**orior**	**orīrī**	**ortus sum**	I arise
mixed (like **capior**)	**morior**	**morī**	**mortuus sum**	I die
	patior	**patī**	**passus sum**	I suffer
	ēgredior	**ēgredī**	**ēgressus sum**	I go out
	ingredior	**ingredī**	**ingressus sum**	I go into
	prōgredior	**prōgredī**	**prōgressus sum**	I advance
	regredior	**regredī**	**regressus sum**	I go back

(the last four are compounds of **gradior, gradī, gressus sum** I step; compare **gradus, -ūs** a step)

---

verbs

cēlō, cēlāre I hide
prohibeō, prohibēre, prohibuī, prohibitum I prevent
coniungō, coniungere, coniūnxī, coniūnctum I join
dēsinō, dēsinere, dēsiī, dēsitum I cease

adjectives

pius, -a, -um pious, good
impius, -a, -um impious, wicked

nouns

mala, -ōrum, n. pl. evils, troubles
terror, terrōris, m. terror
opus est + dat. of person, abl. of thing needed,
e.g. **opus est mihi auxiliō** I need help
(there is need of help for me)
pēs, pedis, m. foot

Scintilla dēspērat

omnēs Venusīnī valdē ānxiī fiēbant. cotīdiē nūntiī peiōrēs Rōmā afferēbantur; rēspūblica in bellum cīvīle lābēbātur, sīcut Flaccus praedīxerat.

5 Scintilla in casā sedēbat cum tabellārius ingressus epistolam eī trādidit. signum continuō frēgit epistolamque celeriter perlēgit; terrōre commōta ululāvit. Flaccus iam ad agrum profectus erat sed cum clāmōrēs uxōris audīvisset, ad casam recurrit. ingressus 'quid passa es, cārissima?' inquit. illa 'ō mī vir, Quīntus Athēnīs

Venusīnī the people of Venusia

praedīxerat had foretold
tabellārius postman

ululāvit shrieked

19

discessit; Brūtum in Asiam secūtus est.' Flaccus 'quid dīcis,
10 cārissima?' inquit; 'num vult mīlitāre fīlius noster?' illa 'lībertātem
populī Rōmānī dēfendit, ut dīcit; ō diem nigrum! ō dī immortālēs,
servāte fīlium nostrum. ō Flacce, Decimum arcesse; ille nōs
adiuvābit.'

Flaccus 'Quīntus nōn iam puer est,' inquit, 'sed vir fortis et
15 bonus; officium suum perficere dēbet. nōn possumus eum
prohibēre lībertātem populī Rōmānī contrā tyrannōs dēfendere.
sed, sī tibi placet, Decimum arcessam ut rem eī prōpōnāmus.'

Flaccus ad Decimī aedēs festīnāvit. occurrit eī Brundisium
profectūrō sed eī persuāsit ut sēcum Venusiam redīret. casam
20 ingressī Scintillam ūbertim flentem invēnērunt. Decimus ad eam
accessit et 'nōlī flēre, Scintilla,' inquit; 'Quīntus sine dubiō mox
Athēnās regressus in Acadēmīā iterum studēbit. bellum nōn diū
gerētur. Quīntus tamen imprūdēns est, sī Brūtō sē coniūnxit;
Antōnius enim mīlitiae perītissimus est cōpiāsque meliōrēs habet.
25 cum Caesaris percussōrēs vīcerit, sine dubiō rempūblicam
restituet. nunc reīpūblicae opus est virō fortī quī pācem cīvibus
reddet. ego ipse Brundisium iam profectūrus sum ut Antōniī
exercituī mē coniungam.'

Flaccus, cum haec audīvisset, sē continēre nōn poterat. 'quid
30 dīcis, perfide?' inquit; 'tū in animō habēs in exercitū illīus tyrannī
mīlitāre? nihilne cūrās dē lībertāte? abī! nōlī unquam posteā in
hanc casam ingredī.'

Decimus sē vertit et tacitus ēgressus est. Flaccus ad Scintillam
accessit et cōnābātur eam cōnsōlārī. illa tamen flēre nōn dēsiit;
35 'quot mala patiēmur!' inquit; 'cīvēs cum cīvibus, patrēs cum fīliīs
pugnābunt. quot mātrēs fīliōs suōs lūgēbunt! saeviet Mars impius
tōtum per orbem terrārum.' haec locūta ad terram cecidit,
exanimāta.

profectūrō about to set out
ūbertim copiously, in floods

percussōrēs assassins
restituet will restore

continēre to restrain
perfide traitor!

lūgēbunt will mourn for
saeviet Mars Mars (god of war) will
  rage; exanimāta in a faint

A scene of fighting from Trajan's column

Respondē Latīnē

1 cūr Venusīnī ānxiī fīēbant?
2 cūr tam commōta erat Scintilla?
3 quōmodo cōnātus est Decimus Scintillam cōnsōlārī?
4 cūr Flaccus Decimō tam īrātus erat? quid eī dīxit?

Fābella: Quīntus Pompēiusque ad disciplīnam mīlitārem īnstituuntur

Personae: **Lūcīlius, Pompēius, Quīntus**

intrant Quīntus Pompēiusque currentēs; sarcinās gravissimās ferunt et scūta et gladiōs. sequitur Lūcīlius.

                                                  sarcinās packs

Lūcīlius: festīnāte, iuvenēs; nōn iam philosophiae in Acadēmīā
5   studētis. currite.
Pompēius: nōn longius currere possum.
Lūcīlius: cōnsistite!
Quīntus (*anhēlāns*): quīnque mīlia passuum iam cucurrimus,   **anhēlāns** panting
           Lūcīlī; cōnfectī sumus. sub arbore sedeāmus paulīsper
10   et quiēscāmus.

arma in terrā dēpōnunt sedentque sub arbore.

Lūcīlius: iam satis quiēvistis, iuvenēs. surgite. nōn tempus est
           morārī. ecce, hostēs in nōs prōgrediuntur. nōnne eōs
           vidētis? in illā silvā sē cēlant.
15 **Pompēius:** quid dīcis, Lūcīlī? nūllōs hostēs videō.
Lūcīlius: hostēs cēlātī sunt. cavēte, nē in īnsidiās cadātis. quid   **īnsidiās** ambush, trap
           facere dēbētis?
Quīntus: dēbēmus explōrātōrēs praemittere cautēque prōgredī,   **explōrātōrēs** scouts
           gladiīs strictīs.   **gladiīs strictīs** with swords drawn
20 **Lūcīlius:** euge, Quīnte. explōrātōrēs praemittite, nē imprōvīsī   **euge** good!; **imprōvīsī** off your guard
           capiāminī, cautēque prōcēdite.

Quīntus cautē prōgreditur gladium vibrāns. Pompēius sequitur,   **vibrāns** brandishing
parvā vōce murmurāns.

Pompēius: quam stultus est hic lūdus! Lūcīlius īnsānit; cōnātur nōs
25   labōre cōnficere.

ubi ad silvam adveniunt, Quīntus maximā vōce clāmat
virgultaque gladiō ferit.   **virgulta** (n. pl.) undergrowth

Quīntus: ecce, Lūcīlī. hostem occīdī; reliquī fūgērunt.
Pompēius: ecce, Lūcīlī. vulnerātus sum; morior.
30 **Lūcīlius:** cōnsistite, iuvenēs. redīte ad mē. curre, Pompēī. nōlō
           alteram vītem in tergō tuō frangere.   **vītem** vine staff

Quīntus Pompēiusque ad Lūcīlium currunt.

Lūcīlius: satis lūsistis, iuvenēs. nōn omnīnō inūtilēs estis. tīrōnēs   **inūtilēs** useless; **tīrōnēs** recruits
           peiōrēs vīdī, rārō tamen. ad castra redeāmus ut lēgātō   **rārō** seldom, not often
35   vōs commendem. iam dextrō pede contendite. ō Quīnte,
           sinistrō pede profectus es. eheu! numquam mīles fīēs.

THE ROMAN ARMY – 2

A Roman army would generally cover fifteen to twenty miles in a day when it was on the move. This meant that it would take about fifty-four days to march from Rome to the Channel ports. However, far greater distances could be achieved in forced marches if necessary.

An army would have to create a temporary camp every evening when it was on the move. The soldiers would dig a ditch (*fossa*) around a square site and pile up the displaced earth behind the ditch to form a mound (*agger*) and a rampart (*vāllum*). They would build a palisade, made up of the stakes they took with them on the march, on top of this. (They would each carry a spade and two or three stakes.)

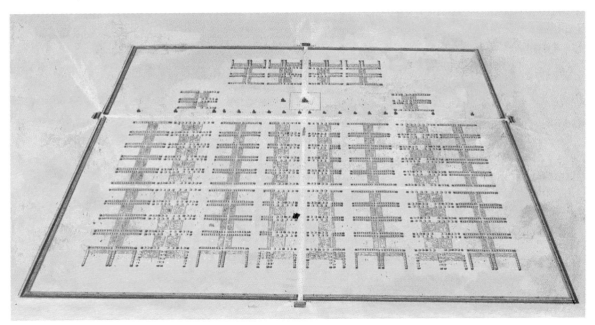

A Roman camp

The general's tent (*praetōrium*) was, as we have seen in the last chapter, at the centre of the camp, where the main thoroughfares from north to south and from east to west met. Here the standards (*signa*) and the treasury of the legions were stored, and young aristocrats, who were accompanying the general in order to gain practical experience of fighting, were quartered. The *quaestōrium*, the quarters of the paymaster where hostages, prisoners and booty were kept, was next to the *praetōrium*. On the other side of the *praetōrium* was an open space called the forum. This was the centre of camp life. Here the general would deliver speeches to his men, give rewards and administer punishments. Here too makeshift shops would suddenly spring into existence.

Now we come to the siege of an enemy town.

When the Romans were confronted with a really strong town,

they would build vast earthworks to put the attackers on the same level as the defenders. Alternatively, huge wheeled towers could be pushed close to the enemy's walls, hurling forth missiles of various kinds. Meanwhile the walls could be beaten down with a battering ram (*ariēs*) or, if this made little impression, iron hooks could be used to tug at the masonry and dislodge it. The *tormentum* flung large boulders; the *catapulta* shot darts and arrows; the *ballista* hurled stones and wooden beams.

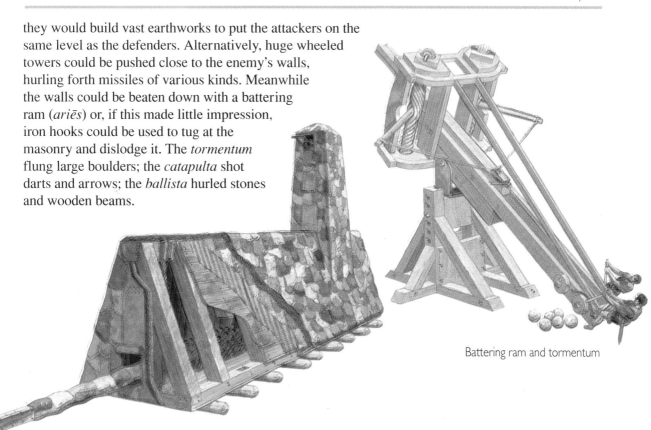

Battering ram and tormentum

A famous formation adopted by the Romans against a besieged town was the *testūdō* (tortoise shell). The soldiers would advance to the walls with their shields locked together over their heads to protect themselves from missiles. They would then try to scale the walls with ladders.

You have already read about a Roman triumph, the reward for a successful general. The valour of ordinary soldiers was rewarded with crowns, collars, bracelets and horse-trappings. On p. 166 we quote an inscription which tells us that a soldier called Silvanus won the lot! The most highly valued award was the civic crown (*corōna cīvica*), granted to soldiers who had saved a Roman citizen's life in battle. When those who had been given this humble crown of oak leaves entered a room, everyone present stood in respect. This is only one illustration of the great honor in which courage was held by the Romans.

From Trajan's column

Imagine yourself in a walled town which is being attacked by the Romans. Describe what happens.

What is going on here?

sōle oriente Quīntus Pompēiusque surrēxērunt armaque induērunt.

armīs indūtīs ad prīncipia cucurrērunt.

Brūtus, **mīlitibus convocātīs**, ōrātiōnem habuit.

ōrātiōne cōnfectā Brūtus mīlitēs dīmīsit.

Notice the phrases in bold print; participial phrases independent of the structure of the rest of the sentence go into the ablative case.

Vocabulary 37

verbs		nouns	
cōgitō, cōgitāre	I think, reflect	**clādēs, clādis**, f.	disaster
praebeō, praebēre,		**cornū, -ūs**, n.	horn; wing of an
praebuī, praebitum	I offer, provide		army
mē praebeō	I show myself		
proelium committō	I join battle	*adjective*	
interficiō, interficere,		**plērīque, plēraeque,**	
interfēcī, interfectum	I kill	**plēraque**	several

Philippī

aliquamdiū Brūtus cum exercitū in Asiā manēbat dum mīlitēs sē
exercēbant et ad bellum sē parābant. Quīntus plērīsque proeliīs
aderat quae in Asiā gessērunt. fortem sē praebuit et strēnuum. in
proeliō quōdam lēgātum legiōnis servāvit, quī summum in

5 perīculum vēnerat.

    paucīs post diēbus, labōribus cōnfectīs, in contuberniō
quiēscēbat cum optiō intrāvit eīque imperāvit ut ad praetōrium
venīret. cum praetōrium animō trepidō intrāvisset, Brūtus surrēxit
eumque cōmiter salūtāvit. 'salvē, Horātī,' inquit; 'optimam fāmam

10 dē tē audīvī; nōn modo fortiter pugnāvistī sed lēgātum legiōnis
ipsum ē perīculō servāvistī. cōnstituī igitur tē tribūnum mīlitum
facere.' hīs dictīs, Quīntum dīmīsit.

strēnuum energetic

contuberniō his tent
optiō an orderly
praetōrium the general's headquarters
trepidō anxious

An army on the march

postrīdiē Brūtus, omnibus cōpiīs convocātīs, ōrātiōnem habuit.
in tribūnal ascendit mīlitēsque salūtāvit. 'commīlitiōnēs,' inquit,

15 'Antōnius Octāviānusque, hērēdēs tyrannī, exercitū maximō
collēctō, nōs oppugnāre parant. iam iter ad Graeciam iniērunt.
necesse est nōbīs in Graeciam contendere ut eīs occurrāmus. itaque
vōs parāte ad iter longum et labōriōsum. hoc tamen meminerīmus:
cum victōriam reportāverimus, lībertāte populō Rōmānō restitūtā,

20 bella cīvīlia cōnfecta erunt.'

mīlitēs Brūtō plausērunt et laetī ad iter sē parāvērunt. paucīs
post diēbus Brūtus omnibus cum cōpiīs ad Graeciam profectus est.
in itinere Cassius eī obviam iit cum duodecim legiōnibus. sīc
Brūtus Cassiusque duōbus exercitibus coniūnctis ex Asiā in

25 Graeciam contendērunt.

Antōniō Octāviānōque prope Philippōs occurrērunt. proeliō
commissō, in dextrō cornū Brūtus Octāviānum vīcit. in sinistrō
Cassius victus est ab Antōniō tantāque clāde acceptā dēspērāvit et
sē interfēcit. Mars anceps fuerat; plūrimī in campō occīsī erant,

30 inter quōs lēgātus ipse decimae legiōnis mortuus erat fortissimē
pugnāns.

tribūnal platform
commīlitiōnēs fellow soldiers
hērēdēs heirs

meminerīmus let us remember
reportāverimus we have won
restitūtā restored
plausērunt (+ dat.) applauded

obviam iit (+ dat.) came to meet
duodecim twelve

Mars anceps fuerat the battle had
been indecisive

Respondē Latīnē

1 cum Quīntus ad praetōrium arcessītus esset,
quid eī dīxit Brūtus?
2 cūr necesse erat in Graeciam contendere?
3 proeliō commissō, quid ēgit Brūtus? quid ēgit
Cassius?
4 quōmodo sē gessit lēgātus decimae legiōnis?

A Roman general addressing his troops

Brūtus vincitur

*Translate the first paragraph of the following passage and answer
the questions on the rest*

tribus post diēbus Quīntus ad praetōrium vocātus est. Brūtus
trīstior vīsus est quam anteā sed Quīntum cōmiter salūtāvit.
'Quīnte,' inquit, 'tribūnus mīlitum factus tē optimē gessistī atque in
illō proeliō exitiālī summam praebuistī virtūtem. lēgātō igitur

5 decimae legiōnis mortuō, tē ipsum legiōnī praeficiō. mox proelium
iterum committēmus. deōs ōrō ut rem melius gerāmus et hostibus
victīs lībertātem populō Rōmānō restituāmus.'

Quīntus ē praetōriō ēgressus nōn rēctā ad Pompēium rediit sed
dē Brūtī verbīs sōlus diū cōgitābat. fīdūciā Brūtī ēlātus est sed

10 magnitūdine tantī officiī sollicitātus.

exitiālī deadly

restituāmus we may restore
rēctā straight
fīdūciā confidence, trust
ēlātus est he was excited
sollicitātus worried

Philippi

haud multō post Brūtus proelium committere coāctus est. prīmum cōpiae eius hostēs summā vī oppugnātōs vīcērunt; Quīntus legiōnem decimam fortissimē dūxit. sed mox Antōnius eōs repulit et cornū sinistrō Brūtī perruptō tōtum exercitum circumdedit. illī
15 territī tergum vertērunt armīsque abiectīs ad castra sua fugiēbant.

perruptō broken through
circumdedit surrounded

1 How did Quintus feel when he was put in command
   of the legion? [4]
2 When the second battle was joined how did Brutus'
   forces fare at first? [3]
3 How did Antony turn the tables on them? [3]
4 What did Brutus' men do? [3]
5 What do you learn from this and earlier chapters
   about the character of Brutus? [4]

BRUTUS AND CASSIUS

Why had Brutus, Cassius and the other conspirators killed Julius Caesar? It was easy for them to say that they had done it to give Rome back the freedom it had lost through the dictatorship of one man. The proud descendant of the Brutus who had driven out the last king of Rome soon issued coins which linked the daggers of the Ides of March with the idea of republican *lībertās*. But, as we have seen, the Roman mob, stirred up by Mark Antony, did not view the assassination in this way. Brutus and Cassius were forced to flee from the city less than a month after they had killed the dictator.

In fact, when the murderers of Caesar talked of freedom, they meant that they wanted to return power to the small number of families who dominated the state. Put like this, their cause does not appear so noble. In any case, the senate had shown that it was incapable of running the Roman state. Sooner or later one powerful man was going to take over. All the conspirators had achieved was to delay this.

History has not passed a generous verdict on Cassius. In *Julius Caesar*, Shakespeare presents him as a near villain with 'a lean and hungry look', drawing a hesitant Brutus into the plot against Caesar. But Cassius, in whose character Shakespeare found generosity and warmth as well as villainy, was certainly sincere in his hatred of tyranny, and he was a resolute and experienced soldier as well. Brutus, his brother-in-law, would have done better if he had taken more of Cassius' advice.

Brutus, however, is the more obviously admirable character. He was a thinker rather than a man of action, and we have seen how he took a deep interest in philosophy when he was in Athens in 44 BC. He discussed philosophical matters with Theomnestus and Cratippus so eagerly that it seemed, even at this critical stage, that he was only interested in study. Yet he showed during this time in Athens that he could fire the young with enthusiasm for his political cause. He was especially pleased by young Marcus Cicero whom he praised highly.

Brutus was a man who always thought he was in the right. But he was undoubtedly sincere. He wrote a book about *virtūs*, which means not just courage but all the qualities which make a good man. He possessed many of these himself, and he died for what he believed.

Shakespeare puts into the mouth of Mark Antony a fine tribute to his enemy Brutus:

This was the noblest Roman of them all:
All the conspirators save only he
Did that they did in envy of great Caesar;
He only, in a general honest thought
And common good to all, made one of them.
His life was gentle, and the elements
So mix'd in him that Nature might stand up
And say to all the world 'This was a man!'

Julius Caesar

Cassius

Brutus

When Julius Caesar saw Brutus, his trusted friend, attacking him amongst the conspirators, he said, 'You too, Brutus?'

How do you think Brutus felt at this moment?

Quīntus scūtō abiectō ē proeliō ad castra fūgit.

hostēs sequentēs in castra irruptūrī erant.

Quīntus comitēs secūtus in silvās cucurrit.

posterō diē Athēnās profectūrus comitēs dormientēs trīstis īnspexit.

The captions introduce the future participle: **irruptūrī** = about to break into; **profectūrus** = about to set out.

Vocabulary 38

verbs		*adjectives*	
cubō, cubāre, cubuī, cubitum	I lie down	**dīrus, -a, -um**	terrible, dire
		rūsticus, -a, -um	rustic, of the country; a countryman
agnōscō, agnōscere, agnōvī, agnitum	I recognize	**memor, memoris** + gen.	remembering, mindful of
prōdō, prōdere, prōdidī, prōditum	I betray	**immemor, immemoris** + gen.	forgetful of
abiciō, abicere, abiēcī, abiectum	I throw away	*adverbs*	
complector, complectī, complexus sum	I embrace	**aliquandō**	sometimes
		noctū	by night
intueor, intuerī, intuitus sum	I gaze at	**paulum**	a little
		quam prīmum	as soon as possible

nouns	
futūra, -ōrum, n. pl.	the future
vāllum, -ī, n.	rampart
difficultās, difficultātis, f.	difficulty
rūs, rūris, n.	the country
rūre	in the country

Quīntus Athēnās fugit

Quīntus, cum Antōnius Brūtī cornū sinistrum perrūpisset, scūtō   **perrūpisset** had broken through
abiectō, ā campō fūgit. ē comitibus paucī hostibus adhūc resistēbant;
plūrēs cum Quīntō ad castra fugiēbant, virtūtis immemorēs, nihil
cūrābant nisi ut quam prīmum ad castra pervenīrent.

5   in castrīs dīram fāmam audīvērunt. Brūtus enim dē futūrīs
dēspērāns in gladium suum incurrerat; mortuus erat. Quīntus, hōc
audītō, penitus commōtus est. sed nōn tempus erat morārī. hostēs   **penitus** deeply
vāllum ascēnsūrī erant; Quīntus clāmōrēs eōrum audīre iam potuit.
comitēs secūtus, quī ex alterā parte castrōrum effugiēbant, in silvās
10   cucurrit.

Quīntus comitēsque cubuērunt, in silvīs cēlātī, diemque trīstēs
exspectābant. Quīntus dormīre nōn poterat; sē suōsque vehementer
reprehendit, quod imperātōrem prōdidissent tergumque vertissent.   **reprehendit** blamed
imperātōre mortuō quid iam factūrus erat? caput saltem servāverat;   **caput saltem** his life at least
15   fēlīcior erat quam multī comitum, quī aut in campō mortuī iacēbant
aut captī in manūs hostium vēnerant. iam nihil cupiēbat nisi domum
redīre et parentēs iterum vidēre; cōnstituit igitur Athēnās sōlus
contendere.

sōle oriente surrēxit, Athēnās profectūrus; comitēs aspexit adhūc
20   dormientēs. paulum dubitāvit, deinde sōlus profectus est. vīgintī
diēs iter labōriōsum faciēbat; interdiū dormiēbat in silvīs cēlātus, nē   **interdiū** in the day time
ab hostibus caperētur. noctū prōcēdēbat per viās dēsertās. aliquandō
rūsticīs occurrēbat, quī plērumque eum cōmiter accipiēbant   **plērumque** usually
cibumque dedērunt.

tandem Athenas procul conspexit

25   tandem Athēnās procul cōnspexit. sōle occidente urbem
ingressus, ad aedēs Theomnēstī festīnāvit iānuamque pulsāvit.
Theomnēstus iānuā apertā Quīntum vix agnōvit sed vultū eius
propius aspectō 'dī immortālēs,' inquit, 'num Quīntum videō? quid
passus es? intrā celeriter.' Quīntus ingressus omnia eī nārrāvit. ille
30 'Quīnte, iēiūnus es. prīmum cēnā, deinde ī cubitum. crās cōgitēmus   **iēiūnus** starving; **ī cubitum** go to bed
quid facere dēbeās.'
    Quīntus diū dormiēbat. merīdiē Theomnēstus eum excitāvit et
'age, Quīnte,' inquit, 'nōn potes in urbe manēre nē Antōniī mīlitēs
tē capiant. quid factūrus es?' Quīntus nihil cupiēbat nisi domum
35 redīre. ad portum igitur profectī sunt ut nāvem quaererent quae ad
Italiam discessūra erat.

Respondē Latīnē

1   cum Antōnius Brūtī cornū sinistrum perrūpisset, quid fēcit
    Quīntus?
2   cum ad castra advēnisset, quid cognōvit Quīntus?
3   in silvīs cēlātus, cūr Quīntus dormīre nōn poterat?
4   quid facere cōnstituit?
5   cūr nōn poterat Athēnīs manēre?

Quīntus in Italiam redit

Translate the first paragraph of the following passage. Read the remainder in Latin several times until you understand it, then summarize what it says in your own words in English

cum Quīntus nāvem cōnscēnsūrus esset, Theomnēstus eum complexus saccum argentī trādidit. 'hoc argentum accipe,' inquit; 'ōlim mihi rependere poteris. iam valē et tē cūrā. dī tē servent.' Quīntus grātiās eī āctūrus erat, sed ille haec locūtus sē verterat et
5 ad urbem festīnābat.

    nautae, iam nāvem solūtūrī, magistrī signum exspectābant, quī Quīntō imperāvit ut festīnāret. ille nāvem vix cōnscenderat cum nautae fūnibus solūtīs in apertum mare rēmigāvērunt. mox vēlīs sublātīs nāvis celeriter prōcēdēbat. itinere sine cāsū cōnfectō,
10 quārtō diē Brundisium advēnērunt.

    Quīntus statim profectus est ut domum quam prīmum advenīret. cum Venusiam accēderet, in summō colle cōnstitit colōniamque dēspexit. summō gaudiō deīs grātiās ēgit quod domum dīlectam tandem vidēret.

15   ad colōniam dēscēnsūrus erat cum colōnum senem prope viam cōnspexit quī agrum labōriōsē colēbat. Quīntus eum agnōvit; Ganymēdēs erat, vetus amīcus patris. accessit eumque salūtāvit. ille vultum eius diū intuitus tandem 'dī immortālēs,' inquit, 'num Quīntum videō? cūr hūc revēnistī? num colōniam intrātūrus es?'
20 Quīntus 'revēnī,' inquit 'ut domum parentēsque revīsam. cūr mē hoc rogās? quid accidit?'

saccum a bag
ōlim some time; **rependere** repay
dī tē servent may the gods preserve
   you

fūnibus the ropes
rēmigāvērunt rowed
vēlis (n. pl.) sails

dīlectam beloved

colonum senem prope viam conspexit

OCTAVIAN RETURNS TO ITALY

Octavian had shot to fame like a meteor. He was only eighteen when Julius Caesar was murdered in March 44 BC. The moment he received the news, he hurried back to Italy from abroad and found on landing that Caesar had adopted him in his will and left him three quarters of his estate. He very skilfully used the fact that he was Caesar's heir to strengthen his position. He now called himself Caius Julius Caesar Octavianus. 'Look at his name,' wrote Cicero, adding, 'then look at his age.'

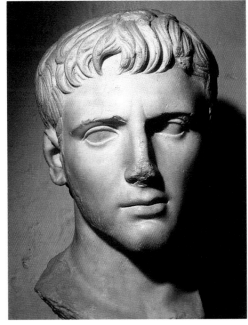

Octavian

His relationship with Caesar's great friend Mark Antony was very tense. Antony thought that he could brush the young man aside, but soon found that this was not possible. At one stage he said resentfully, 'You, boy, owe everything to your name.'

Cicero persuaded the senate that Antony was aiming to become dictator and that they should use Octavian to deal with this threat and then cast him aside. Indeed, Octavian and the two consuls fought two battles with Antony south of the Alps and defeated him. But when the senate then tried to marginalize Octavian, he demanded the consulship and marched on Rome. He was nineteen by now and the minimum legal age was forty-three, but the senate had to give in.

However, it was Antony who, in 42 BC, won the Battle of Philippi and avenged Caesar's death. Octavian had been ill. He said that he had been warned by a friend's dream, and was carried out of his camp only a short time before the enemy overran it. He may have taken refuge unheroically in a marsh.

So Antony had the glory of the great victory and went off to the East to re-establish order and to raise money. Octavian took on the unpopular task of returning to Italy to find land on which to settle the 100,000 veterans of the Philippi campaign.

He caused bitter anger. Large areas were confiscated from eighteen Italian cities to provide homes for the veterans. There were noisy demonstrations against this. Land-owners whose property he had seized flocked to Rome to plead their cause and gained the support of the plebs. Riots broke out and Octavian's life was in danger. Chaos spread throughout Italy. Fights flared up between soldiers and civilians who had resorted to arms themselves. It was a frightening time. Countless small-holders (Quintus' father among them) were forced off their land, and not many were as fortunate as Quintus' fellow-poet Virgil, who may well have got his estate back. Italy became a hungry and desperate country.

Mark Antony

The difficult relationship between Octavian and Antony was now put under new pressure. Antony's wife Fulvia and his brother Lucius raised eight legions and occupied Rome in protest at what Octavian was doing. Octavian soon drove them out and eventually forced them into submission. But then (in 40 BC) Antony himself, returning to Italy from the East, found the port of Brundisium closed against him and laid siege to the city. Octavian marched south with his legions and it looked as if civil war was about to break out yet again. But the soldiers on neither side had the appetite for still more fighting.

A summit conference between Octavian and Antony was arranged, and here they settled their differences. Antony's first wife had recently died and he now married Octavian's sister Octavia. War had been avoided. It looked to some as if a new Golden Age was dawning. Virgil wrote ecstatically:

> Ours is the crowning era foretold in prophecy:
> Born of Time, a great new cycle of centuries
> Begins. Justice returns to earth, the Golden Age
> Returns, and its first-born comes down from heaven above.

Do you feel more sympathy with Antony or with Octavian?

The Golden Age – Mother Earth sits among images of fertility

magister 'cūr sērō advēnistis, puerī?' inquit.
(magister puerōs rogāvit cūr sērō advēnissent.)

indirect question: head verb + ?'s word + subjunctive

magister 'quid facis, Decime?' inquit; 'cūr nōn
labōrās?' (magister Decimum rogāvit quid faceret
et cūr nōn labōrāret.) *head verb = passed imp subjunctive*

magister 'quid facis, Sexte?' inquit; 'cūr nōn
litterās scrībis?' (magister Sextum rogat quid
faciat et cūr litterās nōn scrībat.)

Gāius 'quandō, magister,' inquit, 'nōs dīmittēs?'
(Gāius magistrum rogāvit quandō sē dīmissūrus
esset.)

In the cartoon captions, first the master's words are quoted as he actually spoke – *direct questions*;
then (in parentheses) his words are reported – *indirect questions*. You will see that in indirect
questions Latin (unlike English) uses the subjunctive.

Vocabulary 39

verbs

adimō, adimere, adēmī, adēmptum	I take away
nesciō, nescīre, nescīvī, nescītum	I do not know
queror, querī, questus sum	I complain

nouns

paupertās, paupertātis, f.	poverty
veterānus, -ī, m.	veteran

adverb

forsitan (+ subjunctive)	perhaps
interdum	from time to time
num	whether (introducing indirect questions)

A southern Italian landscape

Quīntus Venusiam revīsit

colōnus Quīntum trīstis aspexit. 'nōnne scīs' inquit 'quid acciderit?
nōnne audīvistī quantam clādem colōnia nostra passa sit?' Quīntus
'quid dīcis?' inquit; 'quid accidit? dīc mihi ubi parentēs meī sint.'
ille 'parentēs tuōs hīc nōn inveniēs. namque abiērunt. age, Quīnte,
5 sub arbore sedē et mē audī. ego omnia tibi nārrābō.
    'Octāviānus, cum ad Italiam ā Graeciā rediisset, legiōnēs
dīmisit; necesse erat agrōs mīlitibus veterānīs dare. cōnstituit igitur
agrōs adimere eīs cīvitātibus quae suās partēs nōn adiūverant
veterānīsque eōs dīvidere. nōs nihil sciēbāmus dē hīs rēbus dōnec
10 decemvirī Venusiam advēnērunt ut agrōs nōbīs adimerent. cīvēs
nostrī vehementer querēbantur; decemvirōs ē colōniā expulimus.
illī tamen rediērunt cum mīlitibus, quibus resistere nōn poterāmus.
    plūrimī cīvēs agrōs perdidērunt, inter quōs erat pater tuus,
Quīnte. aliī hīc mānsērunt, agrīs prīvātī, vītam miseram in
15 paupertāte agentēs, sīcut ego, quī nōn dīves eram sed satis
habēbam; nunc nihil possideō nisi hunc agellum, saxīs carduīsque
plēnum. aliī abiērunt ut meliōrem vītam alibī quaererent, sīcut
pater tuus. trīstia tibi nārrō sed vēra. tōta Italia ēversa est; nec iūs
nec lēgēs valent. squālent arva, abductīs colōnīs. veterānī nōlunt
20 agrōs colere sed dīvitiās ōtiōsī dissipant.'
    Quīntus, angōre commōtus, senem interpellāvit; 'dīc mihi'
inquit 'ubi parentēs inventūrus sim. scīsne quō abierint?' senex
'numquam parentēs tuōs inveniēs, Quīnte. tōta Italia plēna est
cīvibus egēnīs hūc illūc errantibus.'

A Roman farmer

prīvātī (+ abl.) deprived of
possideō I possess
agellum little field; **carduīs** thistles
alibī elsewhere

arva the fields; **squālent** are filthy
dissipant squander
angōre by anguish
interpellāvit interrupted

egēnīs needy

to - huc
this that   wander?

25 hīs audītīs Quīntus summā dēspērātiōne affectus est. diū in terrā sedēbat, lacrimīs per genās cadentibus. tandem senem valēre iussit, quī eum rogāvit quō itūrus esset. ille 'nesciō quō itūrus sim,' inquit; 'hoc sōlum sciō, parentēs tōtam per Italiam quaeram.'

surrēxit collemque dēscendit. sed cum ad portās colōniae 30 advēnisset, cōnstitit. nōluit colōniam intrāre domumque vidēre ab advenīs occupātam. sē vertit et viam iniit quae Rōmam ferēbat.

genās cheeks

advenīs strangers

Respondē Latīnē

1 cūr parentēs Quīntī Venusiā abiērunt?
2 quālem vītam agēbat senex?
3 cum Quīntus senem audīvisset, quid facere cōnstituit?
4 cūr nōluit Quīntus colōniam intrāre?

Quīntus parentēs suōs quaerit

Translate the first two paragraphs of the following passage and answer the questions on the rest

Quīntus iter, quod decem abhinc annōs cum patre tam celeriter fēcerat, iam lentissimē faciēbat. in omnibus vīcīs diū manēbat ut parentēs quaereret. interdum Venusīnīs in viā occurrit quōs ānxiē rogābat num parentēs suōs vīdissent, sed nēmō eī dīcere poterat ubi 5 eōs inventūrus esset.

cum Capuam accēderet, veterī amīcō occurrit; Gāius, quōcum ad lūdum Flāviī ībat, plaustrum dūcēbat quod trahēbant duo bovēs; plēnum erat bonīs omnis modī, super quae sedēbant Gāiī uxor duoque parvī puerī.

decem abhinc annōs ten years ago
vīcīs villages
Venusīnīs people of Venusia

plaustrum a wagon; **bovēs** oxen
omnis modī of every kind

Gaius plaustrum ducebat quod trahebant duo boves

10   Quīntus accurrit Gāiumque salūtāvit. ille, Quīntum intuitus,
'Quīnte,' inquit, 'vix tē agnōvī; nam tē nōn vīdī ex quō Rōmam   **ex quō** since (of time)
cum patre profectus es. quid agis? cūr Capuam contendis?' Quīntus
omnia eī exposuit Gāiumque rogāvit num parentēs suōs vīdisset.
ille respondit, 'nesciō ubi parentēs tuī iam sint. cum decemvirī nōs
15 ex agrīs expulissent, Flaccus Scintillaque nōbīscum Venusiā
profectī sunt. sed cum Beneventum advēnissēmus, nōs paulum ibi
morātī sumus, illī Capuam prōcessērunt. itaque sī Capuam
festīnāveris, forsitan eōs ibi inveniās.'
       Quīntus grātiās eī dedit. 'tū prīmus' inquit 'aliquid spēī mihi   **aliquid spēī** some(thing of) hope
20 praebuistī. vōs Capuam comitābor ut parentēs meōs ibi quaeram.'   **comitābor** I shall accompany

The triumphal arch
at Beneventum

1 When did Gaius last see Quintus?   [2]
2 What had Quintus' parents done, when they were
   driven from their farm?   [2]
3 How did Gaius lose touch with them?   [2]
4 Why did Quintus thank Gaius? What did he plan
   to do next?   [2 + 2]

THE CONFISCATIONS

In these last two chapters Quintus and his family have become the victims of the confiscations which tore the fabric of Italian country life apart. These were begun by the triumvirs after the battle of Philippi in 42 BC and continued right through the thirties into the twenties. Quintus' friend, the poet Virgil, may well have lost his family estate near Mantua. He certainly wrote two poems which convey the desolating sense of loss experienced by the dispossessed.

In one of them Moeris complains to his friend Lycidas that he is now having to work for the new possessor of the farm which he used to own:

Oh, Lycidas, that I should have lived to see an outsider
Take over my little farm – a thing I had never feared –
And tell me, 'You're dispossessed, you old tenants, you've got
   to go.'
We're down and out. And look how Chance turns the tables on
   us –
These are *his* goats (rot them!) you see me taking to market.

In the other poem, Meliboeus laments to Tityrus his loss of his farm to a soldier. (Tityrus has managed to hold on to his land thanks to the intervention of a 'young god' in Rome, presumably Octavian.)

But the rest of us must go from here and be dispersed –
To Scythia, bone-dry Africa, the chalky spate of the Oxus,
Even to Britain – that place cut off at the very world's end.
Ah, when shall I see my native land again? after long years,
Or never? – see the turf-dressed roof of my simple cottage,
And wondering gaze at the ears of corn that were all my
   kingdom?
To think of some godless soldier owning my well-farmed
   fallow,
A foreigner reaping these crops! To such a pass has civil
Dissension brought us: for people like these we have sown our
   fields.
Move onward, little she-goats, onward, once-happy flock!
No more shall I, stretched out in some green dingle here,
Watch you poised far off on the bushy brows of a hillside.
No more singing for me, no taking you to browse,
My little goats, on bitter willow and clover flower.

The confiscations caused devastating unrest. As we saw in the last chapter, a protest backed by Antony's wife and brother led to their occupation of Rome. Octavian drove them out and besieged them in the hill-town of Perusia (Perugia), which was driven by starvation to surrender at the end of the winter of 41/40 BC.

A goatherd milking

Octavian behaved with characteristic ruthlessness to its citizens.

However, when Octavian emerged ten years later as the sole ruler of Italy, which now included Cisalpine Gaul, he saw himself as its patron. He reduced brigandage and improved the roads. The alarming chaos of the civil wars was over, and Italy entered a period of safety and prosperity. All roads may still have led to Rome, but many of the city's leading figures in politics and the arts – the poets Virgil and Horace and the historian Livy among them – came from Italian towns.

Think of a modern situation where considerable numbers of people have been dispossessed. Write ten lines describing the thoughts of one of them as they travel from their homes.

silent lēgēs inter arma ('the laws are silent amid weapons'), wrote Cicero. What do you think he meant?

dum Quīntus dormit, deus Apollō vīsus est eī astāre.

Apollō 'nōlī timēre, Quīnte; ego tē cūrābō,' inquit, et haec locūtus lyram suam eī trādidit.

Apollinī cōnfīsus,* Quīntus Rōmam intrāre ausus* est.

Marcus Quīntusque in hortō sedēre solēbant* vīnum bibentēs.

*see vocabulary

Vocabulary 40

semi-deponent verbs

these verbs are active in form in the present, imperfect and future, but passive in form (but active in meaning, like deponent verbs) in the perfect, pluperfect and future perfect:

audeō, audēre, ausus sum	I dare
gaudeō, gaudēre, gāvīsus sum	I rejoice
soleō, solēre, solitus sum	I am accustomed to
cōnfīdō, cōnfīdere, cōnfīsus sum + dative	I trust in
fīō, fīerī, factus sum	I become, am made

verbs

aestimō, aestimāre	I value
contemnō, contemnere, contempsī, contemptum	I despise
ignōscō, ignōscere, ignōvī, ignōtum + dat.	I pardon, forgive
serviō, servīre, serviī, servītum + dat.	I serve
prōficiō, prōficere, prōfēcī, prōfectum	I make progress, accomplish
suscipiō, suscipere, suscēpī, susceptum	I undertake
ūtor, ūtī, ūsus sum + abl.	I use

nouns

lyra, -ae, f.	lyre
aerārium, -ī, n.	the treasury
fātum, -ī, n.	fate, destiny
respōnsum, -ī, n.	reply, answer
somnium, -ī, n.	dream

adjectives

mīrus, -a, -um	wonderful
turpis, turpe	disgraceful, ugly

adverb

posthāc	after this, hereafter

pronoun

quis, quis, quid	anyone, anything (after **sī, nisi, nē, num**)

deus Apollo

Quīntus amīcō veterī occurrit

Quīntus decem diēs Capuae manēbat parentēs
quaerēns, sed nihil prōfēcit. tandem Capuā trīstis
discessit et viam iniit quae Rōmam ferēbat. in viā
viātōrēs semper rogābat num parentēs vīdissent,
5 sed nēmō eī dīcere poterat quid eīs accidisset.
tandem Rōmam accessit sed urbem intrāre nōn
ausus est; prope viam sedēbat cūrīs cōnfectus;
mox dormīvit.

in somnō deus Apollō vīsus est eī astāre; lyram in manibus
10 ferēbat vultūque benignō Quīntum aspexit. 'Quīnte,' inquit, 'mē
audī. parentēs posthāc numquam vidēbis; nōlī fātō repugnāre.
tempus est novum cursum vītae inīre. dēbēs mihi servīre

repugnāre fight against

Mūsīsque. mihi cōnfīsus Rōmam fortis intrā. ego tē cūrābō.' haec
locūtus lyram Quīntō trādidit; quō factō ēvānuit.

   ēvānuit he vanished

15   Quīntus, cum ēvigilāvisset, somniō gaudēbat. surrēxit
urbemque iniit. nescīvit quid Rōmae factūrus esset, sed Apollinī
cōnfīsus dē futūrīs nōn diūtius timēbat.

   paucīs post diēbus forum trānsībat cum iuvenis quīdam eum
vocāvit. sē vertit et Marcum Cicerōnem vīdit ad sē accurrentem.
20 ille Quīntum complexus 'salvē, Quīnte,' inquit; 'quid agis? ergō
tandem Rōmam redīre ausus es. venī mēcum atque omnia mihi
nārrā quae tibi accidērunt ex quō Philippīs victī sumus.'

    ex quō since

  Marcus eum domum dūxit et cum in hortō sedērent vīnum
bibentēs, 'nārrā mihi' inquit 'quōmodo ē proeliō effūgerīs et quid
25 posteā fēcerīs.' Quīntus omnia eī nārrāvit; Marcus eum intentē
audiēbat, deinde rogāvit quid iam factūrus esset. Quīntus trīstis
respondit; 'nesciō quid factūrus sim. paupertāte marcēscō. opus
quoddam suscipere dēbeō ut pānem mihi comparem.' Marcus
paulīsper tacēbat, deinde 'Quīnte, audī mē,' inquit; 'cōnsilium
30 optimum habeō. nūper quaestor aerāriī factus sum. vīsne mē
adiuvāre? vīsne scrība aerāriī fierī? officia nōn gravia sunt et satis
pecūniae accipiēs. auxiliō tuō, Quīnte, libenter ūtar. sī crās ad
aerārium secundā hōrā vēneris, tē scrībam creābō.'

    marcēscō I'm wasting away
    pānem bread

    quaestor aerāriī quaestor of the
     Treasury
    scrība secretary

  Quīntus Marcī fīdūciā gāvīsus eī grātiās ēgit. 'ō amīce
35 cārissime, tū mihi novam spem praebuistī. mihi valdē placēbit tē in
aerāriō adiuvāre. crās prīmā lūce aderō.' Marcum valēre iussit
domumque festīnāvit ut sē ad nova officia parāret.

    fīdūciā confidence, trust

   postrīdiē prīmā lūce aerāriō adfuit. ā scrībā prīncipālī cōmiter
acceptus est, quod amīcus Marcī erat. ille Quīntō exposuit quid
40 facere dēbēret. officia, sīcut Marcus dīxerat, nōn gravia erant;
tabellās pūblicās cūrāre dēbēbat; respōnsa magistrātibus reddēbat
sī quid rogābant dē rē quādam pūblicā. cotīdiē prīmā lūce aerāriō
aderat; merīdiē negōtiīs cōnfectīs domum redīre solēbat.

    prīncipālī chief

    tabellās pūblicās the public records

The tabularium (Public Record Office),
Rome

43

Respondē Latīnē

1 cuī cōnfīsus Quīntus Rōmam intrāre ausus est?
2 cum Quīntus Marcō occurrisset, quid Marcus eum rogāvit?
3 quōmodo Marcus Quīntum adiūvit?
4 quae officia dēbēbat Quīntus in aerāriō perficere?

senator arrogans

Quīntus ā senātōre malignō vexātur

Translate the first paragraph of the following passage and answer the questions on the rest

Quīntus in aerāriō labōrābat, cum senātor quīdam ingressus eum magnā vōce arcessīvit. Quīntus, negōtiīs occupātus, nōn statim ad eum accurrit. ille, vir nōbilī genere nātus, obēsus erat et arrogāns; querēbātur quod Quīntus nōn statim negōtiīs relictīs ad eum

5 responderat. 'festīnā, scrība,' inquit; 'nōlī morārī. nōn possum tōtum diem cessāre.' Quīntus ad eum festīnāvit; 'salvē, mī senātor,' inquit; 'ignōsce mihi. negōtiīs occupātus eram. quid vīs?'

    ille Quīntum malignē aspiciēns rogāvit quis esset et quō patre nātus esset. Quīntus eī respondit: 'nōmen mihi est Quīntus Horātius

10 Flaccus. pater meus, quī Venusiae habitābat, mortuus est.' hōc audītō ille 'iam meminī,' inquit. 'tū amīcus es Marcī Cicerōnis. nōnne lībertō nātus erās? et tū, fīlius lībertī, tribūnus mīlitum factus es in Brūtī exercitū tōtīque legiōnī imperāre ausus es? nōn mīrum est quod Brūtus victus est, sī fīliōs lībertōrum tribūnōs

15 facere coāctus est.'

    Quīntus, quī tālem contumēliam audīre solitus est, nihil ad haec respondit sed iterum eum rogāvit quid vellet. ille 'nōlō rem agere cum lībertī fīliō. vocā alium scrībam.' Quīntus alium scrībam arcessīvit, quī cum senātōre rem ēgit. ipse in tabulārium recessit,

20 īrātus quod sīc contemptus erat ā tālī virō.

obēsus fat

malignē maliciously

meminī I remember

nōn mīrum est quod it is no wonder that

contumēliam insult(s)
rem agere to do business

tabulārium record office

1 What did the senator ask Quintus? [3]
2 How did he react to Quintus' answer? [7]
3 What did the senator then tell Quintus to do, and why? [3]
4 How did Quintus feel about the senator's behavior? [2]
5 Sum up the senator's character in a few words. [4]

Fābella

Persōnae: Quīntus, Sextus (scrība prīncipālis), Metellus (senātor
        arrogāns), Rūfus (comes eius)

Quīntus in aerāriō labōrat. tabulās pūblicās in ōrdinem dispōnit.

Quīntus: quot tabulae in cōnfūsiōne iacent! nesciō quō hās tabulās   **in cōnfūsiōne** in a muddle

5   pōnere dēbeam. necesse est scrībam prīncipālem
            cōnsulere. (*clāmat*) Sexte, vīsne mē adiuvāre? quō dēbeō   **cōnsulere** consult
            hās tabulās pōnere?

Sextus ad eum accēdit.

Sextus: ecce, Quīnte, hās tabulās in illum pluteum pōnere dēbēs,   **pluteum** shelf

10   ubi locantur cēterae tabulae quae ad respōnsa cēnsōria   **ad respōnsa cēnsōria attinent**
            attinent.   concern the replies of the censors

intrant Metellus Rūfusque.

Metellus: scrība! scrība! venī hūc. volō tē cōnsulere.

Quīntus, quī tabulās in pluteum dispōnit, paulīsper morātur.

15 **Metellus:** festīnā, scrība. nōlī cessāre. heus, iuvenis! nōn possum
              tē tōtum diem expectāre.

Quīntus ad Metellum festīnat.

Quīntus: salvē, mī senātor. ignōsce mihi. negōtiīs valdē occupātus
            eram. quōmodo tē adiuvāre possum?

20 **Metellus:** ad aerārium saepe venīre soleō sed tē numquam anteā
             vīdī. dīc mihi quis sīs et quō patre nātus.

Quīntus: nōmen mihi est Quīntus Horātius Flaccus, mī senātor;
            pater meus, quī Venusiae habitābat, mortuus est.

Metellus: iam meminī. aliquis mihi omnia dē tē dīxit. tū amīcus es

25   Marcī Cicerōnis. nōnne lībertō nātus es? dī immortālēs,
            pater tuus servus erat!

Quīntus: pater meus vir bonus erat et honestus. numquam eius mē   **numquam eius mē paenitēbit** I shall
            paenitēbit.   never be ashamed of him.

Metellus: et tū, fīlius lībertī, tribūnus mīlitum factus es in exercitū

30   Brūtī!

Quīntus: ita vērō, mī senātor. tribūnus mīlitum factus sum   **ita vērō** yes
            Philippīsque legiōnī praefectus.

Metellus: nōn mīrum est quod Brūtus victus est sī fīliōs lībertōrum
            legiōnibus praefēcit. Rūfe, venī hūc. ecce, hic scrība

35   lībertīnō patre nātus est. quid sentīs? nōnne turpe est
            tabulās pūblicās lībertī fīliō committere?

Rūfus: nōn est cūr eum sīc contemnās. sine dubiō iuvenis est   **nōn est cūr** there is no reason why
           strēnuus et ingeniōsus. quid interest sī pater eius lībertus   **quid interest?** what does it matter?
           est? cīvis Rōmānus est atque officia bene perficit.

40 **Metellus:** nōlī nūgās nārrāre, Rūfe. rēs turpissima est et contrā
            mōrem maiōrum facta. ego rem cum fīliō lībertī agere
            nōlō. vocā scrībam prīncipālem.

*Sextus ad Metellum festīnat. Quīntus in aerārium recēdit, valdē
īrātus.*

LATIN POETRY

In this chapter Apollo, god of poetry, has appeared in a dream to Quintus and told him of his poetic mission. In the next chapter you will be reading some of his poetry. It may be of help if we now explain how Latin poetry had developed up to Quintus' time.

The Romans were slow starters as far as literature was concerned. For the first five hundred years of their history they produced nothing which we would recognize as poetry. Only a few hymns, charms and spells survive. Here is a specimen, a lullaby:

> lalla, lalla, lalla.
> ī, aut dormī aut lactā.
> (Lullaby, lullaby, lullaby.
> Come, either sleep or drink your milk.)

It is not unattractive but hardly ranks as poetry.

It was not until it came under the influence of the Greek writers that Roman literature got off the ground. At Orbilius' school Quintus would have had to struggle through the poems of Livius Andronicus (c. 284–204 BC). He was a Greek war-captive and slave and founded the Latin literary tradition by translating Homer's *Odyssey* and Greek tragedies and comedies into Latin. These two forms of literature, epic (long narrative poems on elevated themes) and drama, were developed by a succession of Roman writers over the next two hundred years.

Tragedies and comedies were performed at the festivals which occurred at intervals throughout the year. Rome, where there were five major drama festivals taking up fourteen days in all, produced at least one really great dramatist, Plautus (c. 254–184 BC). Twenty comedies by him, all of them with Greek settings, survive. They are still performed today and remain very funny, containing a large element of knock-about farce and a splendid gallery of characters. Ennius was another writer for whom the Romans, including Virgil, had great respect. He lived from c. 239 to 169 BC and has been

called 'the father of Roman poetry'. As well as tragedies and comedies, he wrote an epic – in the same metre as Homer had used – on the history of Rome.

To begin with, the Roman tradition was limited to forms of poetry intended for public performance. Poetry was not considered a vehicle for the expression of personal feelings, which is what most of us expect of it now. Catullus (c. 84–54 BC) was the first great writer to use poetry to express his thoughts and emotions on every subject which occurred to him, from the trivial to the profound. He is the first love poet in Roman literature. He too found his inspiration in Greek models when he broke with the old Roman tradition of epic and drama. He was influenced by the early Greek lyric poets of the seventh century BC and even more by the highly sophisticated Greek poets who founded a new tradition in Alexandria four hundred years later. Neither he nor the other great Roman poets imitated Greek models slavishly. He and the circle of young poets he wrote for, the *poētae novī*, as Cicero contemptuously called them, were highly original. They found in the Greek poets they looked back to an inspiration which freed them from the old Roman tradition, and enabled them to produce an intensely personal type of poetry.

We have mentioned epic, drama and lyric. Another important genre is didactic poetry. Didactic poems aim to teach their readers something. The earliest surviving didactic poem is by a Greek called Hesiod who lived around the same time as Homer. He wrote about farming. Virgil says that Hesiod's poem was the model for his *Georgics*, the poem on farming which he talks about when he appears in our next chapter. The first Roman didactic poem was written by a contemporary of Catullus called Lucretius (c. 98–c. 55 BC) who wrote an amazing poem in six books called *The Nature of the Universe* (*De Rerum Natura*) in which he gives a scientific exposition of Epicurus' philosophy (see Part II, background section to chapter 29). Lucretius intended the pleasure given by poetry to help to 'sell' his useful philosophical message. Horace gives his approval when he says that 'the poet who has mixed the useful with the pleasurable wins every vote, by delighting and advising the reader at one and the same moment'. But such a comment is an inadequate response to the tremendous excitement of Lucretius' poetry. More than any other Roman poet, he overwhelms by the sheer force of his poetic inspiration.

Name one or more English-speaking poets who wrote in the following genres (types of literature) and name some of their poems or plays: epic, drama, lyric, didactic.

If you were a poet, what sort of subjects would you choose to write about?

47

puerī malī sunt.
magister parentibus dīcit puerōs malōs esse.

puerī tabulās abiēcērunt.
magister parentibus dīcit puerōs tabulās
abiēcisse.

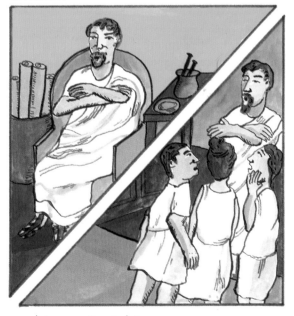

puerī domum remissī sunt.
magister parentibus dīcit puerōs domum remissōs
esse.

magister puerōs pūniet.
magister parentibus dīcit sē puerōs pūnītūrum
esse.

The cartoon captions above first quote the master's words as he actually spoke and then report the
same words after **dīcit** (he says that . . .). How does Latin express such reported statements?

Vocabulary 41

verbs

negō, negāre	I deny, say that . . . not
probō, probāre	I approve of
prōspectō, prōspectāre	I look out at
vītō, vītāre	I avoid
horreō, horrēre, horruī	I tremble at, fear
condō, condere, condidī, conditum	I store away; I found
admīror, admīrārī, admīrātus sum	I wonder at, admire
colloquor, colloquī, collocūtus sum	I talk with
colloquium, -ī, n.	conversation
fruor, fruī, frūctus sum + abl.	I enjoy

nouns

amīcitia, -ae, f.	friendship
aurum, -ī, n.	gold
avis, avis, f.	bird
ovis, ovis, f.	sheep
vallis, vallis, f.	valley

adjectives

beātus, -a, -um	blessed, happy
īnfirmus, -a, -um	weak
levis, leve	light
mortālis, mortāle	mortal

adverbs

modo . . . modo	now . . . now
paulātim	little by little

Quīntus carmina facit

Quīntus iam satis pecūniae accipiēbat ut modicē vīveret; satis ōtiī
fruēbātur ut carmina compōneret. sīc duōs annōs contentus perēgit.
Marcō Cicerōnī saepe occurrēbat quī cognōvit eum carmina
compōnere; ille eum rogāvit ut carmina sibi recitāret. cum ea
5 audīvisset, dīxit Quīntum poētam optimum esse. amīcīs suīs
dīcēbat sē poētam novum invēnisse; illī carmina audīre cupiēbant.
sīc fāma Quīntī paulātim ēmānābat. Quīntus spērābat sē tōtum
librum carminum mox cōnfectūrum esse.

　　ex hīs carminibus ūnum hīc ascrībimus, in quō vītam colōnī
10 rūsticī laudat:

*NB In verse, adjectives are often separated from the nouns they
agree with; you must therefore pay very close attention to word
endings to see which word agrees with which.*

　　'beātus ille, quī procul negōtiīs,
　　　　ut prīsca gēns mortālium,
　　paterna rūra bōbus exercet suīs,
　　　　solūtus omnī faenore.
15　neque excitātur classicō mīles trucī
　　　　neque horret īrātum mare,

ut so that; **modicē** modestly
perēgit passed

ēmānābat was spreading abroad

beātus ille supply **est**
ut prīsca gēns mortālium like the
　ancient race of men
paterna rūra his ancestral farm
bōbus . . . suīs with his oxen
faenore from debt
classicō . . . trucī by the harsh trumpet
mīles as a soldier

49

A pastoral scene

forumque vītat et superba cīvium
    potentiōrum līmina.
aut in reductā valle mūgientium
20   prōspectat errantēs gregēs,
aut pressa pūrīs mella condit amphorīs
    aut tondet īnfirmās ovēs.
libet iacēre modo sub antīquā īlice,
    modo in tenācī grāmine.
25 lābuntur altīs interim rīvīs aquae,
    queruntur in silvīs avēs,
fontēsque lymphīs obstrepunt mānantibus,
    somnōs quod invītet levēs.'

*The poem continues for another forty lines, praising the
tranquillity and simplicity of country life; it ends:*

    haec ubi locūtus faenerātor Alfius,
30   iam, iam futūrus rūsticus,
omnem redēgit Idibus pecūniam,
    quaerit Kalendīs pōnere.

reductā withdrawn, remote
mūgientium of lowing (cattle)
gregēs herds
pressa . . . mella the pressed honey(s)
amphorīs in jars; **tondet** shears
libet he delights to; **īlice** holm oak
tenācī grāmine the clinging grass
rīvīs streams
lymphīs . . . mānantibus with flowing
  water; **obstrepunt** murmur
quod (a thing) which

locūtus supply **est**
faenerātor the money-lender
redēgit called in
Idibus on the fifteenth (of the month)
Kalendīs on the first
pōnere to lend it out (again)

1 Notice that all the poem except the last four lines is in quotes; what does this tell you?
2 How do the last four lines change your impression of the first part of the poem?
3 What would be meant by saying that line 4 (**solūtus omnī faenore**) was ironical?
4 What sort of man was Alfius? Did he really want to become a countryman? What is the significance of **iam, iam futūrus**? (Why is **iam** repeated?)
5 Do you think that there are men like Alfius in the contemporary world? What would be meant by saying that the poem is *satirical*?
6 Whom or what is Horace satirizing?

omnem redegit
Idibus pecuniam

Virgil

Vergilius amīcitiam Quīntī petit

Translate the first paragraph of the following passage and answer the questions on the rest

diē quōdam Quīntus, cum aerāriō discessisset, in tabernā sub arbore sedēbat, cum iuvenis eī nōn nōtus accessit. 'salvē, Horātī,' inquit; 'tē diū quaerō. ego sum Pūblius Vergilius Marō. amīcus quīdam mihi dīxit tē carmina facere. diū cupiō tē cognōscere.'
5 Quīntus surrēxit eumque salūtāvit; respondit sē carmina Vergiliī lēgisse atque ea valdē admīrārī.
    Vergilius eī arrīsit; 'gaudeō,' inquit, 'tē mea carmina probāre. sed quid hodiē factūrus es? an ōtiōsus es? vīsne domum mēcum venīre?'
10 Quīntus gaudēbat Vergilium amīcitiam suam petere eumque domum secūtus est. ad multam noctem in hortō sedēbant inter sē colloquentēs. Quīntus eī recitāvit poēma quod de Alfiō nūper scrīpserat.

ad multam noctem until late at night
poēma (n.) poem

51

A pastoral landscape

Vergilius rīsit et 'ego quoque' inquit 'poēma compōnere cōnor
15 dē rēbus rūsticīs. ea quae tū iocōsē tractās ego sēriō expōnō; nam
de colōnōrum labōribus canō, de rūris pulchritūdine, dē vītā
rūsticōrum innocentī et tranquillā.' Quīntus eum rogāvit ut aliquid
huius carminis sibi recitāret, sed ille negāvit sē carmen eī
recitāturum esse; 'vix quicquam perfēcī,' inquit; 'nēminī haec
20 recitābō dōnec perfecta erint.' tandem Quīntus surrēxit et dīxit sē
dēbēre domum redīre. Vergilius, cum Quīntum valēre iubēret, dīxit
sē colloquiō valdē gāvīsum esse; 'spērō', inquit 'tē saepe hūc
ventūrum esse et carmina tua mihi recitātūrum.'

iocōsē in jest, humorously
tractās you are treating
sēriō seriously

1 What did Quintus recite to Virgil?   [2]
2 What was the poem Virgil was composing about?
   In what way does it differ from Quintus'? Find out what
   Virgil's poem is called.   [2 + 2 +1]
3 Why would Virgil not recite any of this poem to Quintus?   [2]
4 What did he say to Quintus when they parted?   [3]

HORACE

In the last chapter we looked at the literary tradition which Horace
was heir to. Now we must look at his own contribution to this
tradition.

Disregarding Catullus' achievement, Horace claims to be the
first Roman poet to have 'naturalized' Greek lyric poetry, bringing
Greek metres and feelings to Italy. Lyric poetry orginally meant
poetry sung to the accompaniment of the lyre, which was not

unlike our guitar. The early Greek lyric poets had literally sung their poems on love and war and wine to their friends, often at dinner parties. Horace used the metres of these poets, and many of the same themes, but he lived six hundred years later in very different conditions. His poems were intended to be read in private rather than sung to friends on particular occasions, and in this respect they are much more like modern poetry. Just as Catullus was, he was much influenced by the Alexandrian writers.

Horace's first two works, the *Epodes* (from which *Beātus ille* in this chapter comes) and the two books of *Sermones* (= conversation pieces), were published in 35 and 30 BC. The *Epodes* are a collection of poems on love, politics, war and the art of living, while the *Sermones* belong to a genre of literature called satire, the only genre which the Romans invented themselves. In satire, writers in prose or verse or a mixture of the two laugh at the follies and vices of mankind. Horace is highly original in the *Sermones* (which he also called the *Satires*), often laughing at himself as well as others (as in the satire about the bore; see chapter 45). Some years later he wrote the two books of *Epistles* which can be seen as a continuation of the *Satires* and contain his *Art of Poetry*, a didactic poem. A wonderful sense of his highly individual response to life in ancient Rome is conveyed in these works, and at times we have the breathtaking impression of a man talking to us directly across two millennia.

His major work, however, is his *Carmina*, the four books of *Odes*, the first three published in 23 BC, the fourth in 13 BC. Here, as he handles his various verse forms with masterly technical skill, he mingles personal poems on such themes as love, friendship, life and death, poetry, the countryside and the delights of wine, with political poems that reflect his deep anxiety and grateful optimism in a period of considerable uncertainty. He had a passionate belief in the value and permanence of poetry and, as we saw in Part I (chapter 1), proudly claimed that his own work would last for ever:

> I have raised a monument more lasting than bronze and higher than the ruins of the royal pyramids . . . Not all of me shall die.

The pyramid of Sestius

Think of three modern TV programmes which you might describe as 'satirical'. What do they have in common?

What sort of person do you think might disapprove of satire?

Vocabulary 42

FACITIS·VOBIS·SV AVITER·EGO·CANTO·EST·ITA·VALEAS

recepto dulce mihi furere est amico

verbs		*nouns*	
renovō, renovāre	I renew	**convīva, -ae**, c.	guest
habeō, prō certō habeō	I am sure that	**convīvium, -ī**, n.	dinner party
carpō, carpere, carpsī,		**corōna, -ae**, f.	garland, crown
carptum	I pluck, pick	**venia, -ae**, f.	pardon
ēlābor, ēlābī, ēlāpsus sum	I slip out	**silentium, -ī**, n.	silence
		reditus, -ūs, m.	return

(handwritten: battle of Philippi 42 BC)

Pompēius ad patriam revenit

(handwritten: take dat)

paucīs post diēbus Quīntus alterī amīcō veterī in forō occurrit. nam
Pompēium cōnspexit ad palātium festīnantem. accurrit eumque
salūtāvit. 'Pompēī,' inquit, 'tandem in patriam revēnistī? venī
mēcum et mihi nārrā ubi fuerīs, quid fēcerīs, quid iam factūrus sīs.'
(handwritten: vert; I Q - hv, ipronoun subj.)

5 tabernam ingressī vīnum rogāvērunt. cum sēdissent, Pompēius
nārrāvit quid fēcisset et quid iam factūrus esset. *(handwritten: subb \ pluperfect)*

dīxit sē cum cēterīs ē campō Philippōrum effūgisse; diū in *(handwritten: inf.)*
montibus silvīsque sē cēlāvisse; tandem cōnstituisse ad Sextum
Pompēium īre bellumque prō rēpūblicā renovāre. 'ille in Siciliā
10 erat; magnā cum difficultāte eō advēnī. duōs annōs cum eō
mīlitābam, sed ille nihil prōficiēbat prō rēpūblicā, nihil cūrābat nisi

(right margin handwritten: Maecenas - Mayor of Rome)

palātium the Palatium (Octavian's
house on the Palatine)

ut aurum argentumque sibi comparāret. dēnique, cum Octāviānus
veniam inimīcīs suīs prōmīsisset, ego ē castrīs Pompēiī ēlāpsus ad
Italiam nāvigāvī. iam Rōmam tandem regressus ad Octāviānum
15 fēstīnō ut veniam petam.'
    Quīntus 'euge!' inquit; 'gaudeō tē tandem ad patriam revēnisse.
    prō certō habeō Octāviānum veniam tibi datūrum esse. nam valdē
    cupit omnēs inimīcōs sibi conciliāre Italiamque in pācem et ōtium
    redūcere. sed dīc mihi, amīce, quid crās factūrus sīs. vīsne mēcum
20 cēnāre? convīvium faciēmus ut reditum tuum celebrēmus.'

    Pompēius respondit sē ad cēnam libenter ventūrum esse
    abiitque ad Palātium ut Octāviānum quaereret. Quīntus domum
    fēstīnāvit ut omnia ad convīvium parāret. multōs amīcōs ad cēnam
    invītāvit multāsque puellās pulcherrimās. servīs imperāvit ut
25 cibum vīnumque optimum parārent; aliōs ēmīsit quī flōrēs
    carperent corōnāsque facerent.

    convīvium magnificum erat; omnēs convīvae gaudēbant
    Pompēium incolumem Rōmam rediisse; ille laetissimus erat quod
    Octāviānus veniam sibi dederat. omnēs admodum ēbriī factī sunt.
30 tandem Quīntus, silentiō factō, carmen recitāvit quod composuerat
    ut reditum amīcī celebrāret.

conciliāre conciliate, win over

quī . . . carperent to pick

admodum ēbriī extremely drunk

Vocabulary 42a

dōnō, dōnāre	I give
redōnō, redōnāre	I give back
parcō, parcere, pepercī, parsum + dat.	I spare
tangō, tangere, tetigī, tāctum	I touch
mīlitia, -ae, f.	military service, army
patrius, -a, -um	of one's father(s)

Quīntus Pompēiī reditum carmine celebrat

The following is a prose paraphrase of Horace's ode:

ō Pompei, saepe mēcum tempus in ultimum dēducte, Brūtō mīlitiae
duce, quis tē redōnāvit Quirītem dīs patriīs Italōque caelō, Pompei,
prīme meōrum sodālium? cum quō saepe diem morantem merō
frēgī, capillōs nitentēs mālabathrō Syriō corōnātus.
5   tēcum Philippōs et celerem fugam sēnsī, parmulā nōn bene
relictā, cum virtūs frācta est, et minācēs solum mentō turpe
tetigērunt. sed Mercurius celer mē paventem per hostēs āëre dēnsō
sustulit: tē unda in bellum rūrsus resorbēns fretīs aestuōsīs tulit.
    ergō Iovī redde dapem obligātam latusque (tuum) longā mīlitiā
10 fessum sub laurū meā dēpōne, nec parce cadīs tibi dēstinātīs . . .
amīcō receptō dulce est mihi furere.

tempus in ultimum into the last time,
    i.e. danger of death
dēducte voc., agreeing with **Pompei**
Quirītem as a Roman citizen (i.e. no
    longer a soldier)
sodālium of my comrades
merō with undiluted wine
capillōs nitentēs . . . corōnātus
    having crowned my shining hair
mālabathrō Syriō with Syrian
    perfume
parmulā my little shield
nōn bene not well = dishonorably
virtūs virtue = the cause of Virtue,
    Brutus' fight for freedom
minācēs threatening, i.e. those who
    had threatened; **solum** the ground
mentō with their chin(s)
turpe disgracefully, i.e. in disgrace
paventem trembling
āëre dēnsō in a thick mist
resorbēns sucking back
fretīs aestuōsīs on stormy seas
Iovī . . . dapem obligātam the feast
    owed to Jupiter
cadīs tibi dēstinātīs the (wine) jars
    marked out for you
furere to run mad

*Now read the original poem and answer the questions below. The
main difficulty is in the word order, e.g. the first line opens 'ō', but
the vocative **Pompei** does not come until line 5. Remember to read
by the punctuation, not by the line; sense may carry over from
line to line and even from one stanza to the next.*

ō saepe mēcum tempus in ultimum
dēducte Brūtō mīlitiae duce,
    quis tē redōnāvit Quirītem
        dīs patriīs Italōque caelō,

5 Pompei, meōrum prīme sodālium?
cum quō morantem saepe diem merō
    frēgī, corōnātus nitentēs
        mālabathrō Syriō capillōs.

tēcum Philippōs et celerem fugam
10 sēnsī, relictā nōn bene parmulā,
    cum frācta virtūs, et minācēs
        turpe solum tetigēre mentō.

sed mē per hostēs Mercurius celer
dēnsō paventem sustulit āëre:
15   tē rūrsus in bellum resorbēns
        unda fretīs tulit aestuōsīs.

ergō obligātam redde Iovī dapem
longāque fessum mīlitiā latus
    dēpōne sub laurū meā, nec
20   parce cadīs tibi dēstinātīs . . .

                receptō
dulce mihi furere est amīcō.

tetigēre = tetigērunt

Mercurius celer

1 **quis tē redōnāvit?** Horace does not answer this question; can
you suggest an answer?
2 **morantem**: why is the day described as 'lingering'? How did
they fill their time?
3 How does Horace belittle his own performance in the battle?
4 In chapters 35–6 you read of Quintus' actual escape from the
battle. How does he describe his escape in the ode? Why do
you suppose he does this?
5 What image does he use to describe Pompeius' fortunes after
Philippi? How appropriate is it?
6 **obligātam Iovī dapem**: explain what is meant by this phrase.
7 What is Horace's invitation to Pompeius in the fifth stanza?
What is implied by the phrase **cadīs tibi dēstinātīs**?
8 What feelings towards Pompeius does Horace convey in the
poem as a whole?

BOOKS

When we talk about a book in the Roman world, we generally mean a papyrus roll. The papyrus reed is rare today but used to grow in abundance on the banks of the Nile.

How would you convert it into the ancient equivalent of paper? Cut the pith on the papyrus stem into strips and put them side by side horizontally. Wet the layer you have formed with water and add a little glue. Place another set of strips on top of this at right angles to it. Press the two layers together. Allow to dry.

You now have a sheet on which you can write. Next join several of these together, smoothing down the joints carefully, and you have a continuous strip of papyrus. Smooth down the whole surface with pumice; otherwise the ink will blot. All you need to turn it into a book is a pair of cylindrical wooden rollers, preferably with ornamental knobs on, which you fix to each end left and right.

A papyrus fragment

Now it can be written on. You, your secretary or one of your slaves must pick up a pen (either a pointed reed or a sharpened goose quill such as was used until the nineteenth century) and dip it in ink, a black substance made of soot and glue and then diluted. You write from left to right in columns about thirty-five letters wide. You write in capital letters with no word division and little punctuation. Your first task, if you are reading a book, is *ēmendāre* (to correct errors) and *distinguere* (to separate words and punctuate). The papyrus can be as long or as short as you like, but in Horace's day the average length of a book of papyrus was 700 to 900 lines. Presumably this was considered a reasonable size for a scroll.

Now at last you can read your book. You pick up the rollers one in each hand. As you read, you roll it up with your left hand and unroll it with your right. (It is called a *volūmen* from *volvō* = 'I turn, roll'.) If you are a considerate person, when you have finished the book you will re-roll it, since the next reader cannot start on it until the beginning faces outwards again.

You now have the problem of storing the book. You either lay it on a shelf or put it in a cylindrical box, first having made sure that a strip of parchment giving the title is stuck to it. This will either hang down from the shelf or stick out from the box, depending on your method of storage. It is extremely likely to come off. There will be serious difficulty in consulting documents. You can't simply flick through a book as you can today. And you may soon run out of space. Livy's *History of Rome*, for instance, was written in 142 books! There are further dangers in your library. Your books may become damp and rot, or insects may get at them and eat them.

If you wish to re-use a papyrus scroll, a damp sponge will wipe away the ink. The emperor Caligula is said to have forced bad poets to lick out their work with their tongues!

Schoolchildren and adults who wanted to jot down short notes would write not on papyrus but on wax tablets. These consisted of two or more wooden-framed rectangles with waxen inner sections. The frames were tied to each other with leather thongs. You wrote on the wax with a thin pointed stick (a *stīlus*). Later you could rub out the writing using the round or flat head of the *stīlus*. Lovers found these tablets a highly convenient method of communication. Can you suggest why?

There was no real distinction between the roles of publisher and bookseller in the Roman world. Many scribes would be employed as copyists in the large number of bookshops at Rome. If they were dealing with a best-seller, the text would be dictated to a group of scribes and the book would be mass-produced. Cicero's friend Atticus was a famous publisher, running a factory with many slaves who were well trained in all aspects of book production, including making last-minute changes at the author's request.

Sappho

Wealthy Romans like Cicero, an enthusiastic collector of rare books, had excellent private libraries. As you may have seen in Part II, Petronius' *nouveau riche* freedman Trimalchio claimed to have two libraries, one in Latin and one in Greek. And in Horace's day the first public libraries opened in Rome. In the fourth century AD there were twenty-nine public libraries in the city. Libraries were available even in the baths for the pleasure of the bathers.

What were the main difficulties which faced a reader in the Roman world?

Compare book production in the modern world with that practised in Horace's day.

Quīntus in hortō sedēbat carmen meditāns cum incurrit Vergilius.

ille 'venī mēcum, Quīnte,' inquit, 'ad Maecēnātem. tua carmina eum adeō dēlectant ut tē cognōscere cupiat.'

Maecēnās 'salvē, Horātī,' inquit; 'Vergilius dē tē totiēns mihi dīxit ut tua carmina audīre cupiam.'

Quīntus tam verēcundus (shy) erat ut vix quicquam dīcere posset.

Cartoons 2, 3 and 4 contain clauses introduced by **ut** + subjunctive; what are these clauses expressing?

Vocabulary 43

verbs		adjectives	
dīligō, dīligere, dīlēxī, dīlēctum	I love	**indignus, -a, -um** + abl.	unworthy (of)
for, fārī, fātus sum	I speak, say	**prīvātus, -a, -um**	private
nāscor, nāscī, nātus sum	I am born	*adverbs*	
dēsum, dēesse, dēfuī + dat.	I fail	**adeō**	to such an extent, so
		ita	in such a way, so, thus
nouns			
ars, artis, f.	art, skill	*conjunctions*	
honor, honōris, m.	honor, office	**quia**	because
pectus, pectoris, n.	breast, heart	**ut** + subjunctive	that (expressing
pudor, pudōris, m.	shame, modesty		consequence or result)

Quīntus Maecēnātī commendātur

mayor of Rome, wealthy

paucīs post mēnsibus Quīntus in hortō sedēbat carmen meditāns,
cum irrūpit Vergilius valdē ēlātus. 'Quīnte,' inquit, 'venī mēcum;
festīnā. Maecēnās tē exspectat. eī dīxī tē optima carmina
compōnere; carminum tuōrum plēraque eī recitāvī, quae eum adeō
5 dēlectant ut iam tē cognōscere velit.'

    Maecēnās erat vir īnsignis, vetus amīcus Octāviānī; dīves erat
atque nōbilis, quī dīcēbat sē rēgibus Etrūscīs ortum esse. numquam
honōrēs petīverat sed, quamquam eques prīvātus erat, Octāviānus
10 eum tantī aestimābat ut semper eum cōnsuleret dē rēbus maximī
mōmentī. Mūsās colēbat litterīsque studēbat. multōs poētās
adiūverat, quōrum nōnnūllōs in numerum amīcōrum accēperat.

    Quīntus Vergilium secūtus ad aedēs Maecēnātis celeriter
advēnit. cum in tablīnum intrāvissent, Maecēnās ad mēnsam
sedēbat librum legēns. brevī statūrā erat atque obēsus; nōn togam
15 gerēbat sed tunicam solūtam.

nonnullos – 1 ito dies "like a map"

meditāns thinking over, composing
ēlātus excited

eques prīvātus a private knight, i.e.
  he held no office
tantī so highly; **cōnsuleret** consulted
maximī mōmentī of the greatest
  importance

statūrā stature; **obēsus** fat
solūtam loose

PAIN words

A luxurious Roman villa

Vergilius ad eum accessit et 'Maecēnās,' inquit, 'velim commendāre amīcum meum Quīntum Horātium Flaccum. poēta est facētus, ut tibi dīxī, et doctus.' ille Quīntum vultū benignō īnspiciēns 'salvē, Horātī,' inquit; 'Vergilius mihi dē tē totiēns dīxit
20 ut diū tē cognōscere cupiam. dīc mihi aliquid dē parentibus tuīs tuōque cursū vītae.'

Quīntus tam verēcundus erat ut vix fārī posset. pauca tamen verba singultim locūtus, nōn dīxit sē clārō patre nātum esse, sed quod erat nārrāvit. ille pauca respondit Quīntumque mox dīmīsit.
25 Quīntus dolēbat quod sibi ita dēfuisset ut sē indignum amīcitiā tantī virī praebēret. octō mēnsēs praeteriērunt. Maecēnās eum nōn revocāvit. Quīntus putābat sē Maecēnātī nōn placuisse; sed Vergilius dīcēbat Maecēnātem eum dīlēxisse et carmina eius probāre; sed negōtiīs tam occupātum esse ut amīcōs neglegeret;
30 diū Rōmā abesse; sine dubiō Quīntum revocātūrum esse.

nōnō mēnse Maecēnās Quīntum revocāvit iussitque in amīcōrum numerō esse.

velim commendāre I should like to introduce
facētus witty

verēcundus shy
singultim haltingly
quod erat what was (the truth)
dolēbat was upset

Respondē Latīnē

1 quālis erat Maecēnās?
2 cūr Maecēnās Quīntum cognōscere volēbat?
3 cum Vergilius Quīntum Maecēnātī commendāvisset, quōmodo sē gessit Quīntus?
4 cūr putābat Quīntus sē Maecēnātī nōn placuisse?

Maecēnās Quīntum in amīcōrum numerum accipit

Read the following passage and with the help of your teacher translate it

Quīntus ipse dēscrībit quōmodo ā Maecēnāte prīmum acceptus sit; in hōc poēmate dīcit Maecēnātem nōbilem esse sed nōn sē contemnere quod lībertīnō patre nātus sit. 'multī' inquit 'hominēs ignōtōs contemnunt. sī quis honōrēs petit, quaerunt quō patre nātus
5 sit . . .

nunc ad mē redeō lībertīnō patre nātum,
quem rōdunt omnēs lībertīnō patre nātum,
nunc quia sim tibi, Maecēnās, convīctor, at ōlim
quod mihi pārēret legiō Rōmāna tribūnō . . .
10 ut vēnī cōram, singultim pauca locūtus,
īnfāns namque pudor prohibēbat plūra profārī,
nōn ego mē clārō nātum patre . . .
sed quod eram dīcō. respondēs, ut tuus est mōs,
pauca: abeō; et revocās nōnō post mēnse iubēsque
15 esse in amīcōrum numerō. magnum hoc ego dūcō
quod placuī tibi . . .
nōn patre praeclārō sed vītā et pectore pūrō.

rōdunt disparage, run down
convīctor friend

cōram into your presence
īnfāns dumb; **profārī** to say
nātum supply **esse**

magnum hoc ego dūcō I consider this a great thing
nōn patre praeclārō not because of a famous father

addit haec:

sī bonum ingenium habeō,
20   causa fuit pater hīs, quī macrō pauper agellō,
nōluit in Flāvī lūdum mē mittere, magnī
quō puerī, magnīs ē centuriōnibus ortī,
ībant . . .
sed puerum est ausus Rōmam portāre, docendum
25   artēs quās doceat quīvīs eques atque senātor
sēmet prōgnātōs.

causa . . . hīs the reason for this
macrō . . . agellō with a poor little farm

puerum me as a boy
docendum to be taught
quīvīs any
doceat would have taught to
sēmet prōgnātōs (children) born from himself = his own children
prīncipī the emperor
eum paenitēbat was ashamed of

Quīntus patrem suum adeō amābat ut eum semper laudāret grātiāsque eī ageret. cum amīcus esset multīs virīs īnsignibus atque ipsī prīncipī, patris tamen numquam eum paenitēbat.

MAECENAS

Caius Cilnius Maecenas was a key figure in the history of these times. He was probably a few years older than Octavian, born into an equestrian family descended from the Etruscan king Lars Porsinna.

A Roman garden

We have no idea how he came to know Octavian. He must have become his trusted friend by 40 BC, for in that year Octavian asked him to negotiate his first marriage, to Scribonia, sister-in-law of the piratical Sextus Pompeius.

Maecenas showed his diplomatic skills in the same year when he helped to bring about the Peace of Brundisium between Antony and Octavian (see background section to chapter 38) and continued to act as a diplomat on Octavian's behalf throughout the next decade. As you will see in the next chapter, he again tried to bring about peace between Octavian and Antony in 38 BC. Horace says that it was his custom to reconcile quarrelling friends.

But it was not just in personal relationships that he proved helpful to Octavian. He was a shrewd statesman and a resolute leader, and when Octavian went abroad, he left Maecenas behind as his substitute to administer not only Rome but the whole of Italy. He performed this task well. Octavian valued his advice highly, and it is said that it was Maecenas who advised him not to restore the republic but to keep power in his own hands. Maecenas had learned the lesson that the republic could no longer exist without the constant danger of civil war.

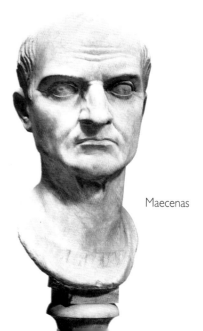

Maecenas

The services to Octavian which we have mentioned make it clear that he was a remarkable man. And yet it is not for these reasons that his name is still so famous. When we call someone a 'Maecenas', we mean he is a great patron of the arts, and that Maecenas undoubtedly was. He gathered around himself some of the most talented poets the world has ever known. He encouraged and fostered the genius of such men as Virgil and Horace, and helped to bring out their gifts, but he also tactfully persuaded them to write in support of Octavian and to suggest that he was bringing a new Golden Age to Rome.

Octavian too was very interested in literature. He was a friend of the poets of Maecenas' circle, he carefully wrote out his own speeches and letters, and he produced many works in prose and some in verse. He frequently attended poetry readings.

Maecenas was an extremely wealthy man. He had a splendid house high on the Esquiline hill. His tastes were wildly extravagant. He delighted in silks, gems and perfumes – and good food: he tried to introduce the flesh of young donkeys onto Roman menus! He loved the theatre and the ballet, wrote bad verses and introduced heated swimming baths to Rome.

His civilizing influence was remarkable. The story goes that

The auditorium of Maecenas

Octavian was once sitting on the tribunal (a public platform) sentencing numbers of people to death. Maecenas was present but could not get near him because of the crowd. So he wrote upon his tablets, 'Get up, you killer' and threw them into Octavian's lap. Octavian immediately left the judgement seat.

Octavian started work on a tragedy about the Greek hero Ajax, who committed suicide by falling on his sword. When asked how he was getting on with the play, he replied, 'Ajax has wiped himself out on my sponge.' What do you think he meant by that?

Maecenas has been called Octavian's Minister of Propaganda. What do you understand by 'propaganda', and do you think Maecenas deserved the title?

Maecēnās Quīntum rogāvit num iter Brundisium
sēcum facere vellet. 'sī festīnābis,' inquit, 'cum
Vergiliō proficīscī poteris.'

Quīntus cognōvit Vergilium iam Brundisium
profectum esse. sī mātūrius (*earlier*) vēnisset, iter
cum Vergiliō fēcisset.

Quīntus Hēliodōrō dīxit, 'nē hodiē proficīscāmur.
sī crās profectī erimus, Arīciam merīdiē
adveniēmus.'

Arīciam vespere advēnērunt. sī celerius
contendissent, merīdiē eō advēnissent.

Notice that in the conditional clauses of captions 1 and 3 the *indicative* is used, in those of captions 2
and 4 the *subjunctive*; how does this affect the meaning of these sentences?

Vocabulary 44

verbs

cantō, cantāre	I sing (of)
careō, carēre, caruī + abl.	I lack, am without
āvertō, āvertere, āvertī, āversum	I turn aside
discurrō, discurrere, discurrī, discursum	I run this way and that
revertō, revertere, revertī, reversum	I turn back
revertor, revertī, reversus sum	I return
comitor, comitārī, comitātus sum	I accompany

nouns

auctōritās, auctōritātis, f. influence, authority

imber, imbris, m. rain

mēns, mentis, f. mind

Oriēns, Orientis, m. the East

nīl = nihil

adjective

absēns, absentis absent

adverb

quidem indeed (emphasizing previous word)

conjunction

namque = nam

Quīntus iter Brundisium facit

diē quōdam Maecēnās Quīntō arcessītō dīxit, 'ego iter facere dēbeō
Brundisium. vīsne tū mē comitārī? Vergilius aderit aliīque amīcī. sī
tū statim proficīsceris cum Vergiliō, ego vōbīs Anxure occurram. **Anxure** at Anxur (see map)
nam tot negōtiīs occupātus sum ut hodiē proficīscī nōn possim.'

5   Quīntus ad Vergiliī aedēs festīnāvit sed cum advēnisset,
cognōvit eum aliīs cum amīcīs iam profectum esse. ad Hēliodōrum
igitur prōcessit; cognōverat enim eum quoque iter factūrum esse.
sed nisi festīnāvisset, sērō advēnisset; namque Hēliodōrum invēnit **sērō** too late

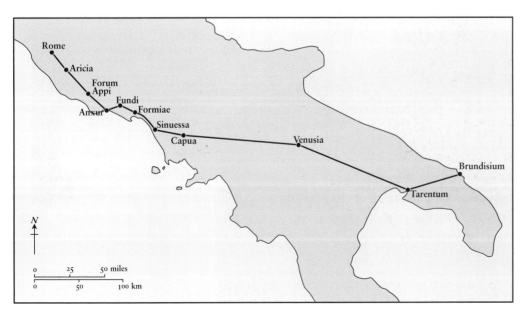

iter Brundisium

iam profectūrum. 'Hēliodōre,' inquit; 'paene merīdiēs est. sī statim
10 discēdāmus, nōn longē ante noctem prōgrediāmur. sī crās māne
profectī erimus, Arīciam merīdiē adveniēmus.' cōnstituērunt igitur
posterō diē proficīscī.

Rōmā igitur māne ēgressī Arīciam contendērunt noctemque in
hospitiō modicō mānsērunt. postrīdiē, cum Forum Appī
15 advēnissent, viās invēnērunt nautīs differtās. Hēliodōrus 'cūr tot
nautae' inquit 'hūc illūc discurrunt? quid faciunt?' Quīntus 'sine
dubiō' inquit 'illī nautae lintrēs regunt per canālem.' ille 'quid dīcis,
Quīnte?' inquit; 'ubi est ille canālis? ego valdē fessus sum. sī
pedibus prōcēdēmus, labōre moriar. ad canālem festīnēmus. sī
20 lintrem cōnscendāmus, iter multō facilius faciāmus.' cōnstituērunt
igitur lintrem cōnscendere, ut dormīre possent dum mūla lintrem
per canālem traheret.

Horātius ipse iter sīc dēscrībit:

ēgressum magnā mē accēpit Arīcia Rōmā
25 hospitiō modicō: rhētor comes Hēliodōrus,
Graecōrum longē doctissimus; inde Forum Appī,
differtum nautīs . . . iam nox indūcere terrīs
umbrās et caelō diffundere signa parābat
. . . dum aes exigitur, dum mūla ligātur,
30 tōta abit hōra. malī culicēs rānaeque palūstrēs
āvertunt somnōs, absentem ut cantat amīcam
multā prōlūtus vappā nauta atque viātor
certātim: [tandem fessus dormīre viātor
incipit, ac missae pāstum retinācula mūlae
35 nauta piger saxō religat stertitque supīnus]
iamque diēs aderat, nīl cum prōcēdere lintrem
sentīmus, dōnec cerebrōsus prōsilit ūnus
ac mūlae nautaeque caput lumbōsque salignō
fuste dolat. quārtā vix dēmum expōnimur hōrā.

Arīciam . . . Forum Appī see map
hospitiō modicō a modest inn
differtās (+ abl.) packed with

lintrēs barges; **regunt** steer, guide
canālem canal

mūla mule

inde Forum Appī then (we walked)
  to Forum Appi
diffundere to scatter
signa the constellations
aes exigitur the fare is collected
ligātur is attached
culicēs mosquitoes
rānae palūstrēs marsh frogs
ut as, while
multā prōlūtus vappā plastered with
  lots of cheap wine
certātim in rivalry
missae pāstum sent to graze
retinācula . . . religat ties the reins
piger lazy
stertit supīnus snores lying on his
  back
cerebrōsus . . . ūnus one quick-
  tempered (passenger)
lumbōs backs
salignō fuste with a willow club
dolat whacks; **dēmum** at last

ad canalem festinemus

40 Quīntus, cum in terram expositus esset, 'hoc iter lentē quidem
cōnfēcimus, Hēliodōre,' inquit, 'sed facile. sī canālis longior esset,
ego in lintre māllem prōcēdere quam pedibus. nunc dēbēmus
Anxur labōriōsē ascendere.' Anxur, quod in summō colle saxīs
candidīs fulgentī situm est, lentē ascendērunt ubi Maecēnātī
45 occurrērunt. inde Sinuessam festīnāvērunt:

postera lūx oritur multō grātissima; namque
Plōtius et Varius Sinuessae Vergiliusque occurrunt.

longum iter atque labōriōsum eōs adhūc manēbat. modo viīs
pessimīs ūtēbantur, modo maximōs imbrēs patiēbantur. Hēliodōrus
50 labōre paene cōnfectus est; sī nōn adiūvisset eum Quīntus, ille
itinere dēstitisset. Venusiam praeteriērunt; Quīntus intrāvisset
domumque veterem vīsisset, sī nōn cognōvisset colōniam iam
advenīs plēnam esse amīcīsque carentem. tandem Brundisium
advēnērunt, portum maximum tōtīus Italiae.

lentē quidem slowly indeed

fulgentī shining

multō grātissima much the most
welcome

dēstitisset (+ abl.) he would have
given up; **advenīs** incomers, strangers

Respondē Latīnē

1 cūr Quīntus cum Vergiliō nōn profectus est?
2 quis erat Hēliodōrus?
3 quōmodo Quīntus Hēliodōrusque iter fēcērunt ā Forō Appī
   ad Anxur?
4 quibus occurrit Quīntus Sinuessae?
5 cūr Quīntus Venusiam nōn intrāvit?

The White Rocks, Anxur

Maecēnās Antōnium cum Octāviānō reconciliat

reconciliat reunites, reconciles

*Translate the first paragraph of the following passage; read the rest
until you understand it thoroughly, then summarize what it says in
your own words*

postrīdiē Quīntus Vergiliusque Maecēnātem ad portum comitātī
valēre iussērunt; ille 'valēte, amīcī,' inquit; 'grātiās vōbīs agō quod
iter mēcum hūc fēcistis; sī sōlus iter fēcissem, taediō periissem.
nunc eādem viā regredī dēbētis. nōlīte cessāre. sī statim
5 proficīscāminī, quīndecim diēbus Rōmam perveniātis.' haec locūtus
nāvem cōnscendit.

taediō from boredom

Maecēnās Athēnās nāvigāre dēbuit ut Antōniō convenīret.
Octāviānus enim eum Athēnās mīserat ut Antōnium, quī inimīcus
fiēbat, sibi reconciliāret. nisi Maecēnās rem summā arte gessisset,
10 reconciliātiōnem nōn effēcisset. tandem tamen Antōniō persuāsit ut
ad Italiam venīret Octāviānumque contrā Sextum Pompēium
adiuvāret.

summā arte with the greatest skill

15 mox tamen Antōnius, ad Orientem reversus, uxōrem suam Octāviam, Octāviānī sorōrem, in Italiam remīsit, Cleopātram, Aegyptī rēgīnam, in Syriam arcessīvit. Octāviānus, sorōre sīc contemptā, tantā īrā commōtus erat ut bellum in Antōnium īnferre cōnstituerit.

20 dum Antōnius cum Cleopātrā in Aegyptō cessat et rēs pūblicās neglegit, Octāviānus ad bellum sē parābat; tōtum populum Italiae sibi conciliābat atque auctōritātem suam paulātim augēbat. in diēs potentior fīēbat.

conciliābat won over
in diēs day by day

Translate the following sentences

1 sī sōlus iter fēcissem, taediō periissem.
2 sī statim proficīscāminī, quīndecim diēbus Rōmam perveniātis.
3 nisi Maecēnās rem summā arte gessisset, reconciliātiōnem nōn effēcisset.

TRAVEL

Quintus and Heliodorus set off along the queen of roads (*rēgīna viārum*), the Appian Way. This, the first of the great Roman roads, was planned by the blind Appius Claudius in 312 BC. Originally it went from Rome to Capua (132 Roman miles) but fifty or so years later it was extended to Brundisium (a further 234 miles). You can still walk down its first ten miles, passing by many family tombs as you go.

The Appian Way

In Horace's day, a network of major roads led to all parts of
Italy. It would soon grow to cover the vast expanse of the empire.
Roman legions – and Roman civilization – could move fast.
How did the Romans build their roads? First of all they established
a course for a section of the road. (In some places each of the
sections was a mile long.) Their roads are famous for their
straightness, especially in Britain and France. They took sightings
from one high place to another or, in wooded or flat country, they
lit fires, the smoke from which served as a guide to the surveyors.

Once they had marked out the course, they dug a trench about a
yard deep. Having beaten the earth hard flat, they crammed large
stones together at the bottom. They set a layer of pebbles,
sometimes binding them with cement on top of these; above the
pebbles they laid sand. The upper layer could now be set on these
firm foundations. If the road was not paved with stone, this might
consist of gravel or small flints. Much would depend on what
material was locally available.

A donkey-drawn vehicle

The surfacing was given a fairly steep camber (of up to one
foot in eight from the centre of the road to the edge) to assist
drainage, and the water would usually run off into ditches dug at
both sides. An embankment (*agger*) would be made where
necessary, for example if a road had to be raised above a marsh.
Roman roads were built to last – and last they did.

There were four ways of travelling by road. You walked. Or
you rode a horse or mule. Or you went in a wheeled vehicle. The
commonest of these, the four-wheeled *raeda*, was not particularly

A raeda

quick. On his journey to Brundisium, Quintus covered only twenty-four miles on the day when he took one. The *cisium*, a light two-wheeled vehicle drawn by two horses, was not so comfortable but went much faster. If you changed horses, you could try to beat the record of two hundred miles in twenty-four hours.*

The fourth and most comfortable means of tranport was the litter (*lectīca*), a portable couch with curtains carried by up to eight slaves. This was used mostly for short journeys in town. It was slung on straps which passed over the bearers' shoulders. The straps were easily detachable in case you wanted to beat an incompetent bearer! *Lectīcae* were so comfortable that they could be used as ambulances.

There were hotels on the main routes. Quintus had no difficulty in finding a smallish one (*modicum hospitium*) in Aricia. But the grasping hotel keepers whom he tells us he found in Forum Appi were typical of their kind. With any luck a friend of yours would live on or near the road and you could stay the night with him.

Land travel had its problems, but most Romans preferred it to a sea voyage. For one thing, in most ships it was only safe to sail on the Mediterranean between March and November, and Seneca complains vigorously about being sea-sick. Passengers would go to a harbor and ask if any ship was sailing to their destination or near by. They would have to be prepared to travel on deck since the smaller ships had cabin space only for the captain and his mate. Even if they had to wait for suitable winds before they set sail, once they were on the move they could travel extremely fast, up to 100 to 120 miles a day. It may have been this factor that caused Octavian to travel by sea whenever he could.

The speed of travel did not change much between Roman times and the nineteenth century when the steam engine was invented. You could travel by land no faster than a horse, and the roads in the Roman empire were better than those in Britain until Victorian times. It took Horace just under a fortnight of admittedly rather leisurely travel to get from Rome to Brundisium, a distance of some 340 miles. Now you can do this comfortably in a day. It took Cicero a day and two nights to sail from Corfu in Greece to Brundisium. The hydrofoil now takes three hours. Longer distances were formidable. It took Cicero the better part of three months to get from Rome to his province of Cilicia (southern Turkey). This journey today might take only two or three days by boat and car, or just a few hours by plane.

List the inventions which have made travel so much faster today. Do you think the world has gained or lost by the increasing speed and its consequences?

*A Roman mile (c. 1665 yards) is slightly shorter than our mile (1760 yards).

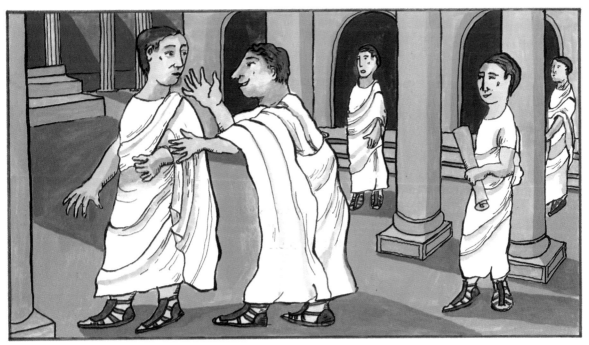

ībam forte Viā Sacrā . . .

Vocabulary 45

verbs

simulō, simulāre	I pretend
āiō (imperf. **āiēbam**)	I say
omittō, omittere, omīsī, omissum	I let go, neglect
arripiō, arripere, arripuī, arreptum	I snatch up
ēripiō, ēripere, ēripuī, ēreptum	I snatch away, rescue
meditor, meditārī, meditātus sum	I think about, meditate
persequor, persequī, persecūtus sum	I follow after, pursue

nouns

invidia, -ae, f.	envy, spite, malice
iūdicium, -ī, n.	law-court, judgement
aestās, aestātis, f.	summer
auris, auris, f.	ear
onus, oneris, n.	burden

adjectives

improbus, -a, -um	wicked, immoral, bad
intimus, -a, -um	innermost, closest

adverbs

iamdūdum	long ago
quōcumque	(to) wherever
tantum	only

pronoun

nescioquis, nescioquid	someone/something or other

conjunction

at	but

maecenas works for octavian agustus

poet loriate — "the poet"

Quīntus ā molestō quōdam vexātur

Chad villa - gifts for poetry — drived by recognition

intereā Quīntus Rōmae habitābat sorte contentus. officia in aerāriō	**molestō** a bore
dīligenter perficiēbat. tot carmina iam scrīpserat ut fāma eius lātius	**sorte** with his lot
ēmānāret. multī ingenium eius laudābant. paucī, invidiā adductī,	**ēmānāret** spread abroad
eum rōdēbant. aliī eum colēbant quod spērābant eum sē adiūtūrum	**rōdēbant** carped at him
esse. sīc aliquis eī dīceret, 'utinam in numerum amīcōrum *wish*	**dīceret** might say; **utinam** I wish!
Maecēnātis accipiar. tū intimus amīcus es eius. possīs igitur mē eī	
commendāre, sī velīs. age, vīsne mē ad eum dūcere?' Quīntus	
respondēre solēbat, 'ignōsce mihi, amīce. nōn ausim hominem vix	**ausim** I would dare
mihi nōtum Maecēnātī commendāre.'	

5

10   fābulam nārrat dē molestō quōdam quī spērābat Quīntum sē
Maecēnātī commendātūrum esse.

ablative absolute

ībam forte Viā Sacrā, sīcut meus est mōs,	
nescioquid meditāns nūgārum, tōtus in illīs.	**nescioquid . . . nūgārum** some nonsense or other
accurrit quīdam nōtus mihi nōmine tantum	**tōtus** wholly engrossed
arreptāque manū, 'quid agis, dulcissime rērum?'	**dulcissime rērum** my dear fellow (sweetest of things)

15

gen pl- partitive genitive

VOCATIVE

dulcis, dulce

adj superlative

The Via Sacra

trans Tiberim ibo

'suāviter, ut nunc est,' inquam, 'et cupiō omnia quae vīs.'
cum adsectārētur, 'num quid vīs?' occupō. at ille
'nōris nōs,' inquit; 'doctī sumus.' hīc ego, 'plūris
hōc,' inquam, 'mihi eris.' miserē discēdere quaerēns,
20 īre modo ōcius, interdum cōnsistere, in aurem
dīcere nescioquid puerō, cum sūdor ad īmōs
mānāret tālōs. 'ō tē, Bōlāne, cerēbrī
fēlīcem!' āiēbam tacitus, cum quidlibet ille
garrīret, vīcōs, urbem laudāret. ut illī
25 nihil respondēbam, 'miserē cupis' inquit 'abīre.
iamdūdum videō; sed nīl agis; usque tenēbō;
persequar hinc quō nunc iter est tibi.' 'nīl opus est tē
circumagī: quendam volo vīsere nōn tibi nōtum:
trāns Tiberim longē cubat is, prope Caesaris hortōs.'
30 'nīl habeō quod agam et nōn sum piger: usque sequar tē.'
dēmittō auriculās, ut inīquae mentis asellus,
cum gravius dorsō subiit onus.

suāviter, ut nunc est very nicely at present (pleasantly as it is now)
adsectārētur he followed
occupō I break in, interrupt
nōris nōs (I want you) to get to know me; **hīc** here, at this point
plūris mihi . . . eris you will be worth more in my eyes
hōc because of this
īre . . . cōnsistere . . . dīcere I went . . . I stopped . . . I said
ōcius more quickly
puerō to his boy = to his slave
sūdor sweat
ad īmōs . . . tālōs to the bottom of my ankles; **mānāret** was flowing
ō tē . . . fēlīcem O Bolanus, lucky in your quick temper! (Bolanus was a man notorious for his quick temper)
quidlibet . . . garrīret was talking some nonsense or other
vīcōs the streets
nīl agis you're doing nothing = you're getting nowhere
usque the whole way
circumagī to be taken out of your way
cubat he is in bed (sick)
quod agam to do (which I must do)
piger lazy
auriculās my ears
inīquae mentis bad-tempered (of bad mind)
dorsō subiit descends on his back

iniquae mentis asellus

molestus ille, sīcut dīxerat, Quīntum usque persequēbātur.
Quīntus cōnātus est eum dīmittere sed nīl ēgit. puerō 'utinam
35 molestum hunc dīmittere possim,' inquit, 'sed ille usque mē tenet.
quid faciāmus? domum quam prīmum festīnēmus.' deinde ille
cōnābātur Quīntō persuādēre ut sē Maecēnātī commendāret. cum
Quīntus negāvisset sē hoc facere posse, 'nōn tibi crēdō,' inquit; 'ad
eum continuō eāmus. nōlim tālem occāsiōnem omittere.'

    nōlim I wouldn't want

40 eō ipsō tempore Quīntī amīcus quīdam eīs occurrit. Quīntus

    occāsiōnem opportunity

eum salūtāvit signumque dedit, oculōs distorquēns, ut sē ēriperet;

    distorquēns twisting, rolling

at ille, quī tōtam rem sēnsit, simulāvit sē nōn intellegere; Quīntum
valēre iussit; fūgit improbus Quīntumque relīquit in manibus
molestī.

45 Quīntus ad summam dēspērātiōnem adductus erat, cum molestī
adversārius quīdam ad eum accurrit magnāque vōce clāmāvit, 'quō

    adversārius adversary (at law)

īs, turpissime? venī in iūs.' in iūdicium eum rapuit. Quīntus 'sīc'

    turpissime you villain! (most base
    person)

inquit 'mē servāvit Apollō.'

Respondē Latīnē

1 quid spērābant multī eōrum quī Quīntum colēbant?
2 cūr Quīntus eōs Maecēnātī commendāre nōlēbat?
3 cum Quīntus amīcō signum dedisset ut sē ēriperet, quid fēcit
   amīcus ille?
4 quōmodo Quīntus tandem servātus est?

Quīntus urbis strepitum effugere cupit

    strepitum din, racket

*Translate the first paragraph of the following passage and answer
the questions below on the second*

Quīntus, sorte contentus, vītam modestam agēbat. virīs dīvitibus
potentibusque, quibus iam amīcus erat, nōn invidēbat. numquam
sibi dīcēbat, 'utinam genere nōbilī nātus essem; utinam senātor
essem!' nōbilēs enim semper negōtiīs officiīsque obstrictī erant,

    obstrictī tied up in

5 ipse ōtiō ita ūtēbātur ut carmina compōnere posset cūrīs solūtus.
illōs, cum per viās urbis ad negōtium quoddam festīnārent, semper
comitābātur turba clientium servōrumque; ipse sōlus incēdēbat
quōcumque īre volēbat. nōnnumquam ad tabernās ībat
quaerēbatque quantī essent holus ac fār; vespere Circum pererrābat

    quantī how much?

10 et Forum; adsistēbat dīvīnīs quae fortūnās praedīcēbant. inde

    holus ac fār cabbage(s) and flour
    adsistēbat (+ dat.) he stood by

domum sē referēbat ad cēnam modestam. deinde ībat dormītum,

    dīvīnīs the fortune-tellers

nōn sollicitus quod crās dēbēbat māne surgere. posterō diē in lectō

    sē referēbat he returned (took
    himself back)

iacēbat ad quārtam hōram; cum surrēxisset, aliquid aut legēbat aut
scrībēbat. 'haec est vīta' inquit 'solūtōrum miserā ambitiōne

    dormītum to bed

15 gravīque.'

    solūtōrum of men free from

sed quamquam contentus erat, strepitū fūmōque urbis saepe
vexābātur. saepe sibi dīcēbat, 'utinam in rūris tranquillitāte
habitārem! sic carmina facilius compōnere possem.' nōnnumquam

cum vēr adesset, amīcōs vocāvit et 'age,' inquit; 'urbis mē taedet; in
20 agrōs discēdāmus ut vēris amoenitāte fruāmur.' aliās 'calōrēs
aestātis' inquit 'ferre nōn possum. quid faciam? velim urbem
effugere rūrisque sōlitūdine gaudēre. in collēs festīnābō.'

mē taedet (+ gen.) I'm tired of
amoenitāte beauty
aliās at other times
calōrēs the heat(s)

ruris tranquillitas

1 What spoiled Quintus' content?   [3]
2 What did he wish, and why?   [4]
3 What did he say to his friends in spring?   [3]
4 Why did he want to escape the city in summer?   [2]
5 Translate the following phrases and explain the uses of
   the subjunctive:
   (a) **utinam habitārem!**
   (b) **discēdāmus**
   (c) **quid faciam?**
   (d) **velim effugere**   [8]
6 What do you learn about Quintus' character in this chapter? [4]

PATRONS AND CLIENTS

As we saw in chapter 23, a Roman who wanted to move up the
social scale had to attach himself to a man of some eminence. He
had in fact to become a client (*cliēns*) to a patron (*patrōnus*).

Soon after sunrise, during the first and second hours of the day,
the great men of Rome held a *salūtātiō*, a ceremony of greeting
when his clients would gather outside their patron's house eager to
be admitted. It was not altogether a one-sided affair since the
patron would gain prestige from the number of morning callers.

To begin with, the *salūtātiō* had been a meaningful business.
The client asked for advice and help from his patron, and the
patron planned political maneuvers and assessed the strength of his
backing with his clients. Later, however, it became a matter simply
of status, and callers were strictly graded.

Clients would often have to get up before daylight to make their
way through the filthy streets to their patron's house. Here they
would wait outside, hoping to give enough satisfaction at the
salūtātiō to receive at least the *sportula*, originally a 'little basket'

containing food but now a kind of dole, a gift in money of 25 asses
(6¼ sesterces), in the afternoon. They were forced to wear the toga,
that expensive form of dress so ludicrously unsuited to the Italian
climate. They were received with contempt by slaves whom they
often had to bribe, and they might fail even to speak to their patron,
as Seneca complains:

> How often will clients find themselves shoved out of the way
> because a patron is either asleep or amusing himself – or is just
> plain rude! How many patrons will inflict a long torture of
> waiting on their clients and then rush past them pretending to be
> in a great hurry! How many of them will avoid exiting through a
> hall crammed with clients and run off through a secret back-
> entrance – as if it were not more offensive to deceive them than
> to shut them out altogether! How many are still half-asleep with
> a stupefying hangover after the night before! Their poor clients
> have broken their own sleep to attend somebody else's, but the
> patrons can scarcely be bothered to raise their lips in an insolent
> yawn and only get the name right after it has been whispered to
> them a thousand times.

If clients did make contact with their patron, they might be
expected to escort him to the forum or the baths. And if they were
invited to dinner – an invitation, writes Juvenal, that only comes
once every two months or more – they were only too likely to be
placed apart from their patron and his real friends and served with
inferior food and drink: while he has mullet and lamprey, you have
eel and pike fed on sewage.

Yet the patron was uneasily aware that his clients did not
necessarily have any affection for him as a person. As Seneca
writes, 'None of them is interested in you, just in what he can get
out of you. It used to be friendship they were after; now it's plunder.
If a lonely old man changes his will, next day the callers will make
for another address.'

Exactly how widespread this degrading ritual was we cannot
know. Much of our evidence comes from the satirical poets Juvenal
and Martial, and satirists are in the business of exaggeration. It is
hard to believe that Maecenas expected Virgil or Horace to gyrate
on this merry-go-round of greetings. Certainly from their
perspective of more than a century later, the satirists looked back on
Maecenas as a model of what a patron should be. Martial writes, 'If
you have a Maecenas, you'll have Virgils too.'

---

*Write an imaginary account of a day in a client's life, making
as much use as possible of the information given in this
background section and in the chapter as a whole.*

*Can you think of any good aspects of the patron–client system?
Are there any similarities to this system in present-day society?*

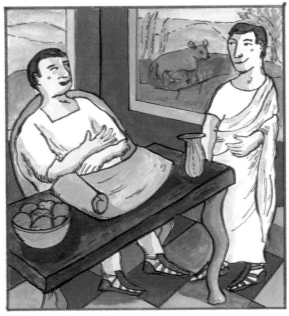

Maecēnās 'Quīnte,' inquit, 'sī crās ōtiōsus eris,
venī mēcum ad collēs Sabīnōs.'

nox iam vēnerat cum ad fundum tandem
advēnērunt. sī festīnāvissent, ante sōlis occāsum
advēnissent.

Maecēnās 'sī celerius equitāvissēmus,' inquit,
'tōtum fundum iam vidēre possēs.'
"would be able to see the whole farm"

posterō diē Maecēnās Quīntum valēre iussit; sī
ōtiōsus fuisset, cum Quīntō in fundō mānsisset.

fruor frui takes + abl.

Vocabulary 46

verbs		adjectives	
optō, optāre	I wish for, pray for		
mereō, merēre, meruī, meritum	I deserve, earn	amplus, -a, -um	large
		vīcīnus, -a, -um	near, neighboring
possideō, possidēre, possēdī, possessum	I possess	fidēlis, fidēle	faithful, loyal
fluō, fluere, fluxī, fluxum	I flow	lēnis, lēne	gentle
offerō, offerre, obtulī, oblātum	I offer	adverbs	
		aliquamdiū	for some time
nouns		simul	together
fundus, -ī, m.	farm		
taurus, -ī, m.	bull, ox	preposition	
vōtum, -ī, n.	vow, prayer	circā + acc.	around, about
frīgus, frīgoris, n.	cold		
mūnus, mūneris, n.	gift		
pecus, pecoris, n.	herd, flock		
seges, segetis, f.	corn crop		

Quīntus rūsticus fit

— degree of difference abl
poeta Laures

paucīs post mēnsibus Maecēnās Quīntum arcessīvit. Quīntus, cum
advēnisset, in tablīnum ductus est. Maecēnās sōlus erat. surrēxit
eīque arrīsit. 'Quīnte,' inquit, 'tē arcessīvī quod dōnum quoddam
tibi offerre velim. iam poēta īnsignis factus es. tibi opus est ōtiō, ut
5 carmina compōnere possīs fūmō strepitūque Rōmae remōtus. sī
domicilium rūre possideās, tranquillitāte fruī possīs. parvum
fundum igitur tibi dōnāre cōnstituī. trīgintā mīlia passuum urbe
abest, in collibus Sabīnīs situs. sī crās revēneris prīmā hōrā, eō
simul ībimus ut fundum īnspiciāmus.' (S)

10 Quīntus semper optāverat rūre habitāre sed vix spērābat sē
unquam fundum possessūrum esse. postrīdiē Maecēnās
Quīntusque prīmā hōrā profectī sunt ut fundum īnspicerent. in
collēs Sabīnōs prōgressī, tandem vallem Dīgentiae iniērunt et sī
festīnāvissent, ante noctem ad fundum advēnissent. sed lentē
15 equitābant, amoenitāte rūris gāvīsī. nox iam aderat cum
advēnērunt.

Quīntus attonitus erat; nam nōn fundus parvus erat, ut dīxerat
Maecēnās, sed rūs modicum. in latere collis vīlla sita est satis
ampla; octō servī aderant quī Quīntum cūrātūrī erant agrōsque
20 cultūrī. tēctō vīcīnus erat fōns aquae iūgis. locus amoenus erat,
prōspectus pulcherrimus. postrīdiē Maecēnās Quīntum circum
omnia dūxit, gāvīsus eum adeō dēlectātum esse.

dēnique 'Quīnte,' inquit, 'sī ōtiōsus essem, hīc manērem tēcum,
sed negōtiīs tam occupātus sum ut crās Rōmam redīre dēbeam. tibi
25 autem licet, sī vīs, hīc manēre.' ille adeō dēlectātus erat ut vix fārī

velim i would like to give you a certain gift.

pere

having been

have I summoned you b/c I would like to give you a certain gift.

you have been made an outstanding poet.

remove **domicilium** a house

smoke and noise in Rome

Dīgentiae of the river Digentia (where the villa lay)
amoenitāte . . . gāvīsī rejoicing in the beauty

rūs modicum a little estate

tēctō vīcīnus near to the house
iūgis ever-flowing
prōspectus the view

tibi . . . licet you may

plup.

Horace's Sabine farm

posset. 'amīce cārissime,' inquit, 'numquam poterō tibi grātiās
dignās reddere. mihi dedistī id quod maximē optāvī.' Maecēnās eī
arrīsit; 'Quīnte,' inquit, 'omnia haec bene meruistī; amīcus fīdēlis
es ac modestus. nisi tē Rōmae retinēre cupīvissem, fundum tibi
30 iamdūdum dedissem.'

posterō diē Quīntus, cum Maecēnātem valēre iussisset, omnia
iterum īnspexit; hortum ingressus sub arbore sēdit et hōs versūs
composuit:

hoc erat in vōtīs: modus agrī nōn ita magnus,
35 hortus ubi et, tectō vīcīnus, iūgis aquae fōns
et paulum silvae super hīs foret. auctius atque
dī melius fēcēre. bene est. nīl amplius ōrō,
Māiā nāte, nisi ut propria haec mihi mūnera fāxīs.

modus agrī plot of land
hortus ubi . . . foret where there
   would be a garden
iūgis aquae of ever-flowing water
paulum silvae a little (of) woodland
auctius more generously
dī = deī (subject of **fēcēre** =
   fēcērunt)
nīl amplius nothing more
Māiā nāte son of Maia = Mercury,
   god of good luck
propria my own, i.e. permanent
fāxīs = faciās

Respondē Latīnē

1 cūr Maecēnās cōnstituit fundum Quīntō dōnāre?
2 cum ad fundum advēnissent, cūr attonitus erat Quīntus?
3 cūr dēbuit Maecēnās Rōmam statim redīre?
4 cum Quīntus Maecēnātī grātiās redderet, quid respondit
   Maecēnās?

Fōns Bandusiae

*Translate the first paragraph of the following passage. Study the
poem with the help of your teacher; when you have thoroughly
understood it, answer the questions below*

Quīntus surrēxit; vīlicum vocāvit et 'sī ōtiōsus es,' inquit, 'velim
fundum īnspicere.' ille eum dūxit prīmum ad vīnētum, deinde
ad olīvētum. dēnique, cum servōs aliquamdiū spectāvissent segetēs
metentēs, collem ascendērunt ad fontem. gelida aqua, splendidior

vīlicum farm manager
vīnētum vineyard
olīvētum olive grove
metentēs reaping; **gelida** cold

fons Bandusiae

5   vitrō, ē cavīs saxīs dēsiliēbat in lacūnam, unde rīvus lēnī murmure
in vallem fluēbat. super fontem erat īlex alta quae umbram grātam
praebēbat et hominibus et pecoribus. hōc locō Quīntus valdē
dēlectātus est. ad vīlicum versus, 'quam amoenus est hic locus!'
inquit; 'quod nōmen est huic fontī?' ille 'nōmen fontī' inquit 'est
10   Bandusia. placetne tibi?' Quīntus 'mihi valdē placet. hīc paulīsper
manēbō.'

    Quīntus in rīpā sedet; aquam spectat in lacūnam dēsilientem
caprōsque in umbrā īlicis iacentēs dum haedī in grāmine lūdunt.
amoenitāte locī excitātus, hoc carmen compōnit:

15   ō fōns Bandusiae, splendidior vitrō,
      dulcī digne merō nōn sine flōribus,
        crās dōnāberis haedō,
          cui frōns turgida cornibus

     prīmīs et Venerem et proelia dēstinat;
20   frūstrā: nam gelidōs īnficiet tibi
        rubrō sanguine rīvōs
          lascīvī subolēs gregis.

     tē flagrantis atrōx hōra Canīculae
     nescit tangere, tū frīgus amābile
25   fessīs vōmere taurīs
          praebēs et pecorī vagō.

     fīēs nōbilium tū quoque fontium,
     mē dīcente cavīs impositam īlicem
        saxīs, unde loquācēs
30   lymphae dēsiliunt tuae.

splendidior vitrō more sparkling than glass; **cavīs** hollow
dēsiliēbat was leaping down
lacūnam pool; **rīvus** stream
īlex (f.) holm oak
quam amoenus how delightful!
caprōs goats; **haedī** kids
crās tomorrow (when there will be a festival in honor of the spring; springs were sacred)
dōnāberis you will be presented with, offered
cui ... prīmīs whose forehead, swelling with its first horns
et Venerem ... dēstinat marks him out for both love and battles = battles of love (goats were notoriously lustful)
īnficiet will stain; **rubrō** red
lascīvī subolēs gregis the child of the playful herd
tē ... tū ... tū Horace invokes the spring
flagrantis ... Canīculae the cruel hour of of the burning Dogstar (the Dogstar rose in late July)
nescit tangere knows not how to touch = cannot touch
amābile welcome to
fessīs vōmere worn out by (tired from) the plough
pecorī vagō the wandering herd
nōbilium ... fontium (one of) the famous springs
loquācēs chattering
lymphae water(s)

1 Describe in your own words the scene Quintus is watching as he composes this poem.

2 What offerings will the spring be given at tomorrow's festival?

3 **frūstrā**: what is the effect of this word in this position?

4 The water is described as **splendidior vitrō** (line 15); what is going to happen to it tomorrow?

5 What seems to be Horace's attitude to the kid?

6 Why was the shade **amābile** to oxen and herds?

7 Horace says the **fōns Bandusiae** will become one of the famous springs (like Castalia, for instance); how will this come about?

8 What do you think the poem is about apart from the spring itself? Is it simply a descriptive nature poem or has it some other dimensions?

HOUSES

We have already taken you to an *īnsula*, one of those squalid, overcrowded tenements where most people had to live in Roman cities. Not surprisingly, the rich lived in very different surroundings.

The wealthy Roman's town house became a by-word for luxury, but to begin with its design had been based on the first Roman dwellings. These were humble one-roomed huts with a hole in the middle of the roof to let in the light and let out the smoke. The chief room of the later houses was called the *ātrium*, the black (i.e. sooty) room.

In earlier days the *ātrium* was the centre of a family's life. Here they ate, and the women spun and did their weaving. Here the family strong-box stood, and the *larārium*, the home of the household gods. The *ātrium* roof sloped downwards and inwards to a rectangular hole (the *compluvium*). There was a pool (the *impluvium*) beneath this to catch the rain and supply the household with water. The room would be pleasantly shady and cool. When darkness fell, it was lit by oil lamps, often on tall bronze stands. Charcoal braziers of bronze, iron or terracotta provided the heat when necessary.

This simple form of house developed into the slightly more elaborate arrangement shown in the House of Sallust at Pompeii (see Plan 1). No two Roman houses were quite the same, but this one is fairly characteristic of its time. Soon, however, the spread of Greek ideas transformed the Italian house. A whole new section was added at the back. This consisted of a pillared courtyard (the *peristȳlium*) enclosing a garden and surrounded by further rooms. Olives, lemons, pomegranates, walnuts, chestnuts and vines, as well as large trees and vegetables, grew in the garden, which contained impressive statues (see Plan 2 for a house of this kind).

A peristylium

There was also the *tablīnum*, a kind of reception room or study for the master of the house between the *ātrium* and the *peristȳlium*.

The *peristȳlium* area came to be the private part of the house and the statues of the gods moved back here with the family. The *ātrium* became comparatively unimportant and in some country houses ceased to exist altogether.

The outside of Roman houses tended to be dull, even forbidding, since they did not look outwards onto the street but inwards onto their beautiful gardens. But the standard of interior decoration was extremely high, with fine frescoes, stucco and mosaics. (Plan 3 brings together all the usual features of the layout of a Roman house.)

The Romans had a deep love of landscape. The country villas of the extremely rich would break away from the normal pattern, with terraces and garden rooms designed to face outwards towards the view. The seaside pleasure villas around the Bay of Naples, the playground of the rich, were elaborately and extravagantly built to take full advantage of their situation. The luxury villas of the very wealthy, with their beautiful gardens and breathtaking views, were delightful and relaxing. A substantial villa has been excavated which may have been Horace's. It had twelve rooms, including a hall, two dining-rooms and a bath with a hypocaust (underground heating system). The walls still stand up to two feet high in places. It had a walled garden, covering about half an acre, which had a pool in the middle and a colonnade round the sides. The estate supported

A reconstruction of a luxury villa

five families and the farm was worked by eight slaves under the supervision of a farm manager (*vīlicus*). There is a spring which can be identified with the *fōns Bandusiae*, and a stream.

Most country villas, however, were working farms. When the owner visited from the city, he would have to fit in as well as he could. The *vīlla rūstica* at Boscoreale is characteristic of such buildings (see Plan 4). Here there were wine and oil presses and a threshing floor. The wine was taken from the presses to ferment in great vats (3 on the plan) which were open to the sun and air.

> *What room is there in the* vīlla rūstica *which you would expect to find in a normal house but cannot in our plans?*
>
> *Discuss some of the differences between the ways the very rich and the very poor lived in Italy. How far has the situation changed in the modern world? There is no need to limit the discussion to Italy.*

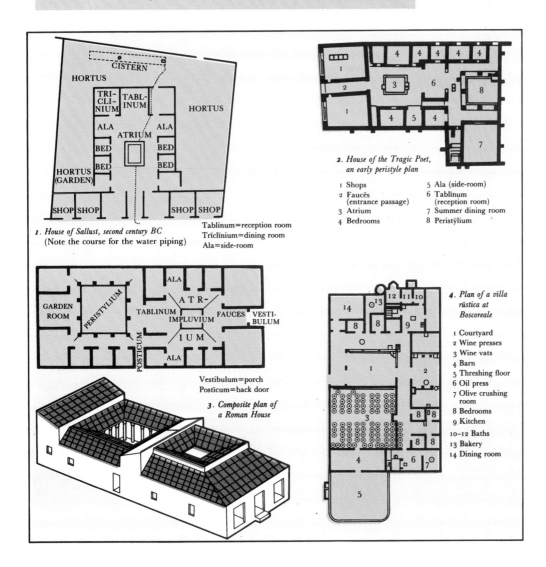

1. *House of Sallust, second century BC*
(Note the course for the water piping)

Tablīnum=reception room
Trīclinium=dining room
Ala=side-room

2. *House of the Tragic Poet, an early peristyle plan*

1 Shops
2 Faucēs (entrance passage)
3 Atrium
4 Bedrooms
5 Ala (side-room)
6 Tablīnum (reception room)
7 Summer dining room
8 Peristȳlium

Vestibulum=porch
Posticum=back door

3. *Composite plan of a Roman House*

4. *Plan of a vīlla rūstica at Boscoreale*

1 Courtyard
2 Wine presses
3 Wine vats
4 Barn
5 Threshing floor
6 Oil press
7 Olive crushing room
8 Bedrooms
9 Kitchen
10–12 Baths
13 Bakery
14 Dining room

Chapter 47 Actium

'Venus, mother of Aeneas, presenting him with arms forged by Vulcan', Nicholas Poussin

Vocabulary 47

verbs

accūsō, accūsāre	I accuse
collocō, collocāre	I place, position
equitō, equitāre	I ride (a horse)
putō, putāre	I think
obsideō, obsidēre, obsēdī, obsessum	I besiege
cōnfugiō, cōnfugere, cōnfūgī	I flee for refuge
trāiciō, trāicere, trāiēcī, trāiectum	I throw across
dominor, dominārī, dominātus sum + dat.	I am master of, I control

conjunction

autem	but

nouns

clēmentia, -ae, f.	mercy, clemency
morbus, -ī, m.	disease
odium, -ī, n.	hatred
classis, classis, f.	fleet
famēs, famis, f.	hunger
mulier, mulieris, f.	woman
scelus, sceleris, n.	crime
fluctus, -ūs, m.	wave

preposition

apud + acc.	at, in, at the house of, with

adverb

ōlim	once (in the past); some time (in the future)

Actium

dum Quīntus in fundō Sabīnō quiēscit, rēspūblica in bellum cīvīle
iterum rapiēbātur. Octāviānus Antōniusque, cum alter alterum
scelerum accūsāret gravissimōrum, plūs odiī inter sē in diēs
concipiēbant. tandem Octāviānus ad bellum apertē sē parāvit. tōta
5 Italia in verba eius iurāvit atque eum ducem bellī poposcit. eī
senātōrēs quī Antōniō favēbant Rōmā ēgressī ad Antōnium
cōnfūgērunt.

    Antōnius autem Octāviam, quam iamdūdum Rōmam remīserat,
repudiāvit et Cleopātram uxōrem suam esse prōnūntiāvit. quae
10 cum cognōvissent senātōrēs, statim bellum Cleopātrae indīxērunt.

    Antōnius sine morā plūrimās cōpiās collectās ad Graeciam
dūxit ut Octāviānō occurreret. Octāviānus autem, Maecēnāte
Rōmae relictō quī Italiam administrāret, Brundisium profectus est
cum Agrippā, quī optimus erat ducum suōrum. cum cōpiās trāns
15 mare in Graeciam trāiēcisset, castra apud Actium collocāvit haud
procul ab Antōniī castrīs.

cum since; **alter alterum** the one the
  other, i.e. each other

concipiēbant harbored, felt

in verba eius iurāvit swore
  allegiance to him

repudiāvit divorced

indīxērunt declared

trāiēcisset had taken across,
  transported

Actium

Agrippa, proeliō cum Antōniī classe commissō, hostēs ita vīcit
ut marī dominārētur. Antōnius, cum mīlitēs eius terrā marīque
obsessī et famē et morbō morerentur, tandem ērumpere coāctus
20 est. legiōnibus ūndēvīgintī in lītore relictīs ut castra dēfenderent,
classem ē portū dūxit, Cleopātrā sequente.

    quattuor diēs tantae tempestātēs erant ut proelium committere
nōn possent. quīntō diē, cum mare esset tranquillum, classis
utraque ad proelium prōdiit. diū aequō Marte pugnābant, cum
25 subitō Cleopātra nāvem suam vertit classemque Aegyptiam in
fugam dūxit. quae cum vīdisset, Antōnius gubernātōrī suō

ērumpere to break out
ūndēvīgintī nineteen

aequō Marte on equal terms

gubernātōrī helmsman

A Roman warship from Actium

imperāvit ut rēgīnam sequerētur. tantō amōre Cleopātrae ardēbat ut honōrem suum salūtemque suōrum minōris aestimāret quam ūnam mulierem.

30   dum Antōnius cum Cleopātrā fugit, classis eius cōpiaeque pedestrēs, cum ā duce dēsertī essent, fortiter tamen hostibus restitērunt; sed tandem spē dēpositā Octāviānō sē dēdidērunt. ille captīvōs hūmānē tractāvit. putābat enim neque Antōnium nec Cleopātram sibi diūtius resistere posse; sē tōtum orbem terrārum
35 iam regere. clēmentiam igitur praebuit ita ut omnēs quī sē dēdiderant līberātōs in exercitum suum accēperit.

salūtem suōrum the safety of his men
minōris aestimāret valued less
cōpiae pedestrēs land forces
cum although

hūmānē tractāvit treated humanely

Respondē Latīnē

1 cūr rēspūblica in bellum cīvīle iterum lābēbātur?
2 cūr senātōrēs bellum Cleopātrae indīxērunt?
3 cūr Antōnius ā proeliō fūgit?
4 quōmodo Octāviānus captīvōs tractāvit?

Vergilius Actium proelium dēscrībit

With the help of your teacher read, understand and translate the following passage

hoc proelium, quō fātum imperiī Rōmānī dēcrētum est, Vergilius in Aenēide sīc dēscrībit:

dēcrētum est was decided

Gods fight alongside Roman soldiers in a sea battle

The scene is represented on a magic shield, which Vulcan had made for Aeneas; around this shield was engraved a series of scenes foreshowing the history of Rome, and in the center the battle of Actium, which decided the fate of the Roman empire.

   in mediō classēs aerātās, Actia bella,
   cernere erat, tōtumque īnstrūctō Marte vidērēs
5   fervere Leucātēn aurōque effulgere fluctūs.

classēs aerātās the bronze-beaked
  fleets (ancient warships had a bronze
  beak at the bows, which was used for
  ramming)

hinc Augustus agēns Italōs in proelia Caesar
cum patribus populōque, penātibus et magnīs dīs,
stāns celsā in puppī . . .
parte aliā ventīs et dīs Agrippa secundīs
arduus agmen agēns . . .
hinc ope barbaricā variīsque Antōnius armīs
Aegyptum vīrēsque Orientis et ultima sēcum
Bactra vehit, sequiturque (nefās) Aegyptia coniūnx.
ūnā omnēs ruere . . .

Here is Cecil Day Lewis' translation of the passage:

Centrally were displayed two fleets of bronze, engaged in
The battle of Actium; all about Cape Leucas you saw
Brisk movement of naval formations; the sea was a blaze of
    gold.
On one side Augustus Caesar, high on the poop, is leading
The Italians into battle, the Senate and People with him,
His home-gods and the great gods.
Elsewhere in the scene is Agrippa – the gods and the winds
    fight for him –
Prominent, leading his column . . .
On the other side, with barbaric wealth and motley equipment,
Is Antony . . .
Egypt, the powers of the Orient and uttermost Bactra
Sail with him; also – a shameful thing – his Egyptian wife.
The fleets are converging at full speed.

*How does Virgil convey the impression that this battle was the
culmination of a righteous war in which Rome defeated the forces
of barbarism?*

DIVORCE

Antony's divorce of Octavia had shattering historical consequences
but was nothing very exceptional in the Roman world. In Horace's
lifetime we frequently hear of senators who have married three or
four times, and women might have children by a succession of
husbands. One Vistilla had six different sons and one daughter by
six different fathers. (Four of the sons became consuls while the
daughter married an emperor.) At the age of fifty-seven Cicero
threw aside Terentia, his wife of twenty-three years, in order to
rebuild his finances by marrying the young and rich Publia.
Terentia bore this with apparent equanimity. She married again
twice and died aged more than a hundred.

 Just as it was extremely easy to get married – to live together as
man and wife was enough and you did not have to go through the

cernere erat it was possible to see
tōtum . . . Leucātēn Leucate is the
  promontory to the south of Actium;
  Vergil means the whole sea round
  Actium
īnstrūctō Marte with warships in
  formation (literally 'with Mars
  (= war) drawn up')
vidērēs you might see
fervere seething (literally 'to seethe')
effulgere gleaming
hinc on this side
Augustus . . . Caesar Octavian, who
  later took the name Augustus
cum patribus with the fathers of the
  state, i.e. the senators
penātibus et magnīs dīs (= deīs) the
  native gods of Rome and the great
  (Olympian) gods
celsā in puppī on the high poop
arduus high, i.e. he stands out
  prominently
agmen agēns leading his line (of
  ships)
hinc on that side
ope barbaricā with barbarian help,
  i.e. with the help of barbarians
Aegyptum . . . vehit carries
  (= brings) Egypt (= Egyptian forces)
vīrēs Orientis the strength of the East
ultima . . . Bactra Bactra is modern
  Afghanistan; it represents the Far East
(nefās) what wickedness!
ūnā . . . ruere are rushing together

elaborate wedding ceremony by which Horatia married Decimus (see Part II, chapter 30) – so it was very straightforward to get divorced. You could leave your partner without discussion or consent. It may have been conventional – and prudent – to give reasons for doing so but there was no legal necessity. When Caesar divorced his wife merely because Publius Clodius had disguised himself as a woman to participate in a religious gathering – the Bona Dea festival, at which she was present – he simply proclaimed, 'Caesar's wife must be above suspicion.' Earlier noblemen had divorced their wives for such frivolous reasons as being seen with a freedwoman, attending the games and even for appearing in public uncovered.

A Roman wedding scene

As for possessions, there was no such thing as joint marital property. If a wife was under the *manus* of her husband (*manus* = the power and protection of a male), everything she had was his. But most wives had exclusive rights to their own property, though they normally had to have a male *tūtor* (= guardian) to see to any legal contract that had to be made. By custom the wife would bring a dowry to her husband, but this normally had to be returned in the case of divorce. These factors might have led husbands to think twice about treating their wives too harshly.

In many ways women were disadvantaged in the Roman world. Yet no Roman woman – or man – found themselves under religious or legal constraints to remain together. Traumatic and costly divorce cases in the courts were not necessary. The financial issues were crystal clear. And there were no painful conflicts over custody of the children, who were automatically under their father's control. A woman could simply walk out of her marriage.

Yet, as we have seen, it was equally easy for her husband to tell her to go: *uxor, vāde forās* ('wife, leave the house'). If he did so, she would have to leave behind her marriage and her children. Even so, the Romans, with their remarkable ability for double-think, professed the ideal of fidelity and life-long commitment and, as inscriptions prove to us, many marriages did last till death.

Would you have preferred to have been a wife (or a husband) in the Roman world or today?

'If you were to find your wife in the act of adultery, you could freely kill her without a trial, whereas if you were to commit adultery, she would not dare lift a finger against you, nor would it be right.' What do you think of this statement, addressed to Roman men?

Bellum Alexandrinum

Cleopātra, verita nē in manūs Octāviānī incideret, mortem sibi cōnscīvit (*inflicted*).

Vocabulary 48

verbs

lateō, latēre, latuī	I lie hidden
comprehendō, comprehendere, comprehendī, comprehēnsum	I seize
dēmittō, dēmittere, dēmīsī, dēmissum	I send down, let down
īrāscor, īrāscī, īrātus sum + dat.	I become angry
suspicor, suspicārī, suspicātus sum	I suspect

nouns

dolus, -ī, m.	trick
triumphus, -ī, m.	triumph
venēnum, -ī, n.	poison
adulēscēns, adulēscentis, m.	young man
carcer, carceris, m.	prison
dēdecus, dēdecoris, n.	disgrace
serpēns, serpentis, m.	serpent
turris, turris, f.	tower

adjective

captīvus, -a, -um	captive

Bellum Alexandrīnum

Octāviānus, postquam Antōnius cum Cleopātrā in Aegyptum fūgit,
eōs lentissimē per Orientem secūtus est. proximō annō dum classis
Alexandrīam nāvigat, ipse exercitum per Syriam dūxit in
Aegyptum. Antōnius adeō dēspērābat ut nōn cōnātus sit Octāviānō
5 resistere Aegyptum ingredientī. proelia prope Alexandrīam terrā
marīque commissa sunt. Antōniī classis mediō in proeliō ad
Octāviānum trānsfūgit; in terrā exercitus eius facile victus est.

    tum dēmum Antōnius timēbat nē, sī in manūs hostium caderet,
captīvus Rōmam dūcerētur. armigerō 'utinam moriar' inquit
10 'antequam tāle dēdecus patiar. sed vereor nē Cleopātra ab hostibus
capiātur. ad urbem festīnēmus.' Alexandrīam regressō eī nūntiātum
est Cleopātram mortuam esse suā manū. quibus audītīs armigerō
suō imperāvit ut sē occīderet. ille autem, adulēscēns fīdēlis, gladiō
strictō nōn Antōnium sed sē ipsum occīdit. Antōnius adulēscentem
15 intuitus in terrā iacentem, 'bene fēcistī,' inquit; 'exemplum mihi
praebuistī. utinam nē ignāvior sim quam tū.' quō dictō gladium
suum strictum in ventrem pepulit.

    ad terram cecidit graviter vulnerātus sed nōndum mortuus. dum
ibi iacet, accurrit Cleopātrae scrība nūntiāvitque rēgīnam adhūc
20 vīvere. quō cognitō, Antōnius mīlitibus imperāvit ut sē ad
Cleopātram ferrent. illa in altā turre sē inclūserat, quam relinquere
nōlēbat, verita nē Octāviānō prōderētur. cum mīlitēs eō advēnissent
Antōnium ferentēs, servōs iussit fūnēs dē fenestrā dēmittere
Antōniumque ad sē tollere. sīc Antōnius in gremiō Cleopātrae
25 mortuus est.

    eō ipsō tempore nūntius advēnit ab Octāviānō missus quī
Cleopātrae persuādēret ut turre relictā sē dēderet. prōmīsit
Octāviānus sē eā ūsūrum esse summā hūmānitāte. illa autem eī nōn
crēdidit nec voluit turrem relinquere. timēbat enim nē Octāviānus
30 vellet sē captīvam per viās Rōmae dūcere. cum triumphum ageret;
quod dēdecus ferre nōn poterat.

trānsfūgit deserted
tum dēmum then at last

eī nūntiātum est it was announced to
  him
armigerō his armor bearer
gladiō strictō his sword having been
  drawn
ignāvior more cowardly
ventrem his belly

scrība secretary

fūnēs ropes; **fenestrā** window
in gremiō in the lap

quī . . . persuādēret to persuade

hūmānitāte kindness, humanity

Respondē Latīnē

1 cum Antōnius in proeliō victus esset, quid timēbat?
2 cum Antōnius armigerō imperāvisset ut sē occīderet, quid
    fēcit ille?
3 Antōniō vulnerātō, quid nūntiāvit scrība Cleopātrae?
4 quōmodo Antōnius ad Cleopātram lātus est?
5 cūr nōlēbat Cleopātra turrem relinquere?

Mors Cleopātrae

*Translate the first two paragraphs of the following passage; study
the verse with the help of your teacher*

Octāviānus, cum urbem Alexandrīam cēpisset, iterum cōnātus est

Cleopātrae persuādēre ut sē dēderet. cum Cleopātra nōluisset
turrem relinquere, dolō eam cēpit. nam dum Cleopātra cum nūntiō
ab Octāviānō missō colloquitur, duōs hominēs mīsit quī in turrem
5 ascenderent; quī scālā ad turrem admōtā per fenestram perrūpērunt
Cleopātramque comprehendērunt.

    Octāviānus Cleopātram captam summā dīligentiā custōdiēbat
veritus nē sē occīderet. illa tamen viam mortis invēnit. senex
quīdam carcerem ingressus custōdēs rogāvit ut sē ad rēgīnam
10 admitterent; dīxit sē dōnum aliquod Cleopātrae dare velle; eīs
ostendit calathum fīcīs plēnum iussitque eōs fīcōs gustāre. illī, nihil
suspicātī, senem ad rēgīnam admīsērunt. Cleopātra dōnō acceptō
senem dīmīsit.

dolō by a trick

scālā ladder; **fenestram** window

viam mortis a way to death

calathum basket; **fīcīs** figs
gustāre to taste

    cum sōla esset, calathum dīligenter īnspexit; sub fīcīs latēbant
duo parvī serpentēs. omnibus praeter duōs ancillās fīdēlēs dīmissīs,
vestīmenta pulcherrima induit omniaque īnsignia rēgālia. deinde
15 serpentēs ē calathō sublātōs ad pectora applicuit. venēnum in
corpus celeriter imbibit. sīc mortua est ultima rēgīna Aegyptī,
mulier et fōrmā pulcherrimā et animō superbō.

praeter (+ acc.) except
ancillās servants
īnsignia rēgālia royal insignia
applicuit applied to
imbibit imbibed, absorbed

Horace wrote an ode on the death of Cleopatra which begins as a
song of triumph in which he calls his fellow Romans to drink and
feast in celebration; but it ends in the following lines, expressing
admiration for her pride and courage

. . . quae generōsius
perīre quaerēns nec muliebriter
   expāvit ēnsem nec latentēs
      classe citā reparāvit ōrās;

5 ausa et iacentem vīsere rēgiam
vultū serēnō, fortis et asperās
   tractāre serpentēs, ut ātrum
      corpore combiberet venēnum,

quae i.e. Cleopatra
generōsius more nobly
muliebriter like a woman
expāvit feared, trembled at
ēnsem sword; **latentēs** hidden, secret
citā swift; **reparāvit** sought, fled to
ausa supply **est**; **et** even
rēgiam her palace
fortis . . . tractāre brave to handle,
  i.e. she had the courage to handle
ātrum black; **asperās** savage
combiberet drank down

dēlīberātā morte ferōcior,
10   saevīs Liburnīs scīlicet invidēns
      prīvāta dēdūcī superbō
         nōn humilis mulier triumphō.

A coin commemorating the capture of Egypt by Octavian

dēlīberātā morte ferocior fiercer as she had planned her death

saevīs Liburnīs . . . invidēns . . . dēdūcī begrudging the fierce Liburnian galleys that she should be led (the swift Liburnian galleys had been responsible for Octavian's victory at Actium; Cleopatra did not intend that they should have the additional satisfaction of capturing her so that she would form part of Octavian's triumphal procession)

scīlicet surely

prīvāta deprived (of her status as a queen)

nōn humilis not humble = extremely proud

CLEOPATRA

Cleopatra was born in 69 BC. She was to be the last ruler of Egypt descended from Alexander's general Ptolemy. She was lively, charming, intelligent, civilized and a brilliant linguist. Such a combination of qualities proved irresistible.

When she was fourteen, her elder sister seized the throne of Egypt from her father. The Roman army regained it for him, the sister was executed and Cleopatra was now joint heir to the kingdom. When she was seventeen, her father died and she succeeded to his throne together with her brother Ptolemy, who was only ten. They were forced to marry, following their family's custom, but they heartily detested each other. Cleopatra's brother's supporters drove her out of Egypt three years later.

She fled to Syria, gathered an army and returned to Egypt to regain her kingdom. Ptolemy's advisers made a bid for the good will of Julius Caesar, but when Caesar arrived in Alexandria, he quarrelled with them. He soon found himself besieged in the palace by the angry mob. Meanwhile Cleopatra, who wished to put her case to him in person, had herself smuggled to him rolled up in a carpet. Caesar was captivated by the enchanting queen who crawled from the bundle at his feet. They became lovers, he gave her back the throne of Egypt, and before long she bore him a child, known as Caesarion.

The next year (46 BC) Caesar, now back in Rome, summoned Cleopatra and Caesarion to the city and installed them in a villa near the Tiber. He went so far as to have a golden statue of her set up in the temple of Venus. But he did not divorce his wife, and when he was assassinated in 44 BC, Cleopatra found herself without a friend in Rome. She returned to Egypt.

Then in 41 BC Mark Antony called her to meet him at Tarsus (in Cilicia in modern Turkey). It was a fateful occasion, and

Shakespeare describes the magic of Cleopatra as she arrived on her elaborate barge:

> The barge she sat in, like a burnish'd throne,
> Burn'd on the water; the poop was beaten gold,
> Purple the sails, and so perfumed, that
> The winds were love-sick with them; the oars were silver,
> Which to the tune of flutes kept stroke, and made
> The water which they beat to follow faster,
> As amorous of their strokes. For her own person,
> It beggar'd all description; she did lie
> In her pavilion – cloth-of-gold of tissue –,
> O'er-picturing that Venus where we see
> The fancy outwork nature.

Once again Cleopatra must have felt herself close to real political power. She soon became Antony's mistress and they passed the winter in a round of wild parties and live ly pranks. She bore him twins, but it is impossible to say how deep their feelings were for each other at this stage. As we have seen, Antony returned to Italy in 40 BC and married Octavian's sister. Cleopatra did not see him again for nearly four years.

Cleopatra

However, in 37 BC Antony abandoned Octavia and renewed his affair with Cleopatra. He was certainly now passionately in love with her. They conducted a marriage ceremony – which had no validity under Roman law – and soon had a third child.

Antony, under the spell of Cleopatra, declared her and her son by Caesar not only rulers of Egypt and Cyprus but 'Queen of Queens' and 'King of Kings'. This may not have meant very much, but Octavian was quick to seize on such un-Roman acts as useful propaganda. Antony, he declared, was 'bewitched by that accursed Egyptian' and wanted to move the capital of the empire from Rome to Alexandria.

Public opinion in Italy rallied behind Octavian and late in 32 BC he declared war on Cleopatra. You have read the rest of the story earlier in Latin. Cleopatra died on the 10th of August at the age of thirty-nine. Octavian killed Caesarion. It was not safe to allow a possible rival to live.

> *It has been said that if Cleopatra's nose had been shorter, the whole history of the world would have been different. What do you think this means?*
>
> *Many people have thought that Antony threw away supreme power over the Roman world because of his love for Cleopatra. If this is true, do you feel that he made the right choice?*

Caesar Augustus

Augustus as priest

Vocabulary 49

verbs

cōnfīrmō, cōnfīrmāre	I strengthen, encourage
dēleō, dēlēre, dēlēvī, dēlētum	I destroy
cēdō, cēdere, cessī, cessum	I yield, give way to
restituō, restituere, restituī, restitūtum	I restore
adiciō, adicere, adiēcī, adiectum	I add to
minor, minārī, minātus sum + dat.	I threaten
assequor, assequī, assecūtus sum	I pursue, catch up, attain

impersonal verbs (see Grammar)

mē iuvat, iuvāre, iūvit (+ inf.)   it delights me = I like to
mihi licet, licēre, licuit (+ inf.)   it is allowed to me = I may
mē oportet, oportēre, oportuit (+ inf.)   it behoves me = I ought to
mihi placet, placēre, placuit (+ inf.)   it is pleasing to me = I decide
mē taedet, taedēre, taeduit (+ gen.)   it wearies me = I am tired of
mihi accidit, accidere, accidit (+ **ut**)   it happens to me

nouns			*pronoun*	
prōvincia, -ae, f.	province		**quis? quid?**	who? what?
exsilium, -ī, n.	exile		**quis, quid**	anyone, anything (after
saeculum, -ī, n.	generation, age			**sī, nisi, num, nē**)
aetās, aetātis, f.	(old) age			
gēns, gentis, f.	race, people		*adjectives*	
cōnsēnsus, -ūs, m.	agreement		**barbarus, -a, -um**	barbarian
fās (indecl.)	right		**ūniversī, -ae, -a**	all
nefās (indel.)	wrong		**validus, -a, - um**	strong

prepositions
ultrā + acc.   beyond
quasi   as if

Caesar Augustus

Antōniō et Cleopātrā mortuīs, Octāviānō placuit in Oriente morārī
ut rēs ibi compōneret. nisi haec fēcisset, sine dubiō bella
redintegrāta essent. prōvinciās igitur imperiī Rōmānī praesidiīs   **redintegrāta essent** would have been
validīs cōnfirmāvit; foedera cum rēgibus fīnitimīs fēcit, nē bella in   renewed
5 fīnibus imperiī fierent. tandem, omnibus rēbus compositīs, eī licuit   **fīnitimīs** neighboring
Rōmam redīre.

    senātus populusque eum summō gaudiō summīsque honōribus
accēpērunt. omnēs crēdēbant bella cōnfecta esse neque umquam
posteā cīvēs cum cīvibus pugnātūrōs esse. multī dīcēbant, 'hic vir,
10 alter Rōmulus, Rōmam dē integrō condidit; hic sōlus imperium   **dē integrō** afresh
nostrum servāvit; nōs oportet eum quasi deum colere.'

    illō tempore Octāviānus, sī rēx fierī voluisset, facile hoc
assecūtus esset; sed sciēbat nōmen rēgis populō Rōmānō odiō esse;   **assecūtus esset** would have attained
'rēgēs plūrimōs abhinc annōs expulimus,' inquit; 'nōn nunc nōs   this; **odiō esse** was hateful to
15 oportet rēgēs restituere.' cum omnium rērum iam potītus esset,   **potītus esset** (+ gen.) had won control
dīxit tamen in senātū sē velle rempūblicam restituere populōque   of
lībertātem reddere. multīs post annīs, cum aetāte prōvectus   **aetāte prōvectus** advanced in age
moritūrus esset, testāmentum ēdidit, in quō haec verba scrīpsit: 'in   **testāmentum ēdidit** published a will
cōnsulātū sextō et septimō, postquam bella cīvīlia exstīnxeram, per   **cōnsulātū sextō et septimō** 28/27 BC
20 cōnsēnsum ūniversōrum potītus omnium rērum, rempūblicam ex   **exstīnxeram** I had extinguished,
meā potestāte in senātūs populīque Rōmānī arbitrium trānstulī.'   ended
    senātōrēs eī plūrimās grātiās ēgerunt sed eum ōrāvērunt nē   **arbitrium** control
reīpūblicae dēesset nēve imperium dēpōneret. plūribus honōribus   **onerāvērunt** burdened him, heaped
eum onerāvērunt; inter alia cēnsuērunt ut nōmine Augustō   on him
25 appellārētur; quod nōmen adeō eum dēlectāvit ut ex eō tempore sē   **cēnsuērunt** voted

appellāret Caesarem Augustum. tandem precibus senātōrum cessit imperiumque accēpit quō plērāsque prōvinciās administrāret. numquam tamen sē imperātōrem appellābat sed prīncipem.

30   verbīs igitur rempūblicam restituit, rē vērā omnibus auctōritāte adeō praestābat ut potentiam semper augēret. plūrimī cīvium hunc statum rērum libenter accēpērunt; bellōrum enim omnēs taeduit et verēbantur nē, nisi ūnus Rōmam regeret, bella cīvīlia iterum fierent. sī quis nōbilium potentiam eius aegrē tulit, aut tacēbat, aut, sī tacēre nōn potuit, in exsilium recēdere eī licuit.

35   sed quamquam, bellīs cīvīlibus exstīnctīs, pācem populō Rōmānō reddiderat, Augustō ipsī nec pāce neque ōtiō ūtī licuit. nam bella multīs cum gentibus externīs suscipere necesse erat. ultrā fīnēs imperiī Rōmānī habitābant gentēs barbarae quae prōvinciīs semper minābantur. sēnsit imperium Rōmānum
40 numquam tūtum fore, nisi fīnēs ad flūmina Rhēnum Dānuviumque prōtulisset. ut haec efficeret, multōs annōs aut ipse aut aliī ducēs mīlitābant multāsque gentēs imperiō Rōmānō adiēcit.

     poētae semper canēbant Augustum et mare trānsitūrum esse ut gentēs Britanniae vinceret et exercitum in Parthōs ductūrum esse,
45 nē clādem ā Crassō acceptam relinqueret inultam. Augustō autem nōn placuit haec facere. numquam dēsiit pācem petere neque ūllum bellum iniit nisi pugnāre necesse erat. in Oriente foedus cum Parthīs fēcit. nūllam clādem accēpit nisi, cum senex esset, in Germāniā, ubi trēs legiōnēs duce Vārō in īnsidiās lāpsae omnīnō
50 dēlētae sunt. hanc clādem semper maerēbat Augustus, quī in somnō, ut dīcunt, saepe clāmābat, 'ō Vāre, legiōnēs redde!'

precibus . . . cessit gave in to the prayers of
imperium a command
imperātōrem emperor
prīncipem leading citizen
praestābat (+ dat.) he excelled

aegrē tulit could not bear

externīs foreign

fore = futūrum esse
Rhēnum the Rhine
Dānuvium the Danube

inultam unavenged

nisi except

maerēbat mourned

Respondē Latīnē

1 cūr Octāviānus in Oriente tam diū morātus est?
2 cum tandem Rōmam rediisset Octāviānus, quōmodo ā senātū populōque acceptus est?
3 cum Octāviānus potentiam suam semper augēret, quōmodo cīvēs hunc statum rērum accipiēbant?
4 cūr ipsī Augustō nōn licuit pāce ūtī?
5 cūr nōlēbat Augustus bellum in Britannōs Parthōsque īnferre?

Vergilius Augustum laudat

Translate the first paragraph of the following passage and study the verse passages with the help of your teacher

The breastplate of Augustus

ēloquentiam studiaque līberālia Augustum ā prīmā aetāte exercēre iuvābat. nōn modo et litterīs studuit et ipse poēmata scrīpsit, sed etiam poētās semper fovēbat, in prīmīs Vergilium, quem in numerō amīcōrum intimōrum habēbat; crēdēbat enim Vergilium sē
5 adiuvāre posse, sī novum statum rērum in carminibus laudāret.

studia līberālia liberal studies

fovēbat encouraged

Vergilius autem putābat omnēs bonōs oportēre Augustum laudāre, quod pācem Italiae tandem reddidisset; vīderat enim rempūblicam bellīs continuīs lacerātam, vīderat fās atque nefās versum, vīderat imperium Rōmānum paene in exitium adductum. sīc scrīpserat

10 cum bellum cīvīle adhūc saevīret:

... fās versum atque nefās: tot bella per orbem,
tam multae scelerum faciēs, nōn ūllus arātrō
dignus honōs, squālent abductīs arva colōnīs,
et curvae rigidum falcēs cōnflantur in ēnsem

15   ... saevit tōtō Mars impius orbe ...

nunc Vergilius crēdēbat Augustum sōlum pācem cōnservāre posse. in Aenēidos prīmō librō, Iuppiter, cum fātōrum arcāna Venerī aperit, dīcit Augustum ōlim saeculum aureum gentibus lātūrum esse pācemque tōtum per orbem terrārum restitūtūrum:

20 nāscētur pulchrā Trōiānus orīgine Caesar,
imperium Oceanō, fāmam quī terminet astrīs ...
aspera tum positīs mītēscent saecula bellīs:
dīrae ...
claudentur Bellī portae; Furor impius intus

25 saeva sedēns super arma ...
        ... fremet horridus ōre cruentō.

CAESAR AUGUSTUS

When Octavian returned from the East in 29 BC the undisputed master of the Roman world, he stopped at Atella near Naples on his way to Rome. It was here that Virgil read him the four books of the *Georgics*, with Maecenas taking over when his voice gave out.

In the great passage from the first book of this poem (we have quoted from it above), Virgil lamented the decades of civil strife which you have read so much of in this course. Warfare had taken the farmers from the land and made them soldiers, straightening their scythes into hard swords and choking the abandoned fields with weeds. Right and wrong were turned upside down and countless wars tore the world apart. Evil was everywhere rampant and impious Mars raged throughout the world. It was as if a driver had lost control of his horses and his chariot was hurtling him along to destruction.

Virgil here captures the desperation felt by his generation in these years of apparently endless slaughter of Roman by Roman. He brilliantly conveys the impression of a world on the brink of chaos. By the time he read these lines to Octavian, the Gates of War in the temple of Janus had been closed for the first time in more than two hundred years. Peace had now been established throughout the empire. To Virgil and his contemporaries it must have seemed almost too good to be true.

---

lacerātam torn to pieces

versum turned upside down

faciēs faces, types

arātrō for the plow

squālent are squalid, unkempt

arva (n. pl.) fields

curvae ... falcēs curved sickles

cōnflantur are beaten

rigidum ... in ēnsem into unbending sword(s)

Aenēidos of the *Aeneid*

arcāna (n. pl.) secrets

Caesar = Augustus (the Julian family, to which Augustus belonged through his adoption by Julius Caesar, claimed descent from Iulus, the son of Aeneas; and so 'he will be born a Trojan from a noble ancestry')

imperium ... astrīs (born) to bound his empire by the Ocean, his glory by the stars

aspera ... saecula the rough generations = the generations of violence

positīs laid aside

mītēscent will grow gentle

dīrae ... Bellī portae the gates of the temple of Janus were closed only when there was peace throughout the Roman empire; Augustus closed them in 29 BC, signifying the beginning of an era of peace

fremet shall growl; **cruentō** bloody

Soon the senate voted Octavian the name of Augustus (which means 'worthy of honor and reverence'). In 17 BC Horace wrote his *Carmen Saeculare*, ushering in a new Golden Age. Eight years later the Ara Pacis (the Altar of Peace) was dedicated on the banks of the Tiber. This magnificent sculptured monument shows not only the people of Italy with the family of Augustus in solemn procession, but also the Italian countryside restored to fertility in a new era. A contemporary poet called Ovid wrote:

> My poem leads us to the Altar of Peace . . .
> Peace, be present, your hair elegantly bound with the garland of Actium:
>   remain in gentleness throughout the world.
> Let us have no enemies: we shall gladly do without a reason for a triumph.
>   You, Peace, will bring our generals greater glory than war.
> Let soldiers carry arms only to keep arms in check,
>   and let the savage trumpet never be blown except in ceremonies.
> Let the ends of the earth shudder in fear of the descendants of Aeneas;
>   if any land does not fear Rome very much, then let it love her.
> Priests, add incense to the flames on the Altar of Peace
>   and let the white victim fall, its forehead stained with blood;
> and ask the gods, who are eager to grant pious prayers,
>   to make the house which guarantees peace, last in peace for ever.

The celebration is sincere. But Rome was no longer a republic. Augustus was called not *rēx* but *prīnceps* ('leading citizen'). However, total power lay in his hands and in his hands alone; and a dynasty had been established ('the house which guarantees peace'). A hundred years later Tacitus, the greatest of the Roman historians, wrote:

Augustus and Rome

> The state had been completely transformed. There was no trace anywhere of the old free Roman character. Equality no longer meant anything. Everyone was at the emperor's beck and call.

What do you think of Augustus? What aspects of his personality have come across to you?

Do you think that the establishment of peace compensated for the loss of liberty?

Would you rather live under a peaceful and well-ordered monarchy or dictatorship or a war-torn and disordered democracy?
If you prefer to live in a democracy, with political equality and freedom, what lessons can you learn from the fall of the Roman republic?

Chapter 50 Augustus Quīntum in amīcitiam suam accipit

Līvia ipsa suā manū lānam faciēbat; numquam dēerat in officia mātrōnae Rōmānae perficiendō.

Vocabulary 50

verbs

dēsīderō, dēsīderāre	I miss, long for
mūtō, mūtāre	I change
mīror, mīrārī, mīrātus sum	I wonder at, admire

nouns

causā + gen.	for the sake of
scrība, -ae, m.	secretary
dēsīderium, -ī, n.	longing

adjectives

maestus, -a, -um	sad
modestus, -a, -um	moderate, modest
praesēns, praesentis	present
similis, simile	like

Augustus Quīntum in amīcitiam suam accipit

Maecēnās Vergiliusque Quīntum Augustō commendāverant; mox ille quoque in numerum amīcōrum prīncipis receptus est, quī adeō eum dīligēbat ut eum scrībam suum facere vellet. epistolam enim ad Maecēnātem scrīpsit in quā haec dīcit: 'anteā ipse sufficiēbam scrībendō epistolās ad amīcōs: nunc occupātissimus et īnfirmus Horātium nostrum ā tē cupiō abdūcere. veniet ergō et nōs in epistolās scrībendō adiuvābit.'

5

sufficiēbam scrībendō I was sufficient for writing = I was capable of writing

A Roman secretary

Maecēnās Quīntō arcessītō dīxit quid vellet Augustus. 'tē
oportet' inquit 'prīncipī pārēre, sed nōn crēdō haec tibi placitūra
10 esse.' ille gaudēbat prīncipem adeō sibi cōnfīdere tantumque
honōrem sibi obtulisse, sed praesentem cursum vītae mūtāre nōluit.
cum Maecēnātis verba audīsset, 'cāre amīce,' inquit, 'sī prīncipī
pāream, nōn satis ōtiī habeam ad carmina compōnendum, neque
possim fundum revīsere meditandī causā. nōlim igitur haec facere.'

15 ille 'nōlī tē vexāre,' inquit; 'fortis estō. dīc eī tē tantō honōre
indignum esse; dīc tē nōn satis valēre ut tantum opus suscipiās.
scītō eum virum prūdentem esse et hūmānum; rem intelleget; nōn
tibi īrāscētur.'

Quīntus igitur prīncipī respondit sīcut Maecēnās monuerat. ille
20 excūsātiōnem eius aequō animō accēpit neque dēsiit eum in
numerō amīcōrum habēre.

Quīntus ad palātium saepe ībat carmina Augustō atque uxōrī
eius Līviae recitandī causā. mīrābātur quam modestē vīverent.
Līvia exemplum mātrōnae Rōmānae praebuit. mulier erat casta
25 virōque fīdēlis, fōrmā īnsignī et ingeniō acūtō; neque dēerat in
officia mātrōnae Rōmānae perficiendō; familiam ipsa regēbat;
lānam ipsa suā manū faciēbat. ab Augustō semper amābātur, quī in
hīs verbīs dēfēcit: 'Līvia, nostrī coniugiī memor vīve, et valē.'

meditandī causā to reflect

scītō know! be assured!

aequō animō with calm mind,
 patiently
palātium the palace (Augustus' house
 on the Palatine hill)
casta chaste

dēfēcit died; **coniugiī** of our marriage

Respondē Latīnē

1 quid facere volēbat Augustus?
2 cūr nōlēbat Quīntus haec accipere?
3 quid eum monuit Maecēnās?
4 cum Quīntus ad palātium īret,
  quid mīrābātur?
5 quōmodo Līvia exemplum
  mātrōnae Rōmānae praebuit?

Livia

Quīntus caelebs manet

Translate the first paragraph of the following passage. After studying the poem with the help of your teacher, answer the questions below it

caelebs bachelor

vixi puellis nuper idoneus

Quīntus ipse numquam uxōrem dūxerat; mālēbat mātrimōniō līber vīvere artem colendī causā. multās tamen puellās amāverat, ā multīs amātus erat, multa carmina scrīpserat amātōria. in hīs carminibus numquam amōre flagrāre vidētur, sed aut puellam aut 5 aliōs amātōrēs aut sē ipsum lēniter irrīdet. nam rēs hūmānās spectat quasi cōmoediam, quae rīsum potius excitāre dēbet quam lacrimās. saepe sī locum sēriō tractāre incēpit, trīstitiā expulsā in iocum rem vertit. cum carmen legere incipis, scīre nōn potes quō tē ductūrus sit. cum iam senior fieret, puellās sīc valēre iubet:

10   vīxī puellīs nūper idōneus
    et mīlitāvī nōn sine glōriā;
        nunc arma dēfunctumque bellō
            barbiton hic pariēs habēbit,

    laevum marīnae quī Veneris latus
15   custōdit. hīc, hīc pōnite lūcida
        fūnālia et vectēs et arcūs
            oppositīs foribus minācēs.

    ō quae beātam dīva tenēs Cyprum et
    Memphim carentem Sīthoniā nive,
20   rēgīna, sublīmī flagellō
            tange Chloēn semel arrogantem.

dūxerat (in mātrimōnium) had married
flagrāre to burn; **irrīdet** mocks
quasi cōmoediam as a comedy
potius rather; **sēriō** seriously
in iocum into a jest
puellīs . . . idōneus suitable for girls, i.e. a lad for the girls
dēfunctum bellō which has finished its warfare
barbiton (acc.) lyre (for serenading)
hic pariēs this wall (i.e. the wall of the temple of Venus, where he is hanging up his weapons)
laevum . . . latus the left-hand side
marīnae sea-born (Venus was born from the foam of the sea)
lūcida fūnālia shining torches
vectēs crowbars; **arcūs** bows
oppositīs . . . minācēs which threatened (threatening) closed doors
ō . . . Cyprum = ō dīva (goddess)
  quae Cyprum tenēs: Cyprus was

1 This poem is a dramatic monologue, that is to say Horace alone speaks but a scene is hinted at in which other actors take part. Using the hints provided by the poem, describe the scene he envisages and the action which takes place (note especially **hīc, hīc pōnite**; to whom is he speaking?)

2 When a soldier retired, he would dedicate his weapons to Mars by hanging them on the temple wall. To whom does Horace dedicate his weapons and what are these weapons?

3 How are we to suppose Horace used these weapons? What strikes you about the order in which they are listed?

4 The last verse shows a sudden change of direction. Explain what Horace means in ordinary words.

5 How seriously did Horace intend the reader to take this poem?

Venus' birthplace and a center of her worship

Memphim another center of Venus' worship, in Egypt, where the climate was very hot, free from the snow of the north (**Sīthoniā**)

sublīmī flagellō with uplifted whip (i.e. 'lift your whip and . . .')

Chloēn accusative of Chloe, the girl who has been proud (**arrogantem**) towards Horace

semel just once (take with **tange**)

VIXI PUELLIS

Read these two translations of *Vīxī puellīs*. Which of them strikes you as the better?

In love's wars I have long maintained
Good fighting trim and ever gained
    Some glory. Now my lyre
    And veteran sword retire.

And the left wall in the temple of
The sea-born deity of love
    Shall house them. Come, lay here,
    Lay down the soldier's gear –

The crowbar, the far-blazing torch,
The bow for forcing past the porch.
    Here is my last request:
    Goddess, ruler of the blest

Venus marina

Cyprus and Memphis, shrine that knows
No shiver of Sithonian snows,
    Whose whip bends proud girls' knees –
    One flick for Chloe, please.

James Michie (1965)

Paphos, in Cyprus, where Venus was born from the sea

Till now I have lived my life without complaints
from girls, and campaigned with my share of honours.
Now my armour and my lyre – its wars are over –
    will hang on this wall

which guards the left side of Venus
of the sea. Here, over here, lay down my bright torches,
the crowbars and the bows that threatened
    opposing doors.

O goddess, who rule the blessed isle of Cyprus,
and Memphis never touched by Sithonian snow,
lift high your whip, O Queen, and flick
    disdainful Chloe, just once.

            David West (1995)

mīrābar quidnam vīsissent māne Camēnae
ante meum stantēs sōle rubente torum.

quidnam why?; **Camēnae** the Muses; **torum** bed

Vocabulary 51

verbs

incitō, incitāre	I urge on, incite
doleō, dolēre, doluī, dolitum	I feel pain, suffer
recēdō, recēdere, recessī, recessum	I go back, retire

nouns

doctrīna, -ae, f.	teaching, doctrine
praeceptum, -ī, n.	advice, precept
sōlācium -ī, n.	comfort
precēs, precum f. pl.	prayers
voluptās, voluptātis, f.	pleasure
plausus, -ūs, m.	applause

pronoun

quisquis, quicquid	whoever, whatever

adjectives

hodiernus, -a, -um	today's
suprēmus, -a, -um	last, highest
tūtus, -a, -um	safe
mollis, molle	soft

adverbs

nōnnumquam	sometimes
semel, bis, ter	once, twice, three times

Maecēnās poētās fovet

Maecēnās Vergilium Horātiumque in numerō amīcōrum
intimōrum habēbat, sed aliōs quoque poētās fovēbat incitābatque
ad carmina compōnenda. interdum plērōsque amīcōrum domum
suam vocābat ad recitātiōnēs audiendās. inter aliōs Sextus
5   Propertius nōnnumquam hīs recitātiōnibus aderat, poēta ingeniō
fervidō, quī plūrima carmina ad puellam suam scrībēbat, Cynthiam
nōmine. Cynthiae diem nātālem sīc celebrat: dīcit Mūsās sōle
oriente sē vīsisse ut puellae diem nātālem eī memorent:

    mīrābar quidnam vīsissent māne Camēnae
10   ante meum stantēs sōle rubente torum.
    nātālis nostrae signum mīsēre puellae
      et manibus faustōs ter crepuēre sonōs.
    trānseat hic sine nūbe diēs, stent āëre ventī,
      pōnat et in siccō molliter unda minās.
15   aspiciam nūllōs hodiernā lūce dolentēs,
      et Niobae lacrimās supprimat ipse lapis . . .

interdum from time to time

fervidō burning, passionate
diem nātālem birthday
memorent bring to mind, remind of

rubente growing red
mīsēre = mīsērunt
faustōs . . . crepuēre sonōs clapped
  happy sounds
stent may they stand still
āëre in the air
siccō the dry shore
minās their threats
Niobae . . . lapis the stone of (= which
  was) Niobe (Niobe was turned to
  stone after Apollo and Artemis had
  killed her children, and ever
  afterwards wept continuously)
supprimat may she suppress, stop

The Muses

    poēta alter, Albius Tibullus, Horātiī erat amīcus, quī saepe dē
rēbus rūsticīs canēbat cursūque vītae ūtēbātur et negōtiīs et dīvitiīs
carentī.
20   Horātius epistolam ad eum scrīpsit cum in regiōnem Pedānam
recessisset ad carmina scrībenda philosophiaeque studendum; ille
Stōicōrum praecepta sequēbātur, quī dīcēbant virum sapientem
bonumque oportēre dē nihilō cūrāre nisi virtūte. Horātius autem ad
doctrīnam Epicūrī inclīnābātur, quī assevērābat summum bonum
25 hominibus esse voluptātem. Albius saepe trīstis erat et querulus. in
hāc epistolā Horātius cōnābātur eum cōnsōlārī, in animum
revocandō quot bona deī eī dedissent:

regiōnem Pedānam a district in
  Latium where Tibullus was born
inclīnābātur inclined to
assevērābat asserted that, maintained
  that . . .
summum bonum the highest good
querulus plaintive, querulous

Albī, nostrōrum sermōnum candide iūdex,
quid nunc tē dīcam facere in regiōne Pedānā?
30 scrībere quod Cassī Parmēnsis opuscula vincat,
an tacitum silvās inter rēptāre salūbrēs,
cūrantem quidquid dignum sapiente bonōque est?
nōn tū corpus erās sine pectore. dī tibi fōrmam,
dī tibi dīvitiās dedērunt artemque fruendī . . .
35 omnem crēde diem tibi dīlūxisse suprēmum.
grāta superveniet quae nōn spērābitur hōra.
mē pinguem et nitidum bene cūrātā cute vīsēs,
cum rīdēre volēs, Epicūrī dē grege porcum.

nostrōrum sermōnum of my *Satires*
candide iūdex honest critic
quid . . . dīcam? What am I to
say/think?
quod something which
Cassī Parmēnsis Cassius of Parma
was a minor poet
opuscula little works (poems)
rēptāre that you are strolling
salūbrēs health-giving
dīlūxisse has dawned
grāta superveniet . . . hōra the hour
(time) will supervene pleasing, i.e.
there will be an extra pleasure in the
time unexpectedly granted him
pinguem fat; **nitidum** sleek
bene cūrātā cute with my skin well
cared for = in good condition
dē grege porcum a pig from the sty

Epicuri de grege porcus

1 What sort of man was Tibullus, on the evidence of this poem?
2 What advice does Horace give to Tibullus?
3 How does Horace paint his own character? Why does he
describe himself as **Epicūrī dē grege porcum**?
4 If you had retired home to study philosophy, would you have
been pleased to get this letter?

Mors Vergiliī

Translate the following passage

tempus fugiēbat; et Quīntus et Vergilius iam seniōrēs erant.
Vergilius, quī numquam rēctē valuerat, iam saepe aegrōtābat. in
Graeciam tamen iter fēcit ad monumenta vīsenda. sed cum
Athēnās advēnisset, Augustō occurrit ab Oriente redeuntī, quī eī
5 persuāsit ut sēcum Rōmam redīret. in itinere morbō correptus
Brundisiī mortuus est. corpus eius Augustus ad Campāniam rettulit
cūrāvitque Neāpolī sepeliendum.
    Quīntus, cum Vergilius ad Graeciam profectūrus esset, carmen
scrīpserat in quō deōs ōrāvit ut Vergilium servārent. nāvem quae

rēctē valuerat had enjoyed good
health

corpus . . . cūrāvit . . . sepeliendum
arranged for his body to be buried
Neāpolī at Naples

10 eum ferēbat invocāvit:

> nāvis, quae tibi crēditum
> dēbēs Vergilium, fīnibus Atticīs
> reddās incolumem precor,
> et servēs animae dīmidium meae.

15 Vergilius ad fīnēs Atticōs incolumis advēnerat, sed precēs
Quīntī vānae fuerant. mortem amīcī cārissimī sine fīne lūgēbat.

invocāvit invoked, called on

crēditum dēbēs the ship owed
(**dēbēs**) Virgil to Horace because
Virgil had been entrusted (**crēditum**)
to it

fīnibus Atticīs the boundaries/shores
of Attica

animae dīmidium meae half of my
soul

The tomb of Virgil

THE ROMAN EMPIRE

When Cleopatra, the last of the Ptolemies, killed herself in 30 BC,
the Hellenistic era was finally over. The Greek civilization which
Alexander the Great and his heirs had spread around the eastern
Mediterranean – and far further to the east – still continued to
flourish, but it was now ruled by Romans. Their empire extended
from the Pillars of Hercules (the Straits of Gibraltar) in the west to
Cilicia and Syria in the east, from Gaul in the north to North
Africa and Egypt in the south.

A publicanus

The provinces of this vast empire were
administered by governors who had held
magistracies in Rome. Ex-consuls were allocated
more important provinces than ex-praetors. Their
authority was more or less unlimited, though any
Roman citizen had the right to appeal to Rome, a
right exercised most famously by St Paul.

What was it like to live in this empire? The
taxes levied were not excessive by the standards
of the time. But the system could be abused, and
the tax-gatherers (*pūblicānī*) were often hated
figures. In Asia they were the agents of the

equitēs of Rome, who fiercely resisted any attempts to protect the provincials from their extortionate demands.

Much depended on the decency and sense of honor of the governors. Some of them were notoriously rapacious. The most infamous vulture of all was Verres, the governor of Sicily who had begun his career of looting early: when on a governor's staff in Pamphylia, he had stolen a celebrated statue of a lyre-player from Aspendos. There would be many grasping staff accompanying the governor, only too eager to fleece the provincials. Yet a strong governor could keep his men under control. The poet Catullus applies a crudely abusive word to Caius Memmius whom he accompanied to the latter's province of Bithynia. Memmius made it impossible for him to come back a penny the richer.

Verres

Certainly many governors were prosecuted for extortion when they returned to Rome. Yet by then the damage to the provincials had been done. In any case an upper-class Roman jury could find itself reluctant to condemn one of their own number. And the punishment could be far from severe. The disgraced Verres fled from Rome before Cicero's onslaught in 70 BC, but he survived until 43 BC when Mark Antony had him eliminated so that he could get hold of his collection of Corinthian bronzes.

The benefits of peace, celebrated at Rome in the course of the following chapter, were shared by the provincials, but only at this stage of Roman history, a fairly late one in the acquisition of the empire. While the provinces had long been prevented from warring upon each other, it was Augustus who first planned a workable system of frontiers and ensured that they were adequately guarded. In the 30s BC he had eliminated piracy in the Mediterranean with enormous economic benefits to the whole empire, and it was he who finally brought to an end the civil wars which had sucked many provinces into the fighting – and into financing it. He took in hand the key provinces and insisted on higher and more consistent standards of government throughout the empire. Things continued to improve. A fascinating exchange of letters exists between the younger Pliny, governor of Bithynia in the second century AD, and the emperor Trajan who had sent him there. As he seeks Trajan's advice about engineering projects – should he dig a canal? – or civic ones – should he form a fire brigade? – or religious ones – what should he do about the Christians? – Pliny shows a high-minded and conscientious concern for the provincials in his charge. The historian Edward Gibbon remarks of this era:

> If man were called to fix the period in the history of the world during which the condition of the human race was most happy and prosperous, he would, without hesitation, name that which elapsed from the death of Domitian [AD 96] to the accession of Commodus [AD 161].

Yet this may well be too sunny a view. Without doubt the Romans showed remarkable toleration of local cultures, languages, law and – perhaps most surprisingly of all – religion. While they encouraged provincials to move into urban centers, they took no interest in or responsibility for their day-to-day life and they were left to administer and see to the upkeep of their own cities. Thus there was at least the appearance of freedom. But the historian Tacitus writes with pungent scorn of the corrupting effect of Romanization on the local culture of the British. It became, he felt, a symptom of enslavement:

> Even our manner of dress became a distinction, and togas were frequently worn. Gradually they turned aside to the kind of things that make vice appealing, meeting in porticoes, baths and stylish dinners. In their innocence they called this civilization when it was simply a part of their slavery.

But what were the alternatives? In a persuasive speech, King Agrippa urges the Jews not to rebel after the appalling brutality of Florus, the Roman governor of Judaea:

> Your present enthusiasm for liberty comes too late. You should have struggled not to lose that liberty in days gone by. For slavery is a harsh experience and it is right to strive to avoid it. But once a man has accepted the yoke, if he then strives to cast it off, he is simply a rebellious slave, not a lover of freedom. There was a time when you should have done everything in your power to keep out the Romans. That was when Pompey invaded this country. But our ancestors and their kings failed to do so . . .
>
> Look at the Athenians, who to preserve the liberty of the Greeks once gave their city to the flames. Before their pursuit the haughty Xerxes, who sailed over the land and trod the sea . . . fled on a single ship like a runaway slave. Those men who by tiny Salamis broke the immense might of Asia, are now slaves to the Romans, and the city that led Greece takes its orders from Italy . . .
>
> Some of you may think that you will fight the war under special conditions and that the Romans will show moderation when they beat you. On the contrary, they will make you an example to the rest of the world, they will burn the holy city to the ground and exterminate your race. Even the survivors will find no place of refuge, since everybody in the world has the Romans as their masters – or fears that they will have them.

Would you prefer to be free and uncivilized to being civilized but the subject of another nation?

The growth of the Roman empire

date of acquisition (BC)

241	Sicily (taken from Carthage after the First Punic War)	81	Cisalpine Gaul (Gaul this side of the Alps)
238	Sardinia and Corsica (seized from Carthage)	75–64	Bithynia, Pontus, Syria, Cyrene, Crete (after Rome's eastern campaigns)
201	Spain (taken from Carthage after the Third Punic War – not finally conquered until the time of Augustus)	58	Cyprus
		52	Transalpine Gaul extended to the English Channel (Caesar's conquests)
146	Greece (Macedonia and Achaea) (after armed intervention and the sack of Corinth)	46	Numidia
		30	Egypt (annexed by Augustus)
	North Africa (Carthage razed to the ground)	25	Galatia (annexed by Augustus)
		15	Raetia, Noricum (northern frontier of the empire finally extended to the Rhine and the Danube west of Vienna)
133–129	Asia (bequeathed to Rome by Attalus of Pergamum)		
121–120	Transalpine Gaul (Gaul across the Alps)	13–AD 9	Pannonia, Moesia (Roman control established up to the Danube from Switzerland to the Black Sea)
102	Cilicia	AD 6	Judaea

The Roman empire

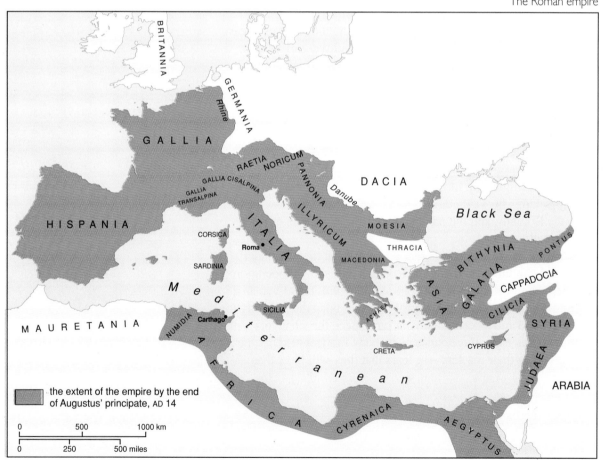

the extent of the empire by the end of Augustus' principate, AD 14

The Ara Pacis

Vocabulary 52

verbs

celebrō, celebrāre	I celebrate
ōrnō, ōrnāre	I adorn
appāreō, appārēre, appāruī, appāritum	I appear, am seen
precor, precārī, precātus sum	I pray

nouns

āra, -ae, f.	altar
modus, -ī, m.	way, kind, sort
omnī modō	in every way
initium, -ī, n.	beginning
sacrificium, -ī, n.	sacrifice
rēligiō, rēligiōnis, f.	reverence, piety

adjectives

aureus, -a, -um	golden
prīscus, -a, -um	old, old-fashioned
sānctus, -a, -um	holy
sapiēns, sapientis	wise

Pāx et prīnceps

omnibus bellīs tandem cōnfectīs, portae templī Iānī clausae erant,
quod significābat pācem esse tōtum per imperium Rōmānum.
Augustō igitur placuit novum saeculum cōnsecrāre lūdīs
saeculāribus celebrandīs. Quīntum ad sē vocāvit et 'Quīnte,' inquit,
5 'ut scīs, lūdōs sānctissimōs parāmus, quī novum saeculum
indūcant. omnia nōbīs facienda sunt ut haec summā rēligiōne
perficiāmus. cūrābō āram magnificam faciendam, in quā sculptōrēs
Pācis mūnera illūstrābunt. carmine quoque sacrō novum saeculum
celebrandum est. tibi, amīce cārissime, hoc carmen scrībendum
10 est.' Quīntus gaudēbat prīncipem ingeniō suō tantum cōnfīdere
domumque festīnāvit ad carmen meditandum.

quod significābat which
meant/signified that
lūdīs . . . celebrandīs by celebrating
the secular games

Carmen saeculāre

tandem vēnit tempus lūdōrum. trēs diēs tōtus populus Rōmānus
fēriās agēbat. lūdī summā rēligiōne summāque sānctitāte celebrātī
sunt. prīmō diē Augustus cum Agrippā sacrificia fēcit in monte
Capitōlīnō Iovī Optimō Maximō Iūnōnīque rēgīnae. tertiō diē
5 sacrificia Apollinī Diānaeque facta sunt in Palātīnō. eā nocte, cum
sacerdōs sacrificia rīte cōnfēcisset, chorus puerōrum puellārumque
carmen Horātiī cantāvit:

fēriās agēbat had a vacation

rīte duly

    Phoebe silvārumque potēns Diāna,
    lūcidum caelī decus, ō colendī
10   semper et cultī, date quae precāmur
      tempore sacrō,

Phoebe Apollo, the sun god
Diāna Apollo's sister, goddess of
hunting and the moon goddess
potēns (+ gen.) powerful over, ruling
lūcidum decus shining glory
ō colendī semper O ever to be
worshipped

Phoebus Apollo

quō Sibyllīnī monuēre versūs
virginēs lēctās puerōsque castōs
dīs, quibus septem placuēre collēs,
    dīcere carmen . . .

15

iam Fidēs et Pāx et Honōs Pudorque
prīscus et neglēcta redīre Virtūs
audet, appāretque beāta plēnō
    Cōpia cornū . . .

Sibyllīnī . . . versūs the Sibylline
Books were books of prophecies
(written in verse), consulted on key
occasions

monuēre = monuērunt, here
followed by accusative and infinitive
'warned (us) that maidens . . . should
sing (**dīcēre**) . . .'

lēctās chosen

Fidēs Faith, Loyalty (here personified
as a deity)

Cōpia Plenty

plēnō . . . cornū with her
full/overflowing horn (of
abundance); on the Ara Pacis Copia
is represented as pouring out plenty
from a vast horn

pleno Copia cornu

20   sīc Horātius novum saeculum celebrat, nōn modo pāce
celebrandā sed omnibus illīs virtūtibus prīscīs revocandīs, quibus
frētī Rōmānī urbem ab initiīs parvīs ad tantum imperium
prōtulerant. rēspūblica, bellīs exstīnctīs, iam saeculum aureum
initūra erat. haec tōtī populō Rōmānō celebranda erant.

quibus frētī relying on which

Respondē Latīnē

1 cūr clausae erant portae templī Iānī?
2 quid facere cōnstituit Augustus ut novum saeculum
    cōnsecrāret?
3 quandō carmen Horātiī cantātum est?
4 quās virtūtēs revocāvit Horātius in carmine suō? cūr eī placuit
    hās virtūtēs revocāre?

SOME GLIMPSES OF AUGUSTUS

Some hundred years after the death of Augustus, his biography was written by Suetonius, who was for some time the secretary to the emperor Hadrian and thus had the enormous advantage of access to the imperial archives. The following passages are excerpts from this biography.

Augustus

As Marcus Cicero escorted Gaius Caesar to the Capitol, he happened to tell his friends a dream he had had the night before. He had dreamed that a boy of noble features had been let down from the sky by a golden chain, had stood at the doors of the temple and been given a whip by Jupiter. Then he suddenly caught sight of Augustus who had been unknown to most people before his uncle Caesar had summoned him to the ceremony. 'That,' he said, 'is the very youth whose image appeared to me in my dream.'

When he was sixteen, after receiving his *toga virīlis*, he was awarded military prizes at Caesar's African triumph although he had been too young to take part in the war. Not much later, when his uncle went to Spain to fight against Pompey's sons, though he had only just recovered from a serious illness, he followed him with a tiny escort along roads held by the enemy, even suffering shipwreck, and won great favor with Caesar who quickly formed a high opinion of his character over and above the keen commitment with which he had made the journey.

When he joined with Antony and Lepidus in the Second Triumvirate, he finished the Philippi war, weakened with illness though he was, in two battles. In the first of these he was driven out of his camp and barely managed to escape to Antony's wing. He showed no moderation after the victory but sent Brutus' head to Rome to be thrown before the statue of Caesar and used violent language to the most distinguished captives, not even sparing them insulting taunts. For instance, when one of them asked humbly for burial, he is said to have replied, 'That will be up to the carrion birds!' When two others, a father and a son, begged for their lives, he is said to have ordered them to cast lots to decide which of them should be spared, and in fact to have seen both of them die since the father was killed because he had offered his own life for his son, and the latter then committed suicide.

There are many great illustrations of his mercy and moderation. It would be tedious if I were to give the full list of political enemies whom he not only pardoned but even allowed to hold high office.

If any cohorts broke in battle, he ordered every tenth man to be killed and fed the rest on barley instead of wheat.

Since the city was not adorned as befitted the grandeur of its empire and was liable to flooding and fires, he so improved it that he could justifiably boast that he had found it brick and left it marble.

For more than forty years he stayed in the same bedroom in his house on the Palatine hill both in winter and in summer. Although he found that the city was bad for his health in the winter, he continued to spend that season there. If ever he planned to do something on his own or without interruption, he had a private room at the top of his house which he called 'Syracuse' – Archimedes of Syracuse had had a similar study – or his 'little workshop'. He used to hide away here or in the house of one of his freedmen in the suburbs. However, if he fell ill, he would sleep at Maecenas' house.

One can tell how simple his furniture and household goods were from the couches and tables which still exist. Most of these are scarcely grand enough for a private citizen. They say that he always slept on a low bed with a plain covering.

He was a very light eater and generally ate plain food. He was particularly fond of coarse bread, tiny fishes, fresh hand-pressed cheese and green figs of the second crop. He would eat even before dinner, whenever and wherever he felt hungry. Here are some quotations from his own letters: 'I ate some bread and dates in my carriage' and 'While I was on my way back from King Numa's Palace in my litter, I ate an ounce of bread with a few hard-skinned grapes.'

He was also by nature a very abstemious drinker. The historian Cornelius writes that he never drank more than three units over dinner at Mutina. In later life, when he indulged himself more generously, he would not exceed a pint, or if he did, he would vomit it up.

He always wrote down his more important statements to individuals, even to his wife Livia, and read them out from a notebook. He was afraid that he would say either too much or too little if he spoke off the cuff.

On the last day of his life, he repeatedly asked whether talk of his illness was causing any public disturbance. Then he called for a mirror and ordered his hair to be combed and his sagging jaws to be set straight. Next he summoned his friends and asked them if they thought that he had played his part in the comedy of life with a good enough grace. And he added the tag:

> If I have pleased you kindly signify
> Appreciation with a warm goodbye.

How do you respond to the character of Augustus? Do these excerpts from Suetonius all seem to be about the same man? If not, does this puzzle you?

Quintus rusticus

fūmus strepitusque (*noise*) urbis Quīntō odiō erant.

cum ad fundum recesserat, ipse suā manū saxa ex agrīs movēbat.

sī multum pluēbat, vītēs (*vines*) eī summae cūrae erant.

ipse ūvās cum vīlicō (*farm manager*) carpēbat, quī magnō auxiliō eī erat.

Vocabulary 53

verbs

pōtō, pōtāre	I drink
peragō, peragere, perēgī, perāctum	I finish, accomplish
prōpōnō, prōpōnere, prōposuī, prōpositum	I put foward, propose, explain
polliceor, pollicērī, pollicitus sum	I promise
tueor, tuērī, tuitus sum	I protect

nouns

cor, cordis, n.	heart
hospes, hospitis, c.	host, guest
salūs, salūtis, f.	safety; greetings; health
sors, sortis, f.	lot, fate
ūsus, -ūs, m.	use

adjectives

ambō, ambae, ambō	both
modicus, -a, -um	moderate, small
nocturnus, -a, -um	nocturnal, at night

adverb

quid?	why?

Quīntus rūsticus

Quīntus, ut senior fīēbat, plūs temporis in fundō suō manēbat. nam negōtiōrum eum taeduit et strepitus fūmusque urbis eī odiō adhūc fīēbant. saepe cum in urbe manēret, sibi dīcēbat:

> ō rūs, quandō ego tē aspiciam? quandōque licēbit
> 5   nunc veterum librīs, nunc somnō et inertibus hōrīs,
>   dūcere sollicitae iūcunda oblīvia vītae?

per aestātem in collibus habitāre mālēbat, veritus nē aegrōtāret, sī Rōmae manēret. plūrimī enim febre corripiēbantur, sī calōrēs aestātis in urbe patiēbantur.

10   Quīntus igitur aestāte in fundō perāctā, cum vēnerat brūma, ad mare dēscendēbat et prope Neāpolim hiemābat. temperiēs enim illīus locī salūtī eius magnō ūsuī erat. vēre ineunte, cum flārent Zephyrī et prīma hirundō Italiam revīsisset, nūntium ad Maecēnātem mittēbat quī dīceret sē mox Rōmam reditūrum esse.

eī odiō . . . fīēbant were becoming hateful to him

veterum librīs by books of the ancient (authors)
inertibus hōrīs hours of laziness
dūcere to enjoy
oblīvia (n. pl.) forgetfulness
aegrōtāret he might fall ill
febre by fever; **calōrēs** the heat(s)
brūma winter
hiemābat he spent the winter
temperiēs the temperate climate
salūtī eius to his health
flārent were blowing
Zephyrī the Zephyrs (the west winds of spring); **hirundō** (nom.) swallow

The Bay of Naples

15 aestāte quādam, ad fundum suum Rōmā itūrus, Maecēnātī
pollicitus erat sē rūre quīnque diēs tantum mānsūrum esse; deinde
Rōmam regressum Maecēnātem revīsūrum. sed, cum ad fundum
advēnisset, tam contentus erat ut Rōmam redīre nōllet tōtumque
Sextīlem rūre manēret. epistola igitur ad Maecēnātem eī scrībenda
20 erat, quā cōnfitērētur sē mendācem fuisse; amīcum ōrat ut veniam
sibi det:

> quīnque diēs tibi pollicitus mē rūre futūrum,
> Sextīlem tōtum mendāx dēsīderor. atquī
> sī mē vīvere vīs sānum rēctēque valentem,
25 > quam mihi dās aegrō, dabis aegrōtāre timentī,
> Maecēnās, veniam . . .
> quodsī brūma nivēs Albānīs illinet agrīs,
> ad mare dēscendet vātēs tuus et sibi parcet
> contractusque leget; tē, dulcis amīce, revīset
30 > cum Zephyrīs, sī concēdēs, et hirundine prīmā.

Sextīlem August

quā cōnfitērētur to confess (by which
he might confess); **mendācem** a liar

dēsīderor I am missed, I am missing
atquī and yet
sānum sound, healthy
**quam . . . dabis . . . veniam = veniam
quam . . . das, dabis**
quodsī but if, but when; **nivēs** snows
illinet spreads; **vātēs tuus** your poet
contractus huddled up (because of the
cold); **concēdēs** you allow (me to)

ipse vinum faciebat

Quīntus, cum in fundō Sabīnō manēret, rē vērā rūsticus fīēbat.
servōs ēmīsit quī segetēs meterent. puerōs dēsignāvit quī ovēs
custōdīrent. ipse suā manū saxa ex agrīs movēbat, ipse ūvās
carpēbat vīnumque faciēbat. vīnum quod in suō fundō fēcerat
35 hospitibus offerēbat; sīc cum Maecēnātem ad cēnam vocāret, dīxit:

> vīle potābis modicīs Sabīnum
> cantharīs, Graecā quod ego ipse testā
> conditum lēvī . . .

sī rārō pluēbat, segetēs Quīntō cūrae erant; sī grandinēs in
40 vīnētum ruēbant, prō ūvīs timēbat. fundus enim eī tantopere cordī
erat ut semper laetus eum revīseret, semper trīstis esset cum
Rōmam redeundum esset.

quī . . . meterent to reap
dēsignāvit he appointed

vīle . . . Sabīnum cheap Sabine wine
modicīs . . . cantharīs from little cups
quod (wine) which
Graecā . . . testā conditum stored in
a Greek jar; **lēvī** I sealed

pluēbat it rained; **grandinēs** hailstones
vīnētum vineyard
tantopere cordī erat was so dear to
him

Respondē Latīnē

1 cūr mālēbat Quīntus in collibus manēre per aestātem?
2 quid faciēbat cum brūma vēnerat?
3 cūr Maecēnātī dīxit Quīntus sē mendācem fuisse?
4 quōmodo sē gerēbat Quīntus cum in fundō suō manēret?

Mūs rūsticus et mūs urbānus

Translate the following passage

tālī vītā plānē contentus erat neque aliīs invidēbat quī dītiōrēs sē
erant. fābulam nārrāvit quā nōs monēret nē nimium optārēmus. in
hāc fābulā rūsticō mūrī persuādētur ut amīcum urbānum vīsat
urbisque gaudia gustet:

5 . . . ōlim
rūsticus urbānum mūrem mūs paupere fertur
accēpisse cavō, veterem vetus hospes amīcum.

mūs rūsticus optima dē horreō paupere prōtulit quibus hospitem
superbum dēlectāret; ille ea fastīdiōsē accepta vix gustāvit.

10 tandem ūrbanus ad hunc 'quid tē iuvat' inquit, 'amīce,
praeruptī nemoris patientem vīvere dorsō?
vīs tū hominēs urbemque ferīs praepōnere silvīs?
carpe viam, mihi crēde, comes; terrestria quandō
mortālēs animās vīvunt sortīta, neque ūlla est
15 aut magnō aut parvō lētī fuga: quō, bone, circā,
dum licet, in rēbus iūcundīs vīve beātus;
vīve memor, quam sīs aevī brevis.' haec ubi dicta
agrestem pepulēre, domō levis exsilit; inde
ambō prōpositum peragunt iter, urbis aventēs
20 moenia nocturnī subrēpere.

mūs, mūris (m.) mouse
dītiōrēs richer
gustet taste
fertur is said
cavō in his hole
optima (n. pl.) his best (fare)
dē horreō from his store
fastīdiōsē disdainfully
gustāvit tasted
ad hunc (said) to him
quid tē iuvat? why does it please
  you? = why do you choose?
praeruptī nemoris . . . dorsō on the
  ridge of a steep wood
vīs tū . . . praepōnere won't you/
  wouldn't you prefer
carpe viam start the way, i.e. get
  going
comes as my companion, i.e. with me
terrestria quandō since earthly
  creatures
mortālēs animās . . . sortīta allotted
  mortal souls
lētī fuga escape from death
quō . . . circā therefore

mures Romani

media nox iam vēnerat cum domum dīvitem intrāvērunt. mūs
urbānus hospitem in lectō locāvit dapēsque magnificās eī prōpōnit:

ille cubāns gaudet mūtātā sorte . . .
. . . cum subitō ingēns
25 valvārum strepitus lectīs excussit utrumque.

currēbant per tōtum conclāve, territī; simul domus personuit
canibus.

. . . tum rūsticus 'haud mihi vītā
est opus hāc' ait et 'valeās: mē silva cavusque
30 tūtus ab īnsidiīs tenuī sōlābitur ervō.'

quam sīs aevī brevis of how short a
 life you are, i.e. how short-lived you
 are
pepulēre = pepulērunt drove, struck
levis exsilit leaps up light(ly)
prōpositum . . . iter their intended
 journey; aventēs longing
subrēpere to creep under
locāvit placed; dapēs (f. pl.) feast
cubāns reclining
valvārum strepitus the banging of
 the doors; excussit shook off
conclāve (n. acc.) dining-room
personuit echoed; valeās goodbye!
tenuī . . . ervō with a little vetch
sōlābitur will comfort me

THE TOWN MOUSE AND THE COUNTRY MOUSE

We here give the complete story of the town mouse and the
country mouse:

rusticus urbanum murem mus
paupere accipit cavo

Once upon a time
a country mouse is said to have welcomed to his humble hole
a mouse from the city – a friend and guest of long standing.
He was a rough fellow, who kept a tight hand on his savings,
though he didn't mind relaxing when it came to a party.
Anyhow, he drew freely on his store of vetch and long oats,
then brought a raisin in his mouth and bits of half-eaten bacon,
hoping, by varying the menu, to please his finicky guest.

The latter would barely touch each item with his dainty teeth,
while the master of the house, reclining on a couch of fresh
straw, ate coarse grain and darnel, avoiding the choicer dishes.
At last the townsman spoke: 'Look, old man, why on earth
do you want to eke out a living on a cliff edge in the woods?
You ought to give up this wild forest in favour of the city
and its social life. Come on back with me now: I mean it.
All earthly creatures have been given mortal souls;
large or small they have no means of escaping death.
So my dear chap, while there's still time, enjoy the good things
of life, and never forget your days are numbered.' His words
prodded the peasant into action. He hopped nimbly from his
house, and then the pair completed the journey, hurrying on
to creep within the city wall under cover of darkness.
Night had reached the middle of her journey across the heavens
when they made their way into a wealthy house. Covers steeped
in scarlet dye shimmered expensively on ivory couches,
and close by, piled in baskets, were several courses
left from a great dinner earlier on that evening.
Inviting the peasant to relax on the red material, the host
bustled about, like a waiter in a short jacket, serving
one course after another, not forgetting the house boy's
duty of testing everything he brought with a preliminary nibble.
The other was lying there, thoroughly enjoying his change of
  fortune
and playing the happy guest surrounded by good cheer,
when suddenly the doors crashed open and sent them scuttling
  from their places.
They dashed in fright down the long hall, their fear turning
to utter panic when they heard the sound of mastiffs baying
through the great house. Then the countryman said: 'This isn't
  the life
for me. Goodbye: my hole in the woods will keep me safe from
sudden attack, and simple vetch will assuage my hunger.'

(translation by Niall Rudd)

How is each of the two mice characterized? And how are the contrasts between the town and the country brought out in this passage? Would it be right to call the town mouse an Epicurean?

Introducing this story, Horace describes it as an 'old wives' tale'. What evidence is there that the story is told tongue-in-cheek? What is the point of this element of humor?

Can you think of any other authors who use stories about animals to point morals?

D·M
Q·HORATIO FLACCO
ANNOS VIXIT·LVII
MVLTIS·ILLE
BONIS·FLEBILIS
OCCIDIT

Vocabulary 54

verbs

aegrōtō, aegrōtāre	I am ill
volvō, volvere, volvī, volūtum	I roll, turn over
coepī, coepisse*	I began
meminī, meminisse* + gen. or acc.	I remember
ōdī, ōdisse*	I hate
oblīvīscor, oblīvīscī, oblītus sum + gen. or acc.	I forget

nouns

senecta, -ae, f.	old age
tumulus, -ī, m.	mound, tomb
opēs, opum, f. pl.	wealth
pietās, pietātis, f.	piety
pulvis, pulveris, m.	dust
quiēs, quiētis, f.	quiet
tellūs, tellūris, f.	land, earth
maiōrēs nostrī	our ancestors
vīs (acc. **vim**; abl. **vī**), f.	force, violence
aciēs, aciēī, f.	line of battle, battle

adjectives

cūnctus, -a, -um	all
frīgidus, -a, -um	cold
invīsus, -a, -um	hated
līberālis, līberāle	generous, liberal

conjunction

simul ac/atque	as soon as

* **coepī, meminī, ōdī**: these verbs are 'defective', i.e. they have no present forms:

meminī (perfect) = I remember
meminerō (future perfect) = I shall remember
memineram (pluperfect) = I remembered

Indomita mors

Quīntus, ut senior fīēbat, saepe trīstis erat; iam mors et ipsī et
amīcīs imminēre vidēbātur. in carmine quod ad amīcum quendam,
Postumum nōmine, scrīpsit haec dīxit:

eheu, fugācēs, Postume, Postume,
5   lābuntur annī nec pietas moram
        rūgīs et īnstantī senectae
            adferet indomitaeque mortī . . .

die quōdam, sub īlice sedēns super fontem Bandusiae, tempora
praeterita in animō volvere coeperat. amīcōs veterēs in animum
10 revocāvit; vīvōrum meminerat, quōrum Maecēnās iam aegrōtābat
Pompēiusque in vīllā marī vīcīnā senēscēbat; neque vērō
mortuōrum oblīvīscēbātur, Marcī Cicerōnis, quī cōnsul factus erat
ac prōcōnsul Asiae, Vergiliī, quī diem obierat Aenēide nōndum
cōnfectā, sorōris parentumque, quōs etiam nunc dēsīderābat,
15 amīcōrum multōrum quī in bellīs cīvīlibus perierant.
    vēr aderat; sōl fulgēbat; aura levis arborēs movēbat; aqua
frīgida lēnī murmure ē fonte fluēbat. omnia pulchra erant, omnia
quiētem ac tranquillitātem fovēbant. Quīntus tamen trīstis erat. id
carmen cōnficere cōnābātur quod multōs abhinc annōs dē reditū
20 vēris scrīpserat et dē gaudiīs quae vēr sēcum fert. nunc et senior
factus erat et sapientior. cognōverat omnia pulchra
celeriter praeterīre, vītam brevem esse, mortem ūniversōs
manēre, nēminem ex īnferīs redīre:

diffūgēre nivēs, redeunt iam grāmina campīs
25   arboribusque comae;
mūtat terra vicēs, et dēcrēscentia rīpās
        flūmina praetereunt.

Grātia cum Nymphīs geminīsque sorōribus audet
        dūcere nūda chorōs.
30 immortālia nē spērēs, monet annus et almum
        quae rapit hōra diem.

frīgora mītēscunt Zephyrīs, vēr prōterit aestās
        interitūra simul
pōmifer autumnus frūgēs effūderit, et mox
35   brūma recurrit iners.

damna tamen celerēs reparant caelestia lūnae:
        nōs ubi dēcidimus
quō pater Aenēās, quō Tullus dīves et Ancus,
        pulvis et umbra sumus.

The three Graces

pulvis et umbra sumus

40   quis scit an adiciant hodiernae crāstina summae
        tempora dī superī?
    cūncta manūs avidās fugient hērēdis, amīcō
        quae dederis animō.

    cum semel occideris et dē tē splendida Mīnōs
45   fēcerit arbitria,
    nōn, Torquāte, genus, nōn tē fācundia, nōn tē
        restituet pietās.

    īnfernīs neque enim tenebrīs Diāna pudīcum
        līberat Hippolytum,
50   nec Lēthaea valet Thēseus abrumpere cārō
        vincula Pērithoō.

    carmen cōnfēcerat; surrēxit et in vīllam lentē rediit. vix līmen trānsierat cum vīlicus lacrimīs per genās cadentibus ad eum accurrit. 'domine,' inquit, 'nūntium trīstissimum accēpī: mortuus
55 est Maecēnās.' Quīntus, quamquam diū cognōverat Maecēnātem graviter aegrōtāre, angōre perculsus est. tacitus tablīnum intrāvit amīcumque intimum, quī eum totiēns adiūverat, quī semper benignus fuerat, semper līberālis, diū sōlus lūgēbat. posteā cognōvit Maecēnātem in testāmentō suō ad Augustum hoc
60 scrīpsisse: 'Horātiī Flaccī ut meī estō memor.' Quīntus omnēs amīcōs cārissimōs iam perdiderat; vītae eum taeduit. paucīs post mēnsibus ipse diem obiit; sepultus est in monte Esquilīnō prope tumulum Maecēnātis.

diffūgēre = diffūgērunt grāmina (n.
    pl.) the grass; **vicēs** its
seasons **dēcrēscentia**
growing smaller **geminīs**
twin, two; **almum . . . diem**
    = hōra quae almum diem
rapit the
    hour which carries off the
kindly day **mītēscunt**
Zephyrīs grow mild before
    the west winds
prōterit comes on the heels
    of **interitūra** about to perish
simul = simul ac; **pōmifer** fruitful
frūgēs its fruits; **brūma . . . iners**
    inactive winter, i.e. winter when
    nothing stirs; **damna . . . caelestia**
    the losses in the heavens; **celerēs . . .**
    lūnae the swiftly passing moons (=
    months); **reparant** repair, make good
quō pater Aenēās supply **dēcidit**
Tullus . . . et Ancus the third and
    fourth kings of Rome; **an** whether
hodiernae . . . summae to today's
    total; **crāstina . . . tempora**
    tomorrow's times = tomorrow
hērēdis of your heir; **amīcō . . . animō**
    to your dear soul, i.e. your dear self
Mīnōs the judge of the underworld
arbitria judgements; **Torquāte** the
    friend to whom Horace wrote this
    poem; **fācundia** your eloquence
īnfernīs . . . tenebrīs from the
    darkness of the underworld
Hippolytum a devotee of the virgin
    huntress goddess Diana; Venus had
    him killed by a sea monster
nec . . . valet has not strength to/cannot
abrumpere strike off
Lēthaea . . . vincula the chains of
    Forgetfulness (Lethe was one of the
    rivers of the underworld; when the
    dead drank from it, they forgot the
    world above)
Pērithoō Theseus and Perithous went
    down to the underworld to carry off
    Persephone but were caught and

DEATH

There was a high rate of infant mortality in the Roman world and those who survived childhood would die on average between the ages of forty and fifty. Death was a threat that was constantly present.

People on the point of death would be laid on the bare earth. Their closest relations would catch their final breath with a kiss and close their eyes. Then those present would call out their name loudly, either to recall the soul or to reawaken its powers. Next came the preparation of the body. It was washed with warm water, dressed in its best clothes and laid out on public display in the *ātrium*. A small coin was placed under its tongue to pay Charon, the ferryman who would punt it across the river of the dead to a kind of rest in the shadowy afterlife in the underworld. The women of the house would mourn loudly, beating their breasts and tearing their clothes and their hair. And a branch of pine or cypress was put in front of the house to warn passers-by that a corpse lay inside. Undertakers (*libitīnāriī*) would oversee the arrangements. Theirs was a profitable profession but they were held in such contempt that their civil rights were reduced.

A Roman funeral

Pipers led the funeral procession which moved to the sound of flutes and brass instruments. Behind the bier came torch-bearers (originally all funerals had taken place at night) and the hired female mourners, who would howl noisily, together with the dead person's family. There was an element of mockery too. Dancers and clowns capered through the processions, singing ballads in which they jeered at the dead. When the emperor Vespasian died, the chief clown dressed up to look like him and joked about his famous stinginess.

However, the overall impression of an important man's funeral was profoundly serious, as Polybius, a Greek who lived in the second century BC, conveys in this description:

Whenever one of their famous men dies, he is carried at his

funeral to the so-called *rōstra* in the forum. Sometimes he is displayed in an upright posture, more rarely he reclines. When all the people are standing around, a grown-up son, if one is still alive and happens to be present, or, if not, some other relative, goes up onto the *rōstra* and speaks about the virtues of the dead man and the successful achievements of his life. As a result of this the crowd recalls these deeds to their minds and recreates them before their eyes, and this applies not only to those who shared in those achievements but to everyone. They are moved to such sympathy that the loss seems not to belong to the mourners alone but to the whole people.

Afterwards they bury the corpse and perform the usual customs and then they place the image of the dead man in the most conspicuous place in the house, enclosing it in a wooden shrine. The image is a mask which looks exactly like the dead man in features and complexion. At public sacrifices they display these images and decorate them with the utmost care, and when any distinguished member of the family dies, they bring them to the funeral, putting them on those who seem to be most like the originals in stature and appearance. These wear togas with a purple border if the deceased was a consul or praetor, an entirely purple one if he was a censor and one embroidered with gold if he had celebrated a triumph or achieved something similar. They ride in chariots preceded by the *fascēs*, the axes and the other insignia appropriate to the original's status in his life – and when they reach the *rōstra* they all sit down in rank on chairs of ivory. You could not easily find a finer sight for a young man who is eager for fame or virtue. For who could fail to be inspired by the sight of the images of men famous for their virtue all sitting together as if alive and breathing? What spectacle could be finer than this?

A Roman nobleman carrying the busts of his ancestors

The rich were likely to be cremated on a pyre. Offerings of clothes, ornaments, weapons and even food were thown onto the flames. When the pyre had burnt down, the ashes were cooled with wine and a relative or friend would collect the bones and put them in an urn. The urn was then placed in one of the fine tombs which lined the streets leading into the city. The urns containing the ashes of less wealthy citizens were placed in a *columbārium*, literally a pigeon nesting-box but generally used of a niche in a tomb. The corpses of the poorest citizens or of slaves would either be buried in cheap coffins in public cemeteries or thrown unceremoniously into communal pits.

Compare a Roman funeral with a funeral in the modern world. How different are the funerals of different religions in the modern world? How important is it that a funeral should have a religious aspect?

Grammar and exercises

Chapter 34

The subjunctive mood

Consider the different ways in which the verbs are used in the following sentences:

(a) He is helping us.   statement
      Is he helping us?   question
(b) Help us!   command
(c) Let us help him.   exhortation (= encouragement)
      Let him help us.   3rd person command
      May he help us!   wish
      He may help us.   possibility

These different ways of using the verb are called *moods* (Latin **modus** = way).
In Latin:

(a) statements and questions are in the *indicative* mood;
(b) commands are in the *imperative* mood;
(c) exhortations, 3rd person commands, wishes and possibilities are in the *subjunctive* mood.

You have already learned the indicative and imperative moods. You now have to learn the subjunctive.

The present subjunctive

1st		2nd	3rd	3rd **-iō**	4th	**esse**
par-em	*I may prepare*	mone-am	reg-am	capi-am	audi-am	sim
par-ēs	*etc.*	mone-ās	reg-ās	capi-ās	audi-ās	sīs
par-et		mone-at	reg-at	capi-at	audi-at	sit
par-ēmus		mone-āmus	reg-āmus	capi-āmus	audi-āmus	sīmus
par-ētis		mone-ātis	reg-ātis	capi-ātis	audi-ātis	sītis
par-ent		mone-ant	reg-ant	capi-ant	audi-ant	sint

Note that the subjunctive endings for 1st conjugation verbs are **-em, -ēs, -et**, etc. For all the other conjugations the endings are **-am, -ās, -at**, etc. (except for **sum** and compounds, and **volō, nōlō, mālō**, which are irregular).

Exercise 34.1

Give the present subjunctive (1st person singular) of

    vocō, dormiō, dēfendō, festīnō, faciō, studeō, adsum

You must watch verb endings with great care; the change of one letter alters the meaning, e.g.

    dūcimus   we lead, are leading   **dūcēmus**   we shall lead   **dūcāmus**   let us lead

Exercise 34.2

Translate the following verb forms

1	dīcimus	5	veniat	9	iuvant	13	habeāmus
2	dīximus	6	venit	10	iūvērunt	14	habēmus
3	dīcēmus	7	veniet	11	iuvābunt	15	habuimus
4	dīcāmus	8	vēnit	12	iuvent	16	habēbimus

The present subjunctive is used in main clauses to express all three of the meanings listed under (c) above; thus **parēmus** can mean:

(1) let us prepare (exhortation)
(2) may we prepare! (wish)
(3) we may prepare (possibility)

We deal with wishes and possibilities later (chapter 45). At present we only use the first of these three meanings (exhortations and 3rd person commands). This is called the *jussive subjunctive*:

> **ad lūdum festīnēmus.**   Let us hurry to school.
> **nē domī maneat.**   Let him not stay at home.

Note that the negative is **nē**.

Exercise 34.3

Translate

1 fortiter pugnēmus.
2 nē fugiāmus.
3 statim ad castra redeant.
4 amēmus patriam; pāreāmus senātuī.
5 puerī dīligenter labōrent.

Clauses of purpose

The subjunctive is found in many types of subordinate clause, e.g. clauses expressing *purpose*. These are introduced by **ut**, if positive, **nē** = lest, if negative:

> **collem ascendimus <u>ut</u> templum <u>videāmus.</u>**
> We are climbing the hill <u>so that we may see</u> the temple/<u>to see</u> the temple.
> **festīnāmus <u>nē</u> sērō <u>adveniāmus.</u>**
> We are hurrying <u>lest we arrive</u> late/<u>that we may not arrive</u> late/<u>so as not to arrive</u> late.

Notice that English often uses the infinitive to express purpose; Latin *always* uses **ut/nē** + subjunctive.

Exercise 34.4

Translate the following sentences

1 festīnāmus ut tē adiuvēmus.
2 Quīntus Delphōs iter facit ut Apollinis fānum (*shrine*) videat.
3 hominēs ab omnibus partibus Graeciae Delphōs veniunt ut deī ōrācula petant.
4 multī iuvenēs Athēnās nāvigābunt ut in Acadēmiā studeant.
5 ad theātrum convenīte, iuvenēs, ut Theomnēstum audiātis.
6 puerī ad lūdum festīnant nē sērō adveniant.
7 puellae domum celeriter redībunt nē parentēs vexent.
8 māter fīliam revocat nē in perīculum cadat.

The sequence of tenses

If the verb in the main clause is present, imperative, future or 'perfect with have', the verb in the **ut/nē** clause will be in the *present subjunctive*; if the verb in the main clause is in a past tense, the verb in the **ut/nē** clause will be in the *imperfect subjunctive*, as in English:

We are coming so that we *may* help you. (present subjunctive)
We came so that we *might* help you. (imperfect subjunctive)

The imperfect subjunctive

The imperfect subjunctive is formed from the present infinitive, e.g. infinitive: **parāre**; imperfect subjunctive: **parārem**. This applies to all verbs of all conjugations.

parāre		monēre	regere	capere	audīre	esse
parārem	*I might prepare*	monērem	regerem	caperem	audīrem	essem
parārēs		etc.	etc.	etc.	etc.	etc.
parāret						
parārēmus						
parārētis						
parārent						

Exercise 34.5

Translate

1 festīnābāmus ut tē adiuvārēmus.
2 Quīntus Delphōs iter fēcit ut Apollinis fānum vīseret.
3 hominēs ab omnibus partibus Graeciae veniēbant ut deī ōrācula peterent.
4 multī iuvenēs Athēnās nāvigābant ut in Acadēmiā studērent.
5 iuvenēs ad theātrum convēnerant ut Theomnēstum audīrent.
6 puerī ad lūdum festīnābant nē sērō advenīrent.
7 puellae domum celeriter rediērunt nē parentēs vexārent.
8 pater epistolam ad fīlium mīsit ut eum dē perīculō monēret.
9 Marcus ad Macedoniam abierat ut cum Brūtō mīlitāret.
10 Brūtus exercitum comparāverat ut lībertātem populī Rōmānī dēfenderet.

Notice that in purpose clauses the reflexives **sē** and **suus** refer to the subject of the main verb, e.g.

> **puerī dīligenter labōrābant ut magister <u>sē</u> mox dīmitteret.**
> <u>The boys</u> worked hard that the master might dismiss <u>them</u> soon.
> **puella domī manēbat nē māter <u>sē</u> culpāret.**
> The girl stayed at home lest her mother might blame her.

Exercise 34.6

Translate the following verb forms (translate the present subjunctive as may, *e.g.* **parēmus** = *we may prepare; the imperfect subjunctive as* might, *e.g.* **parārēmus** = *we might prepare)*

1	cape	4	captus est	7	ductī sumus	10	dūcet	13	vocāmur
2	cēpī	5	caperet	8	dūcerem	11	vocētis	14	vocāret
3	capiāmus	6	dūcat	9	dūxistī	12	vocātus eram	15	vocābimur

Exercise 34.7

In the following sentences put the verbs in parentheses into the correct form of the subjunctive; then translate, remembering to observe the 'sequence of tenses' (see p. 129 above)

1 Quīntus Pompēiusque iter faciunt ut Delphōs (vidēre).
2 collem ascendēbāmus ut templum Apollinis (īnspicere).
3 diū hīc manēbimus ut omnia (spectāre).
4 tandem Delphīs discessērunt ut Athēnās (redīre).
5 ubi Athēnās rediērunt, Marcus abierat ut cum Brūtō (mīlitāre).
6 epistolam Quīntō relīquerat, in quā scrīpserat: 'in Macedoniam festīnāvī ut lībertātem cum Brūtō (dēfendere).'

Exercise 34.8

Translate into Latin

1 Quintus hurried to the Academy to see his friends.
2 I shall make a journey to Delphi to visit the temple of Apollo.
3 Many men were waiting near the door of the temple to hear the oracle.
4 Quintus woke Pompeius at first light, lest they arrive at the temple late.
5 We have come to Delphi to learn the truth.
6 They have waited in Delphi three days to hear the oracle.
7 The girls were working hard so that the master might praise them.
8 The boys are working hard so that the master may not punish (**pūnīre**) them.

P.S.

What do the following pairs of words mean?

ubi? ubīque
unde? undique
quis? quisque
uter? uterque

Chapter 35

Indirect command

Direct command: **domum redī!**   **mē adiuvā!**   **nōlīte lūdere!**
                           Return home!   Help me!   Don't play!

Indirect command:

pater puerō imperat ut domum redeat.   The father orders the boy to return home.
senex puerum rogat ut sē adiuvet.   The old man asks the boy to help him.
magister puerīs imperāvit nē lūderent.   The master forbade the boys to play.

The construction is the same as that for clauses expressing purpose: **ut/nē** + subjunctive after verbs such as I order, I ask, I beseech, I persuade, I encourage.

English usually uses the infinitive to express indirect command but Latin always uses **ut/nē** + subjunctive except after **iubeō (iubēre, iussī, iussum)** (I order) and **vetō (vetāre, vetuī, vetitum)** (I forbid), with which the infinitive is used.

As in purpose clauses, the reflexives **sē** and **suus** refer to the subject of the main verb.

The sequence of tenses

The rules given for purpose clauses apply equally to indirect command, e.g.

pater fīlium rogat ut sē adiuvet.   Father asks his son to help him.
pater fīlium rogāvit ut sē adiuvāret.   Father asked his son to help him.
pater fīliō persuādēbit nē domum redeat.   Father will persuade his son not to return home.
pater fīliō persuāserat nē domum redīret.   Father had persuaded his son not to return home.

Remember that if the main verb is a true perfect ('perfect with have'), the subjunctive in the **ut/nē** clause is present, e.g.

hōs iuvenēs ad lēgātum dūcō; <u>vēnērunt</u> ut cum Brūtō <u>mīlitent</u>.
I am taking these young men to the legate; they <u>have come</u> that they <u>may serve</u> with Brutus.
puer in agrō manet; patrī <u>persuāsit</u> nē sē domum <u>remittat</u>.
The boy is staying in the field; he <u>has persuaded</u> his father <u>not to send</u> him back home.

Exercise 35.1

Translate

1   māter fīliae imperāvit nē in viā lūderet.
2   fīlia mātrem rogāvit ut sē ad forum dūceret.
3   māter fīliam iussit in casā manēre et sē iuvāre.
4   puella patrī persuādet ut sē ad forum dūcat.
5   puella mātrī dīxit, 'in casā nōn manēbō; patrī enim persuāsī ut mē ad forum dūcat.'
6   māter virō dīxit, 'quid facis, mī vir? tē rogāvī nē fīliam ad forum dūcerēs.'
7   vir eius respondit, 'puella mihi persuāsit ut sē mēcum dūcam.'

8 māter virō dīxit, 'puella pessimē sē gessit. tē moneō nē eī sīc indulgeās (*spoil* + dat.).'

9 pater tamen fīliam nōn vetuit sēcum venīre.

Exercise 35.2

Turn the following direct commands into indirect commands after **imperāvit**, *and translate, e.g.*

magister 'solvite nāvem, nautae,' inquit.   **magister nautīs imperāvit ut nāvem solverent.**
The captain ordered the sailors to cast off the ship.

1 Quīntus 'ad urbem festīnā, Pompēī,' inquit.

2 centuriō 'venīte mēcum, iuvenēs,' inquit, 'ad prīncipia legiōnis.'

3 Rūfus Quīntum excitāvit et 'surge, Quīnte,' inquit.

4 Rūfus eōs ad Lūcīlium dūxit et 'Lūcīlī,' inquit, 'docē hōs iuvenēs aliquid disciplīnae mīlitāris.'

5 Lūcīlius Pompēiō saepe dīcēbat: 'nōlī cessāre, Pompēī.'

Exercise 35.3

Translate into Latin

1 Quintus persuaded the soldier to lead him to Brutus' camp.

2 The soldier asks Quintus not to hurry, because he is tired.

3 When they reached the camp, a centurion said, 'Come with me to see the legionary commander.'

4 The centurion said, 'These young men have come to serve with Brutus.'

5 The commander told (= ordered) Rufus to look after them.

6 Rufus has persuaded Quintus not to leave the camp.

The pluperfect subjunctive

This tense is formed by adding the following endings to the perfect stem:

-issem	parāv-issem	monu-issem	rēx-issem	audīv-issem	cēp-issem
-issēs	etc.	etc.	etc.	etc.	etc.
-isset					
-issēmus					
-issētis					
-issent					

cum ad portum Ephesī advēnissent, ad urbem festīnāvērunt.
When they had arrived at the port of Ephesus, they hurried to the city.

Note that **cum** = 'when' usually takes the subjunctive (imperfect or pluperfect) when the verb is in a past tense (for exceptions to this rule, see chapter 47).

Exercise 35.4

Match the following verb forms to the English translations below (the pluperfect subjunctive may be translated as 'might have', e.g. **parāvissēmus** *we might have prepared)*

1	rēxissent	6	dormīte	11	videāmus
2	regimus	7	dormīvī	12	vidēbimur
3	regāmus	8	dormiēs	13	vidērētis
4	regēmus	9	dormiāmus	14	vīsī sunt
5	regerēmus	10	dormīre	15	vīdisset

I slept, you might see, they might have ruled, sleep! let us rule, we shall be seen, to sleep, we shall rule, you will sleep, we might rule, they were seen, we may see, let us sleep, he/she might have seen, we rule

Exercise 35.5

Translate

1 Quīntus, cum ad nāvem rediisset, continuō dormīvit.
2 cum ad portum advēnissēmus, ad urbem festīnāvimus.
3 cum in forō manērēmus, multōs mīlitēs vīdimus.
4 cum mīles quīdam nōs ad Brūtī castra dūxisset, tribūnō mīlitum occurrimus nōbīs nōtō.
5 tribūnus, cum nōs vīdisset, hilariter nōs salūtāvit.

Passive forms of the subjunctive

To form the present and imperfect subjunctives passive, change the active person endings to corresponding passive forms; thus:

Present subjunctive:

active	passive	active	passive		
par-em	par-er	mone-am	mone-ar		
par-ēs	par-ēris	mone-ās	mone-āris		
par-et	par-ētur	mone-at	mone-ātur		
par-ēmus	par-ēmur	mone-āmus	mone-āmur		
par-ētis	par-ēminī	mone-ātis	mone-āminī		
par-ent	par-entur	mone-ant	mone-antur		
reg-am	reg-ar	audi-am	audi-ar	capi-am	capi-ar
reg-ās	reg-āris	audi-ās	audi-āris	capi-ās	capi-āris
etc.	etc.	etc.	etc.	etc.	etc.

Imperfect subjunctive:

active	passive	active	passive		
parār-em	parār-er	monē-rem	monē-rer		
parār-ēs	parār-ēris	monē-rēs	monē-rēris		
parār-et	parār-ētur	monē-ret	monē-rētur		
etc.	etc.	etc.	etc.		
reger-em	reger-er	audī-rem	audī-rer	caper-em	caper-er
etc.	etc.	etc.	etc.	etc.	etc.

The pluperfect subjunctive passive is formed by changing the pluperfect indicative (e.g. **parātus eram**) to the corresponding subjunctive form (e.g. **parātus essem**):

parātus essem	monitus essem	rēctus essem	audītus essem	captus essem
parātus essēs	etc.	etc.	etc.	etc.
parātus esset				
parātī essēmus				
parātī essētis				
parātī essent				

Exercise 35.6

Change the following active subjunctive forms into corresponding forms of the passive

1 mittāmus
2 mitteret
3 mīsissent
4 amētis
5 amārem

6 amāvissēs
7 custōdiant
8 custōdīvisset
9 custōdīret
10 cēpissēmus

Exercise 35.7

Translate

1 Brūtus Caesarem occīdit nē populus Rōmānus ā tyrannō regerētur.
2 cum ab Antōniō oppugnātus esset, Rōma fūgit.
3 Athēnās nāvigāvit nē ab Antōniō caperētur.
4 Athēnīs diū manēbat ut iuvenēs ad suam causam addūceret.
5 Marcō Cicerōnī persuāsit ut sēcum mīlitāret.
6 cum plūrimī iuvenēs ad causam reīpūblicae adductī essent, in Macedoniam festīnāvit.
7 cum pater Marcī ab Antōniī mīlitibus occīsus esset, Quīntus quoque cum Brūtō mīlitāre volēbat.
8 Pompēiō persuāsit ut sēcum ad Asiam nāvigāret.
9 cum Ephesum advēnissent, ad forum festīnāvērunt.
10 cum in forō sedērent, mīlitī cuīdam occurrērunt quī eōs ad Brūtī castra dūxit.

Exercise 35.8

Translate into Latin

1 When Flaccus had returned from the field, he greeted Scintilla who was sitting in the garden.
2 When dinner was ready, she called him into the house.
3 When they were dining, Scintilla said, 'I am anxious. Quintus has not sent us a letter.'
4 When Flaccus had heard this, he said, 'Don't be anxious. Without doubt he will write to us soon.'
5 But Flaccus also was anxious. When he had finished dinner, he went out to see his friends.
6 When he was sitting in the pub (**taberna, -ae,** f.), a messenger arrived from Rome.
7 The messenger said, 'Brutus has persuaded many young men to leave Athens and serve (**mīlitō, -āre**) in his army.'
8 When the words of the messenger had been heard, Flaccus hurried home to tell Scintilla everything.
9 Scintilla wrote a letter to Quintus and begged him not to be led into the war by Brutus.
10 But when Quintus received this letter, he was already serving in Brutus' army.

P.S.

What do the following compounds of **currō** *mean?*

accurrō, circumcurrō, concurrō, dēcurrō, discurrō, incurrō, intercurrō, occurrō, percurrō, praecurrō, prōcurrō, recurrō, succurrō, trānscurrō?

Chapter 36

Deponent verbs

These verbs are passive in form but active in meaning. Review the list of deponent verbs in Vocabulary 36.

Exercise 36.1

Translate

1 patrem iuvāre cōnābimur.
2 eum ad agrum secūtī sumus.
3 in viā cum amīcīs diū colloquēbar.
4 agrum ingressus patrem vocāvī.
5 in agrō diū morābar.
6 vespere domum profectus sum.

The perfect participles of deponent verbs are active in meaning, e.g. **morātus** = having delayed; **veritus** = having feared; **profectus** = having set out; **prōgressus** = having advanced.

    centuriōnem secūtī ad prīncipia advēnimus.
    Having followed the centurion we arrived at headquarters.

(English often says, e.g. 'Following the centurion we arrived . . .', but since the action of 'following' precedes 'arriving', Latin uses the perfect participle.)

> **prīmā lūce profectī merīdiē ad urbem advēnimus.**
> Having set out/setting out at first light we arrived at the city at midday.

Although deponent verbs are passive in form they form a present participle like ordinary verbs, e.g. **sequēns** = following, **cōnāns** = trying, **loquēns** = talking.

The present participle is used when the action of the participle takes place at the same time as that of the main verb, e.g.

> **in forō manēbant cum amīcīs colloquentēs.**
> They stayed in the forum talking with their friends.
> **Quīntō in lītore morantī magister imperāvit ut festīnāret.**
> When Quintus was delaying on the shore the captain told him to make haste.

The present infinitive passive

You will have noted the present passive form of the infinitive in learning the principal parts of deponent verbs:

1st	**cōnor, cōnārī**	to try
2nd	**vereor, verērī**	to fear
3rd	**sequor, sequī**	to follow
3rd **-iō**	**patior, patī**	to suffer
4th	**orior, orīrī**	to rise

From ordinary (non-deponent) verbs, these infinitives are passive in meaning:

1st	**paror, parārī**	to be prepared
2nd	**moneor, monērī**	to be warned
3rd	**regor, regī**	to be ruled
3rd **-iō**	**capior, capī**	to be taken
4th	**audior, audīrī**	to be heard

They are formed by changing final **-e** of active infinitives to **-ī** (**par-āre** active, **par-ārī** passive), except in the 3rd conjugation and 3rd **-iō** conjugation verbs: these infinitives are formed by adding simply **-ī** to the present stem, e.g. **dūc-ō** I lead, **dūc-ī** to be led; **iaci-ō** (stem **iaci-/iac-**) I throw, **iacī** to be thrown.

Exercise 36.2

Translate the following verb forms

1	sequimur	5	secūtī sumus	9	mitte
2	sequēmur	6	sequēbāris	10	mīsī
3	sequāmur	7	sequerentur	11	mittī
4	sequī	8	sequentēs	12	mittēns

13 mittantur	17 verēbantur	21 vereantur
14 mittāmus	18 verērī	22 verēberis
15 mīsērunt	19 veritī	23 veritī sumus
16 missī erant	20 verentēs	24 verēbantur

Exercise 36.3

Translate

1 domum redīre cōnāmur.
2 prūdentēs vidēminī, amīcī.
3 volumus colloquī vōbīscum, puellae.
4 prīmā lūce profectī, merīdiē in urbem ingressī sumus.
5 Brūtum ad Asiam sequī cōnstituī.
6 perīculum veritae fēminae in casā manēbant.
7 multī cīvēs in bellō cīvīlī mortuī sunt.
8 Flaccus ē casā ēgressus ad agrum profectus est.
9 in viā amīcō occurrit quōcum diū loquēbātur.
10 in agrum ingressus, diū labōrābat.
11 puellam in casā morantem māter iussit ad fontem festīnāre.
12 puella statim profecta multās fēminās invēnit prope fontem colloquentēs.
13 aquam celeriter dūxit domumque regrediēbātur cum lāpsa est.
14 mātris īram verita, ad fontem regressa, urnam iterum complēvit (*filled*).

Passive imperatives

	1st **paror**	2nd **moneor**	3rd **regor**	3rd **-iō capior**	4th **audior**
sing.	parāre	monēre	regere	capere	audīre
pl.	parāminī	monēminī	regiminī	capiminī	audīminī

You will notice that the singular of the passive imperative is the same as the present active infinitive, and the plural the same as the 2nd person plural of the passive indicative.

These forms rarely occur from ordinary verbs, since sense does not often require them; you are unlikely to find e.g. **amāre** = be loved (though you might find e.g. **ā mē monēminī** = be warned by me). But they are common from deponent verbs, which have an active sense, e.g.

mē sequere, Quīnte.   Follow me, Quintus.
statim proficīsciminī, amīcī.   Set out at once, friends.

Exercise 36.4

Give the imperatives, active and passive, singular and plural of

1 moneō   2 vertō

Exercise 36.5

Translate

1 venīte hūc, iuvenēs, et mē iuvāre cōnāminī.
2 in urbe trēs diēs morāre, fīlī; deinde domum proficīscere.
3 mē sequiminī ad agrum, puerī; agrum ingressī colōnōs adiuvāte.
4 manē, amīce, et nōbīscum colloquere.
5 nōlīte hostēs verērī, mīlitēs, sed fortiter prōgrediminī.
6 ā mē monēminī, amīcī; nōlīte in perīculum lābī.

Exercise 36.6

Translate into Latin

1 We shall follow Brutus to Asia.
2 Setting out (= having set out) at once, we sailed to Ephesus.
3 When we had arrived, we tried to find Brutus' army.
4 After entering (use **ingredior**) the camp, we met a centurion.
5 He said, 'Follow me to the headquarters (**prīncipia, -ōrum**, n. pl.) of the legion.'
6 We did not delay but followed him at once.
7 We met the commander going out of the headquarters.
8 He said, 'Wait in the headquarters, young men. I shall soon return.'
9 He returned soon and talked with us for a long time.
10 At last he said, 'You seem sensible young men. I shall take you to Brutus. Follow me.'

P.S.

Explain the meaning and use of the following abbreviations

i.e. = id est	ad fin. = ad fīnem	p.a.= per annum
e.g. = exemplī grātiā	ab init. = ab initiō	lb = lībrae
etc. = et cētera	P.S. = post scrīptum	R.I.P. = requiēscat in pāce
a.m. = ante merīdiem	cf. = confer	No. = numerō
p.m. = post merīdiem	et seq. = et sequentia	MSS = manūscrīpta
A.D. = annō Dominī	flor. = flōruit	N.B. = notā bene
A.M.D.G = ad maiōrem Deī glōriam		

Chapter 37

The ablative absolute

So far you have always seen participles agreeing with the subject or object of a verb or with a noun or pronoun which forms some other part of the clause it belongs to, e.g.

cōpiae Cassiī victae ad castra fūgērunt.
The forces of Cassius having been conquered fled to the camp.
(the participle **victae** agrees with the subject **cōpiae**)

Quīntus epistolam perlēctam Pompēiō trādidit.
Quintus handed over the letter, having been read, to Pompeius (i.e. Quintus read the letter and handed it over to Pompeius).
(the participle **perlēctam** agrees with the object **epistolam**)

Quīntō haec rogantī Pompēius omnia dīxit.
To Quintus asking this (i.e. when Quintus asked this) Pompeius told everything.
(the participle **rogantī** agrees with the indirect object **Quīntō**)

But sometimes the participial phrase (i.e. the noun + participle) is independent of the structure of the rest of the sentence, e.g.

Brūtus, hīs dictīs, mīlitēs dīmīsit.
Brutus, these things having been said, dismissed the soldiers (i.e. Brutus said this and dismissed the soldiers/After saying this, Brutus dismissed the soldiers).

dictīs agrees with **hīs**, which is not subject or object of the main verb (**dīmīsit**) but is independent (or, as the grammarians say, 'absolute'); in this case both noun and participle are in the ablative case.
You will notice that English does not often use such absolute participial phrases and you will need to translate them into natural English.

Here are some more examples:

cēnā parātā Scintilla quiēscēbat.
When dinner was ready (dinner having been prepared) Scintilla rested.
Quīntō haec locūtō, Marcus gaudēbat.
When Quintus said these things (Quintus having said these things), Marcus was delighted.
Quīntō in Acadēmiā studente Brūtus Athēnās advēnit.
(While) Quintus (was) studying in the Academy, Brutus arrived at Athens.

(NB Remember that the ablative singular of the present participle ends **-e**.)

Exercise 37.1

Translate the following sentences and explain the use of the cases **collēctum** *(sentence 1),* **collēctus** *(sentence 2),* **collēctō** *(sentence 3)*

1   Antōnius exercitum maximum collēctum ad Graeciam dūcēbat.
2   exercitus maximus ab Antōniō collēctus ad Graeciam contendēbat.
3   Antōnius exercitū maximō collēctō ad Graeciam contendit.

Exercise 37.2

Translate

1   Quīntus, labōribus cōnfectīs, cum amīcīs colloquēbātur.
2   Quīntō cum amīcīs colloquente, centuriō accessit, quī eum ad Brūtum arcessīvit.
3   Brūtus, mīlitibus convocātīs, ōrātiōnem habuit.
4   'hostibus victīs,' inquit, 'lībertātem populō Rōmānō reddēmus.'
5   mīlitēs dīmissī ad iter sē parāvērunt.
6   Scintilla in casā sedente, intrāvit tabellārius (*postman*).

7 Scintilla, epistolā perlēctā, Flaccum vocāvit.
8 Flaccus, clāmōribus eius audītīs, in casam ānxius rediit.
9 Flaccus Scintillam flentem cōnsōlārī cōnātus est.
10 Scintilla dēspērante, Flaccus exiit ut Decimum arcesseret.

Exercise 37.3

In the following sentences put the participial phrases (noun + participle) in parentheses into the correct cases; then translate

1 (Caesar interfectus), Flaccus Quīntō imperāvit ut Athēnās nāvigāret.
2 (longum iter cōnfectum), Quīntus tandem Athēnās advēnit.
3 (monumenta spectāta), Quīntus ad Acadēmīam festīnāvit.
4 Quīntus (Marcus in ātriō vīsus) salūtāvit. (*Be careful!*)
5 (Marcus in tabernā bibēns), Quīntus dīligenter studēbat.
6 (Quīntus Theomnēstum audiēns), Marcus in tabernā bibēbat.
7 Marcus (epistola ā patre scrīpta) Quīntō trādidit. (*Be careful!*)
8 Quīntus (epistola perlēcta) Marcō reddidit.

Exercise 37.4

Translate the following verb forms

1	audītus	7	loquēns	13	monēbō
2	audiēbātur	8	loquētur	14	monuimus
3	audīrent	9	loquere	15	monerētur
4	audīrī	10	locūtus est	16	moneāmus
5	audiēmur	11	loquēbātur	17	monēminī
6	audiāmus	12	loquī	18	monitus

Exercise 37.5

Translate into Latin (in these sentences use the ablative absolute, e.g. Quintus, after writing a letter to his parents, went to sleep = Quintus, a letter having been written to his parents, went to sleep = **Quīntus epistolā ad parentēs scrīptā dormīvit***)*

1 After greeting her mother Horatia entered the house.
2 Scintilla prepared dinner and called Flaccus.
3 Flaccus, seeing his daughter, rejoiced.
4 When dinner was finished, they talked for a long time.
5 At last Horatia left her parents and returned home.

Exercise 37.6

Translate into Latin (NB use past participles to translate where there are parentheses; in some of these sentences the participle will agree with the subject or object of the sentence, in others an ablative absolute construction is required; be careful!)

1 (After returning* from Delphi), Quintus and Pompeius sailed to Asia to find Brutus.
2 (When their journey was finished), they hurried to Brutus' camp.

3 (After delaying in Asia for a long time), Brutus led his army into Greece.
4 (When battle was joined), Brutus defeated Octavian.
5 But Cassius, (when he had been defeated by Antony), killed himself.
6 (When Brutus was dead), Quintus fled with his companions.

*use **regredior**

Note that the verb **esse** has no present participle:

> **Cicerōne cōnsule rēspūblica in magnō perīculō erat.**
> (**Cicerōne cōnsule** = Cicero (being) consul = when Cicero was consul, in the consulship of Cicero)

> **Caesare duce Rōmānī Britanniam invāsērunt.**
> (**Caesare duce** = Caesar (being) leader = when Caesar was leader, under the leadership of Caesar)

The two nouns in the ablative form an ablative absolute phrase.

Exercise 37.7

Translate

1 Quīntō puerō plūrimī colōnī Venusiae habitābant.
2 ventō secundō celeriter ad portum advēnimus.
3 cōnsulibus Pompēiō Crassōque Caesar in Galliā mīlitābat.
4 Brūtō duce Quīntus Pompēiusque Philippīs pugnāvērunt.
5 Caesare dictātōre Brūtus cōnstituit rempūblicam līberāre.

P.S.

What is the meaning of the following nouns, all formed from supines of verbs you know?

nārrātor, fautor, scrīptor, lēctor, prōditor?
dēditiō, commendātiō, salūtātiō, monitiō, quaestiō?
cantus, reditus, monitus, rīsus, ascēnsus?

Chapter 38

The future participle

You have already met the future participle several times in the course of your reading, e.g.

> **nāvis discessūra est.**   The ship is <u>about to depart</u>.

It is formed by changing the supine ending **-um** to **-ūrus**:

parāt-um	**parāt-ūrus**	about to prepare
monit-um	**monit-ūrus**	about to warn
rēct-um	**rēct-ūrus**	about to rule
capt-um	**capt-ūrus**	about to take
audīt-um	**audīt-ūrus**	about to hear

It is active in meaning and declines like **bonus, -a, -um.**

NB The future participle of **sum** is **futūrus** = about to be.

Deponent verbs form future participles from the perfect stem:

cōnor, cōnārī, cōnāt-us	**cōnāt-ūrus**	about to try
vereor, verērī, verit-us	**verit-ūrus**	about to fear
sequor, sequī, secūt-us	**secūt-ūrus**	about to follow
patior, patī, pass-us	**pass-ūrus**	about to suffer

Exercise 38.1

Translate the following verb forms

1	profectus	6	mortuus	11	lēgit
2	proficīscī	7	moriēns	12	legit
3	proficīscere	8	moritūrus	13	lēctūrus
4	proficīscuntur	9	moriēbantur	14	lēctus
5	profectūrus	10	morī	15	leget

Exercise 38.2

Translate

1 hostibus sequentibus Quīntus comitēsque ad castra fūgērunt.
2 Brūtō mortuō, Quīntus cōnstituit Athēnās redīre.
3 Athēnās profectūrus, comitēs aspexit dormientēs.
4 cum Athēnās advēnisset, Theomnēstum rogāvit ut sē adiuvāret.
5 Theomnēstus Quīntō Athēnīs morantī persuāsit ut ad Italiam proficīscerētur.
6 Theomnēstus haec locūtus Quīntum ad portum dūxit, ubi nāvem invēnērunt ad Italiam itūram.
7 cum nāvis discessūra esset, Theomnēstus Quīntum valēre iussit.
8 sōle oriente nāvis ē portū profecta est.
9 Quīntus tandem domum reditūrus gaudēbat.
10 cum Venusiam accēderet, multōs advenās (*strangers*) vīdit colōniam ingressūrōs.
11 sōle occidente colōniam initūrus erat.
12 sed nōluit domum suam vidēre ab advenīs occupātam; sē vertit, longum iter Rōmam factūrus.

Exercise 38.3

Translate into Latin

1 Flaccus was about to go to the field, but hearing the shouts of Scintilla he ran back into the house.
2 Entering the house, he found her weeping.
3 After reading Quintus' letter, he tried to comfort her.
4 But he could not persuade her to listen to him.
5 When she could speak, she asked him to send for Decimus.
6 Flaccus set out at once to find Decimus.
7 Having entered his house (use **ingredior**), he found Decimus about to set out for Brundisium.
8 Decimus hurried to the house with Flaccus following.

P.S.

What is the meaning of the following words?

alius, aliter, aliquis, aliquandō, aliquot, aliquotiēns, aliquamdiū, alibī?

Chapter 39

Indirect questions

Questions can refer to present, future or past time, e.g.

What are you doing?	**quid facis?**
What are you going to do?	**quid faciēs?** or **quid factūrus es?**
What have you done?	**quid fēcistī?**

In *indirect questions* Latin uses the subjunctive, e.g.

1 Present: He asks what they are doing.
   rogat quid faciant.

2 Future: He asks what they are going to do.
   rogat quid factūrī sint.

3 Past: He asks what they have done.
   rogat quid fēcerint.

There is no future subjunctive. To express a future in indirect questions, the future participle is used with the subjunctive of **sum,** e.g.

| **nesciō quid factūrus sim.** | I do not know what I am going to do. |
| **nesciēbāmus quid factūrī essēmus.** | We did not know what we were going to do. |

The perfect subjunctive

The perfect subjunctive is the same in form as the future perfect indicative except in the 1st person singular, which ends **-erim**; thus:

1st	**parāv-erim** etc.
2nd	**monu-erim** etc.
3rd	**rēx-erim** etc.
4th	**audīv-erim** etc.
3rd **-iō**	**cēp-erim** etc.
sum	**fu-erim** etc.
possum	**potu-erim** etc.

Indirect questions can be introduced by any of the interrogative words you have met (e.g. **quis? cūr? quandō?** etc.) and also by **num** = whether, e.g.

Quīntus senem rogāvit <u>num</u> parentēs suōs vīdisset.
Quintus asked the old man <u>whether</u> he had seen his parents.

Double questions are introduced by **utrum . . . an** = whether . . . or, e.g.

> **senex Quīntum rogāvit <u>utrum</u> Venusiae mānsūrus esset <u>an</u> parentēs quaesītūrus.**
> The old man asked Quintus <u>whether</u> he was going to stay in Venusia <u>or</u> look for his parents.

utrum . . . necne = whether . . . or not:

> **Quīntus senem rogāvit utrum parentēs suī Venusiā discessissent necne.**
> Quintus asked the old man whether his parents had left Venusia or not.

Sequence of tenses

If the main verb is *primary* (i.e. present, future or perfect with have), the verb in the indirect question clause will be in either the present subjunctive or the perfect subjunctive, or the future participle + present subjunctive of **sum**.

If the main verb is *secondary* (i.e. imperfect, perfect or pluperfect), the verb in the indirect question clause will be in either the imperfect subjunctive or the pluperfect subjunctive, or the future participle + imperfect subjunctive of **sum**.

Exercise 39.1

Translate (in the following sentences all the main verbs are primary)

1 Theomnēstus Quīntum rogat quid passus sit.
2 Theomnēstus Quīntum rogat quid nunc factūrus sit.
3 Theomnēstus Quīntum rogat quō īre cupiat.
4 scīre volumus quandō nāvis discessūra sit.
5 magistrum rogā cūr nāvis nōndum discesserit.
6 nesciō quandō ad portum adventūrī sīmus.
7 Quīntus senem rogat num parentēs suōs vīderit.
8 senex Quīntum rogat utrum colōniam initūrus sit an Rōmam iter factūrus.

Exercise 39.2

Translate (in the following sentences all the main verbs are secondary)

1 Theomnēstus Quīntum rogāvit quid passus esset.
2 Theomnēstus Quīntum rogāvit quid iam factūrus esset.
3 Theomnēstus Quīntum rogāvit quid facere cuperet. *complementary infinitive*
4 scīre volēbāmus quandō nāvis discessūra esset.
5 magistrum rogāvī cūr nāvis nōndum discessisset.
6 nesciēbam quandō ad portum adventūrī essēmus.
7 Quīntus senem rogāvit num parentēs suōs vīdisset.
8 senex Quīntum rogāvit utrum in colōniā mānsūrus esset an iter Rōmam factūrus.

Exercise 39.3

Translate

1 Quīntus, cum Venusiam advēnisset, nesciēbat quid accidisset.
2 senex, cuī prope viam occurrit, eum rogāvit cūr Venusiam rediisset.
3 'nōnne scīs' inquit 'quot mala colōniae nostrae acciderint?'
4 Quīntus senem rogāvit num parentēs suī Venusiae adhūc manērent.
5 senex respondit, 'Venusiā discessērunt. nesciō utrum Rōmam ierint an rūre maneant.'
6 Venusiā relictā Quīntus iter iniit quod Rōmam ferēbat.
7 Rōmam profectus, omnēs quibus occurrit rogāvit num parentēs suōs vīdissent.

Exercise 39.4

In the following sentences put the verbs in parentheses into the correct form of the subjunctive and translate

1 Quīntus, dum iter Rōmam facit, veterī amīcō occurrit quem rogāvit num parentēs suōs (vidēre).
2 ille 'nesciō' inquit 'ubi parentēs tuī (esse).'
3 Quīntus eum rogāvit quandō parentēs suī Venusiā (discēdere) et quō (īre).
4 ille respondit, 'parentēs tuī Capuam contendēbant. sed nesciō utrum Capuae adhūc (manēre) an Rōmam (proficīscī).'
5 Quīntum rogāvit quid factūrus (esse).

Exercise 39.5

Translate into Latin

1 We don't know where the farmer has gone.
2 I shall ask the boys whether they have seen him.
3 'Boys, do you know where the farmer is?'
4 'We asked him whether he was going to return home or stay in the field; but he made no answer (= answered nothing).'
5 Soon we saw the farmer entering the field. We asked him why he had not waited for us.
6 He said, 'I did not know when you wanted to meet me. I went home to have dinner, because I was tired.'

P.S. Miscellanea: Latin phrases in common use today

1 In a mathematical problem, what are the **data**?
2 What is a **post mortem** examination?
3 What is meant by saying a law case is still **sub iūdice**?
4 What are **obiter dicta**? (**obiter** = in passing)
5 What is meant by saying someone is acting **in locō parentis**?
6 What would be meant by saying that something is mine **dē iūre**, yours **dē factō**?
7 What is meant by saying that a law case is adjourned **sine diē**?
8 What is meant by saying that a proposal was passed **nem. con.** (= **nēmine contrādīcente**)?
9 What is an artist's **magnum opus**?
10 What is the meaning of the stage direction **exeunt omnēs**?

Chapter 40

Further uses of the ablative case

1   A few verbs are found with the ablative case, e.g.

ūtor, ūtī, ūsus sum I use, e.g. **gladiō ūsus sum**. I used a sword.
fruor, fruī, frūctus sum I enjoy, e.g. **pāce fruēbantur**. They were enjoying peace.

2   Ablative of comparison

puella prūdentior est puerō = **puella prūdentior est quam puer.**
The girl is more sensible <u>than the boy</u>.
Quīntus diūtius Athēnīs mānsit Marcō = **Quīntus diūtius Athēnīs mānsit quam Marcus.**
Quintus stayed longer in Athens <u>than Marcus</u>.

When two things or persons are compared with each other, instead of **quam** = than, the second thing/person may be in the ablative.

3   Ablative of measure of difference

puella multō prūdentior est. The girl is <u>much</u> more sensible (more sensible by much).
Quīntus paulō diūtius mānsit. Quintus stayed <u>a little</u> longer (longer by a little).

4   Ablative of price and genitive of value

hunc equum centum sēstertiīs ēmī. I bought this horse <u>for a hundred sestertii</u>.
eum maximī aestimō. I value it <u>very highly</u>.

The *ablative* is used when a definite price is stated.
The *genitive* is used to express the value in which someone or something is held.

5   Ablative of origin

vir nōbilī genere nātus = a man born <u>of (from)</u> a noble family.
Quīntus lībertīnō patre nātus est = Quintus was born <u>from a freedman father</u>, i.e. was the son of a freedman.

Exercise 40.1

Translate

1   'vīsne tū hunc equum emere? trīgintā dēnāriīs eum ēmī sed vīgintī dēnāriīs eum tibi vendere volō.'
2   'sī eum tantī aestimās, cūr vīs eum tam vīlī (*cheaply*) vendere?'
3   'eum vīlī vendere volō, quod nunc opus est mihi argentō.'
4   'ego equum multō minōris aestimō quam tū. praetereā equum meliōrem iam habeō.'
5   'equus tuus multō peior est meō. quantī tū meum equum aestimās?'
6   'ego eum parvī aestimō. quīnque dēnāriōs tibi dabō.'
7   'quid dīcis? quīnque dēnāriōs! nōlī nūgās nārrāre. ego volō eum tibi vendere decem dēnāriīs.'
8   'mihi equō nōn opus est, sed quod tibi opus est argentō, ecce, octō dēnāriōs tibi dabō. nesciō tamen quandō tālī equō ūsūrus sim.'

Revise the following verbs (see Reference grammar, pp. 203-4):

sum, esse, fuī
possum, posse, potuī
volō, velle, voluī
mālō, mālle, māluī
nōlō, nōlle, nōluī
ferō, ferre, tulī
eō, īre, iī

subjunctives:	present	imperfect	perfect	pluperfect
	sim	essem	fuerim	fuissem
	possim	possem	potuerim	potuissem
	velim	vellem	voluerim	voluissem
	mālim	māllem	māluerim	māluissem
	nōlim	nōllem	nōluerim	nōluissem
	feram	ferrem	tulerim	tulissem
	eam	īrem	ierim	iissem

eō present participle: **iēns, euntis**

Semi-deponent verbs

A small number of verbs are active in form in the present stem tenses (present, imperfect, future) but passive (deponent) in perfect stem tenses (perfect, pluperfect, future perfect); see Vocabulary 40.

fīō, fierī, factus sum I become, I am made. This verb is used to supply a passive of **faciō** in present, future (**fīam**) and imperfect (**fīēbam**). The infinitive is passive in form. In the perfect stem tenses the passive of **faciō** is used (**factus sum, factus eram, factus erō**), e.g.

puerī miserī fīunt. The children are becoming miserable.
multa scelera ā triumvirīs fīēbant. Many crimes were being done/committed by the triumviri.
Quīntus scrība aerāriī ā Marcō factus est. Quintus was made a secretary of the treasury by Marcus.

Exercise 40.2

Translate the following verb forms

1	gaudēbant	6	solēbas	11	fīēbam
2	gāvīsus	7	solitī sumus	12	facta est
3	gaudēte	8	solent	13	fierī
4	gāvīsī estis	9	ausus	14	fit
5	gaudēre	10	audēbātis	15	factī erant

Exercise 40.3

Translate

1 Quīntus Apollinī cōnfīsus Rōmam inīre ausus est.
2 Quīntus, scrība aerāriī factus, gāvīsus est.
3 cotīdiē ad aerārium festīnāre solēbat ubi officia dīligenter perficiēbat.
4 Quīntus, ā senātōre contemptus, īrātus fīēbat.
5 sed tālia convīcia (*insults*) ferre solitus nōn diū vexātus est.
6 nam verba hominis tam arrogantis nōn magnī aestimāvit.

Exercise 40.4

Translate into Latin

1 We are in the greatest danger. We need help. We dare not attack the enemy.
2 You have never been accustomed to fear the enemy.
3 Surely you have not now become cowards (**ignāvī**)?
4 Use that courage which you have often shown before.
5 You have always been much braver than the enemy.
6 Trusting in the gods, follow me, soldiers, and fight bravely to defend your country.

Exercise 40.5

Change the following verb forms into (a) the imperfect (b) the perfect

1 loquimur
2 gaudent
3 pōnitis
4 fīunt
5 cōnfīdis

P.S.

Review the following adverbs expressing place or motion

place where	motion to	motion from
hīc	hūc	hinc
illīc	illūc	illinc
ibi	eō	inde
ubi?	quō?	unde?

Chapter 41

Indirect statement

You have seen that the construction used for indirect statements is the *accusative and infinitive*. (This construction is occasionally used in English, e.g. I believe him to be wise = I believe that he is wise = **crēdō eum prūdentem esse.**)

In indirect statements, infinitives of all tenses are used, active and passive; these must now be learned:

	active	*passive*
present	parāre	parārī
	monēre	monērī
	regere	regī
	capere	capī
	audīre	audīrī
	esse	
perfect	parāv-isse	parātus esse
	monu-isse	monitus esse
	rēx-isse	rēctus esse
	cēp-isse	captus esse
	audī-visse	audītus esse
	fuisse	
future	parāt-ūrus esse	
	monit-ūrus esse	
	rēct-ūrus esse	
	capt-ūrus esse	
	audīt-ūrus esse	
	futūrus esse/fore	

(The future passive infinitive is rare and is at present omitted.)

Note the future infinitive of **sum: futūrus esse** and the alternative form **fore**.

Deponent verbs have infinitives active in meaning, though the present and perfect are passive in form, e.g.

present	cōnārī	sequī
future	cōnātūrus esse	secūtūrus esse
perfect	cōnātus esse	secūtus esse

Exercise 41.1

Give all infinitives, active and passive (except future passive) of (a) **dō** *(b)* **mittō**.

The accusative and infinitive construction is introduced by verbs such as **dīcō** (I say), **negō** (I deny, say not), **pūtō** (I think), **sciō** (I know), **nesciō** (I do not know), **cognōscō** (I get to know, learn), **crēdō** (I believe), **prōmittō** (I promise), **spērō** (I hope) and a few other verbs such as **gaudeō** (I rejoice that).

The reflexives **sē** and **suus** refer back to the subject of the verb which introduces the indirect statement:

> **<u>Marcus</u> dīcit <u>sē</u> Quīntum adiūtūrum esse.**
> <u>Marcus</u> says that <u>he</u> will help Quintus.

149

puerī dīcunt <u>sē</u> ā magistrō dīmissōs esse.
<u>The boys</u> say that <u>they</u> have been dismissed by the master.

Notice that in the case of the infinitives formed from participles (perfect passive, e.g. **parātus esse**, and future active, e.g. **parātūrus esse**), the participle agrees with the *accusative* (subject) of the infinitive, e.g.

magister dīcit <u>puerōs</u> domum <u>dīmissōs</u> **esse.**   The master says that the boys have been sent home.

fēmina spērat <u>puellās</u> sē <u>adiūtūrās</u> **esse.**   The woman hopes that the girls will help her.
puellae dīcunt <u>sē</u> fēminam <u>adiūtūrās</u> **esse.**   The girls say that they will help the woman.

Exercise 41.2

Translate

1 Quīntus cognōscit parentēs suōs Venusiā discessisse.
2 spērat sē eōs in viā inventūrum esse.
3 Gāius negat sē eōs vīdisse.
4 crēdit eōs Capuam profectōs esse.
5 Apollō prōmittit sē Quīntum cūrātūrum esse.
6 Quīntus tandem scit sē parentēs numquam posteā vīsūrum esse.
7 Marcus dīcit Octāviānum veniam sibi dedisse.
8 Quīntus gaudet sē scrībam aerāriī factum esse.

If the verb introducing the indirect statement is past, English makes the verb in the indirect speech past. But in Latin the tense of the infinitive is that used in the original words, e.g.

Scintilla <u>said</u> that Flaccus <u>was working</u> in the field. (indirect speech)
Scintilla said, 'Flaccus <u>is working</u> in the field.' (direct speech)
Scintilla dīxit Flaccum in agrō <u>labōrāre</u>. (indirect speech)

Scintilla said that he had worked for a long time. (indirect speech)
Scintilla said, 'He <u>has worked</u> for a long time.' (direct speech)
Scintilla dīxit eum diū <u>labōrāvisse</u>. (indirect speech)

Scintilla said that he would return home soon. (indirect speech)
Scintilla said, 'He <u>will return</u> home soon.' (direct speech)
Scintilla dīxit eum mox domum <u>reditūrum esse</u>. (indirect speech)

Exercise 41.3

Translate

1 Quīntus cognōvit parentēs suōs Venusiā discessisse.
2 spērāvit sē eōs in viā inventūrum esse.
3 Gāius dīxit sē Capuam iter facere.
4 Quīntus respondit sē Gāium secūtūrum esse.
5 eī quibus Quīntus in viā occurrit negāvērunt sē parentēs eius vīdisse.

3 Verbs

6 amīcī quibus Quīntus carmina sua recitāverat dīcēbant [ea optima esse.]
7 Quīntus gaudēbat Vergilium amīcitiam suam petere.
8 spērābat Vergilium carmina sua probātūrum esse.
9 Vergilius dīxit sē carminibus Quīntī dēlectātum esse.
10 Quīntus respondit sē Vergiliī carmina valdē admīrārī.

Exercise 41.4

Turn the following sentences into indirect statement after **dīxit** (*or* **negāvit**), *e.g.*

> **puellae laetae sunt = dīxit puellās laetās esse**
> **puellae nōn laetae sunt = negāvit puellās laetās esse**

1 magister īrātus est.
2 Quīntus in Italiam redit.
3 Quīntus parentēs quaesīvit.
4 colōnī ab agrīs expulsī sunt.
5 Quīntus parentēs Venusiae nōn inveniet.

Exercise 41.5

Translate into Latin (remember that the reflexives **sē** *and* **suus** *refer back to the subject of the main clause; and that the tense of the infinitive will be the same as that of the direct words)*

1 Marcus said that he would help Quintus.
2 He said that he had been made quaestor of the treasury.
3 He hoped that Quintus would help him.
4 Quintus rejoiced that Marcus trusted him.
5 Quintus knew that the duties would not be difficult.
6 He hoped that he would write many poems (**carmina**).
7 He told his friends that he had written a few poems.
8 His friends said that his poems were very good.
9 Quintus was content and said that he had never been so happy (= denied that he had ever been so happy).

P.S.

Adjectives formed from verbs ending **-ilis, -bilis** denote passive qualities, e.g.

admīrā-bilis, -e (admīror)	admirable (= to be admired)
crēd-ibilis, -e (crēdō)	believable, creditable
doc-ilis, -e (doceō)	teachable
fac-ilis, -e (faciō)	doable, easy
flē-bilis, -e (fleō)	lamentable, lamented
horr-ibilis, -e (horreō)	horrible
memorā-bilis, -e (memorō)	memorable
mīrā-bilis, -e (mīror)	wonderful
terr-ibilis, -e (terreō)	terrible

Chapter 42

This chapter introduces no new grammar.

Exercise 42.1

Turn the following active verb forms into the corresponding forms of the passive

1	parātis	6	posuit
2	monēre	7	monēte
3	regere	8	tulimus
4	audīvistī	9	fēcērunt
5	caperēmus	10	ēgisset

Exercise 42.2

Translate

1 Quīntus, cum Pompēium in forō cōnspexisset, ad eum accurrit.
2 amīcum salūtāvit rogāvitque quandō Rōmam revēnisset.
3 Pompēius dīxit sē Rōmam revēnisse ut Octāviānī veniam peteret.
4 Quīntus prō certō habēbat Octāviānum eī veniam datūrum esse. *time when*
5 Pompēium rogāvit ut ad cēnam venīret. ille respondit sē posterō diē cum Quīntō libenter cēnātūrum esse. *abl absolute takes dat.*
6 Quīntus servīs convocātīs imperāvit ut omnia ad cēnam parārent.
7 'festīnāte' inquit; 'omnia parāte ut Pompēiī reditum celebrēmus.'
8 plūrimī amīcī Quīntī domum ingressī Pompēium salūtāvērunt.
9 sōle occidente Quīntus amīcīs imperāvit nē domum redīrent.
10 'manēte paulīsper,' inquit, 'ut carmen audiātis quod dē Pompēiī reditū composuī.'

Exercise 42.3

Translate into Latin

1 Pompeius said that for a long time he had hidden (himself) in the mountains.
2 He said that now he had returned to Rome to ask for pardon.
3 Quintus was sure that Octavian would receive him kindly.
4 He asked Pompeius to come to dinner; he said that many friends had been invited.
5 Pompeius promised that he would come.
6 When all the guests had arrived, they enjoyed an excellent dinner and drank much wine.
7 When dinner was finished, Quintus recited the poem which he had written about Pompeius.
8 All the guests, delighted by the poem, praised Quintus.

P.S.

Adjectives ending **-āx** in the nominative singular, formed from the present stem of verbs, denote a habit or tendency, e.g.

loquāx, loquācis	talkative	(loqu-or)
audāx, audācis	daring	(aud(e)-ō)
capāx, capācis	holding	(cap(i)-ō)
rapāx, rapācis	grasping	(rap(i)-ō)
tenāx, tenācis	clinging	(ten(e)-ō)

Chapter 43

Consecutive (result) clauses

> **Quīntus tam verēcundus erat ut vix quicquam dīcere posset.**
> Quintus was so shy that he could scarcely say anything.
> **Quīntus adeō timēbat ut dīcere nōn posset.**
> Quintus was so nervous that he could not speak.

Clauses expressing result are introduced by **ut** + subjunctive, negative **nōn**.

The main clause usually contains one of the words meaning 'so', e.g.

tam (with adjectives and adverbs):
tam fessus erat ut diū dormīret.   He was <u>so</u> tired <u>that</u> he slept a long time.

tantus = so great:
tanta erat tempestās ut omnēs timērent.   The storm was <u>so great that</u> all were afraid.

tot = so many:
tot spectātōrēs aderant ut locum vacuum invenīre nōn possēmus.
There were <u>so many</u> spectators present <u>that</u> we could not find an empty place.

totiēns = so often:
Vergilius dē tē totiēns mihi dīxit ut carmina tua audīre cupiam.
Virgil has spoken to me of you <u>so often that</u> I want to hear your poems.

ita = in such a way:
Quīntus carmen ita recitāvit ut omnēs eum laudārent.
Quintus recited the poem <u>in such a way that</u> all praised him.

(NB In result clauses the reflexive refers to the subject of the **ut** clause; hence in this sentence **eum**, not **sē**.)

adeō = to such an extent, so much:
tua carmina Maecēnātem adeō dēlectant ut tē cognōscere cupiat.
Your poems please Maecenas <u>so much that</u> he wants to get to know you.

Exercise 43.1

Translate

1 Maecēnās tam prūdēns erat ut Octāviānus eī semper cōnfīderet.
2 litterīs adeō studēbat ut multōs poētās adiuvāret.
3 Vergilium tantī aestimābat ut eum in numerum amīcōrum intimōrum accēperit.
4 Vergilius Maecēnātī dē Quīntō totiēns dīxerat ut ille Quīntum cognōscere vellet.
5 cum Vergilius Quīntum Maecēnātī commendāvisset, ille tam verēcundus erat ut fārī nōn posset.
6 Quīntus putābat Maecēnātem sē contemnere.
7 sed Vergilius dīxit Maecēnātem eum dīlēxisse et carminibus eius dēlectātum esse.
8 tandem Maecēnās Quīntum revocātum iussit in numerō amīcōrum suōrum esse.

In result clauses the normal rules of sequence are not necessarily followed; the tenses of the subjunctive can be varied according to the sense, e.g.

tam dīligenter herī labōrābat ut hodiē fessus sit.
◆ He worked so hard yesterday that he is tired today.
Siciliam ita vastāvit ut restituī nūllō modō possit. (Cicero *Verr.* 1.4)
He (has) so plundered Sicily that it can in no way be restored.
(The plundering took place in the past but the result is still present.)

The perfect subjunctive is used to stress the actuality of the event:

Maecēnās Vergilium tantī aestimābat ut eum in numerum amīcōrum intimōrum accēperit.
Maecenas valued Virgil so highly that he accepted him into the number of his closest friends.

Exercise 43.2

Translate into Latin

1 Many men were so foolish that they despised Quintus because he was the son of a freedman.
2 But Maecenas valued highly all who were talented (**ingeniōsus, -a, -um**).
3 He did not ask whether they were the sons of freedmen or nobly born (= born from a noble family).
4 Maecenas was so busy (= occupied by affairs) that he did not call Quintus back at once.
5 But in the ninth month he called him back and told him to be one of his friends.
6 He said that he had been delighted by Quintus' poems; he promised that he would help him.

P.S.

Inscriptions on tombstones throw a great deal of light on the life of ordinary Roman citizens. Once you have mastered the abbreviations used, you will find them easy to read.

Four funerary inscriptions on girls who died young:

1 *Felicius Simplex, centurion of the Sixth Legion, made the following memorial for his little daughter:*

D.M. SIMPLICIAE FLORENTINAE ANIMAE
INNOCENTISSIMAE QUAE VIXIT MENSES DECEM
FELICIUS SIMPLEX LEGIONIS VI CENTURIO PATER
FECIT

(inscribed on a stone coffin found in York)

D.M. = **dīs mānibus** (sacred) to the deified spirits of the dead (this formula often starts funerary inscriptions, followed by the name of the dead person in the dative, or sometimes the genitive, case)

2 *Panathenais made the following inscription for her daughter who died tragically just before her marriage:*

D.M. s(acrum). Callistē vīxit annīs xvi mēnsēs iii hōras vi et sēmisse: nūptūra īdibus Octōbris, moritur iiii īdūs Octōbrēs: Panathēnais māter pia cārae fīliae fēcit.

(from Mauretania in North Africa)

sēmisse half
īdibus Octōbris on 15 October
iiii = ante diem quārtum the fourth day before the Ides (12 October)

3 *The following illustrates how barren and desolate the pagan beliefs about life and death were:*

D.M. sacrum. Aurēliae Vercellae coniugī dulcissimae, quae vīxit plūs minus annīs XVII. 'nōn fuī, fuī, nōn sum, nōn dēsīderō.' Anthimus marītus eius.

plūs minus more or less, approximately
Anthimus . . . supply 'made this monument'

4 *The following is a funerary inscription for a Christian girl, the daughter of a veteran of the Roman army:*

Aurēliae Mariae puellae, virginī innocentissimae, sānctē pergentī ad iūstōs et ēlēctōs in pāce. quae vīxit annōs XVII, mēnsēs V, diēs XVIIII, spōnsāta Aurēliō Damātī diēbus XXV. Aurēlius Iānisirēus veterānus et Sextīlia parentēs īnfēlīcissimae fīliae dulcissimae ac amantissimae contrā vōtum. quī dum vīvent, habent magnum dolōrem. Martyrēs sanctī, in mente habēte Mariam.

(from Aquileia in North Italy)

sānctē pergentī going in holiness
spōnsāta betrothed
contrā vōtum supply
hōc fēcērunt made this monument contrary to their prayers, i.e. they had prayed that she should live

Chapter 44

Conditional clauses

These are clauses introduced by **sī** = 'if' or **nisi** = 'unless/if . . . not', which state a condition on which the truth of the main clause depends, e.g.

1 Simple fact (open) conditions

sī hoc dīcis, errās. If you say this, you are wrong.
sī hoc fēcistī, stultus erās. If you did this, you were foolish.

In these sentences the truth of the main clause is left open, e.g. in the second example the speaker does not say that 'you were foolish' as a fact, but simply says '*If* you did this, you were foolish.' You have already met many sentences of this type; they present no difficulty; both English and Latin use the indicative.

2   Contrary to fact conditional clauses

imperfect

sī pater noster adesset, nōs adiuvāret.
If our father were here, he would be helping us (but he is not here).
sī hoc fēcissēs, stultus fuissēs.
If you had done this, you would have been foolish (but you didn't).

The form of the sentence suggests that the main clause is untrue. In this case Latin uses the subjunctive in both the conditional and the main clauses; English uses the conditional tense 'would/should' in the main clause.
The imperfect subjunctive is used to refer to present time, the pluperfect subjunctive to past time, e.g.

sī prūdēns essēs, hoc nōn facerēs.
If you were wise, you would not be doing this (but you are doing it).
sī festīnāvissent, tempore advēnissent.
If they had hurried, they would have arrived in time (but they didn't hurry).
nisi imprūdēns fuissēs, iam incolumis essēs.
Unless you had been imprudent, you would now be safe.
(**fuissēs** refers to past time, **essēs** to present)

3   Future conditional clauses

These are of two sorts:

(a) Future more vivid, with the indicative (you have often met these), e.g.

sī domum revēneris, omnia tibi nārrābō.
If you come back home, I will tell you everything.

Notice that Latin uses the future or, more often, the future perfect, in the **sī** clause (English appears to use the present).

(b) Future less vivid, when the condition is represented as improbable, e.g.

sī domum reveniās, omnia tibi nārrem.
If you were to return home, I should tell you everything.
or If you returned home . . .

In these the present subjunctive is used in both the **sī** clause and the main clause.

Exercise 44.1

Translate (NB all the following sentences are 'contrary to fact' or 'future less vivid' conditional clauses, using the subjunctive; be sure you get the time reference (present, past or future) right)

1   sī fortiter pugnāvissētis, hostēs vīcissētis.
2   sī pater noster vīveret, cōnsilium nōbīs daret.
3   nisi Quīntus ē campō fūgisset, ab hostibus captus esset. *contrary to fact*
4   sī Quīntus prūdēns esset, in Brūtī exercitū nōn mīlitāret.
5   sī statim proficīscāmur, domum ante noctem adveniāmus. *future less vivid*
6   sī puerī bonī fuissent, magister fābulam eīs nārrāvisset.
7   magister 'puerī,' inquit, 'sī dīligenter labōrētis, fābulam vōbīs nārrem.'
8   māter fīliae 'sī mē adiuvēs,' inquit, 'pater tē laudet.' *present – showawoud*
9   puella 'māter,' inquit, 'sī ōtiōsa essem, libenter tē adiuvārem.'
10 puella, nisi occupāta esset, mātrem libenter adiūvisset.

Exercise 44.2

Translate (NB some of the following sentences are 'simple fact' or 'future more vivid' conditionals with the indicative, others 'contrary to fact' or 'future less vivid' with the subjunctive; be careful)

1   nisi Pompēius cum Sextō Pompēiō mīlitāvisset, iamdūdum (*long ago*) in Italiam rediisset.
2   sī Pompēius tandem redierit, omnēs gaudēbimus.
3   sī Octāviānum veniam rogāvissēs, ille tibi ignōvisset.
4   sī Octāviānus mihi ignōscat, Rōmae maneam.
5   sī mēcum cēnābis, reditum tuum celebrābimus.
6   sī plūs vīnī biberitis, plānē ēbriī eritis. *← fut perf ind*
7   nisi Pompēiī reditum celebrārēmus, tantum vīnī nōn biberēmus.
8   sī Quīntus alterum carmen recitābit, ego abībō.
9   nisi puellae tam pulchrae adessent, iamdūdum abiissem.
10 barbarus es, sī hōc carmine nōn dēlectātus es.

"more of wine"

Exercise 44.3

Translate into Latin; before translating say what sort of conditional you are writing – 'simple fact', 'contrary to fact', 'future more vivid' or 'future less vivid'

1   If you come home soon, I will tell you everything.
2   If you were to set out at once, you would arrive here in two days.
3   If you had not delayed at Rome, I would have met you in Capua.
4   If you waited for me in Capua, you were very foolish.
5   If you were here now, you would be sitting with me under a tree drinking wine.

P.S.

Note the following

quīcumque, quaecumque, quodcumque whoever, whatever   **ubicumque** wherever
quōcumque (to) wherever, whithersoever   **quācumque** by whatever way

Chapter 45

Uses of the subjunctive in main clauses

In main clauses the subjunctive has several uses: jussive (used in exhortations and 3rd person commands); deliberative questions; optative (wishes); potential.

1 Jussive (hortatory)

    ad forum festīnēmus.   Let us hurry to the forum.
    nē domum redeant.   Let them not return home.

You are already familiar with this usage. The negative is **nē**.

2 Deliberative questions

    quid faciāmus?   What are we to do?

The subjunctive (1st person singular or plural) is used in questions when the speaker is wondering what to do.

    utrum hīc maneam an domum redeam?   Am I to stay here or return home?

Exercise 45.1

Translate

1 quid tibi dīcam?
2 quō eāmus?
3 utrum hostibus resistāmus an fugiāmus?
4 quōmodo molestum illum dīmittam?
5 quandō Rōmā discēdāmus?

3 Optative (wishes)

    (utinam) diū vīvās semperque valeās.   May you live long and always be healthy!
    (utinam) pater meus adesset.   I wish my father were here!
    (utinam) pater meus nē Rōmam abiisset.   I wish my father had not gone away to Rome.

NB **1 utinam** (= I wish that) is often used in wishes to make the meaning clear.

2 The tenses of the subjunctive are used as in 'contrary to fact' conditional clauses, i.e. the present subjunctive is used for a wish for the future, the imperfect for a wish for the present and the pluperfect for a wish for the past.

3 The negative is **nē**:

    (utinam) nē in perīculum incidāmus.   May we not fall into danger.

Exercise 45.2

Translate

1 vīvās et valeās!
2 utinam dīves essem.
3 utinam nē mihi haec dīxissēs.
4 deī tē servent.
5 utinam incolumis domum redeās.

4 Potential

| **velim hoc facere.** | I should like to do this. |
| **nōn ausim pugnāre.** | I would not dare to fight. |

This use of the subjunctive is not common except with **velim, nōlim, ausim** (an irregular present subjunctive form of **audeō**). It is a sort of conditional subjunctive with the 'if' clause omitted, e.g. 'I should like to help you (if I could).' The negative is **nōn**.

Exercise 45.3

In each of the following sentences say what type of subjunctive is being used: jussive (i.e. expressing an exhortation or command), deliberative, optative (i.e. expressing a wish) or potential; then translate

1 quid faciam, amīce? quōmodo Octāviānō persuādeam ut mihi ignōscat?
2 ad palātium eāmus. prō certō habeō eum tibi ignōtūrum esse.
3 utinam Octāviānus nōs benignē accipiat.
4 Octāviāne, velim amīcum meum Pompēium tibi commendāre.
5 salvē, Pompēī. utinam nē inimīcōs meōs tam diū adiūvissēs.
6 sed gaudeō tē tandem vēnisse ut veniam rogēs. tibi libenter ignōscō. nōlim enim quemquam pūnīre quī veniam petit.
7 omnēs inimīcitiās dēpōnāmus. utinam posthāc semper pāce fruāmur et concordiā.

Exercise 45.4

Translate into Latin

1 Are we to stay here or hurry home?
2 Let us stay here; we cannot reach home before night.
3 I would not dare travel (= make the journey) by night.
4 I wish we had not set out so late!
5 I wish we were now safe at home!
6 We are in great danger. May the gods preserve us!
7 Let us set out for home at first light.

P.S. Two doctors

1 *The funerary inscription of a successful freedman:*

P. Decimius P(ūbliī) l(ībertus) Erōs Merula, medicus, clīnicus, chīrurgus, oculārius; VIvir. hic prō lībertāte dedit HS L. hic prō sēvirātū in rem p(ūblicam) dedit HS II. hic in statuās pōnendās in aedem Herculis dedit HS XXX. hic prīdiē quam mortuus est relīquit patrimōnium . . .

(from Assisi)

VIvir the *sēvirī* were priests of the cult of Augustus, the highest office a freedman could attain
HS L 50,000 sesterces
in statuās pōnendās for setting up statues; **aedem** temple
patrimōnium a fortune/estate (figure missing)

2 *A surgeon's victim:*

D.M. Euhelpistī līb(ertī): vīxit annīs XXVII mēns(ibus) IIII diēb(us) XI: flōrentēs annōs mors subita ēripuit. anima innocentissima, quem medicī secārunt et occīdērunt. P. Aelius Aug. līb(ertus) Pecūliāris alumnō suō.

anima a soul (**quem** refers to **anima**, masculine, because the soul is that of a man); **secārunt** cut
alumnō suō for his fosterchild (supply 'made this monument')

Chapter 46

A review chapter.

Exercise 46.1

Put the following indicative verb forms into corresponding forms of the subjunctive

1	amāmus	6	sunt
2	dīcēbant	7	volēbant
3	secūtī erant	8	ferēbāmus
4	proficīscimur	9	nōlō
5	gaudent	10	potes

Exercise 46.2

Translate

1 Maecēnās dīxit sē parvum fundum Quīntō datūrum esse.
2 'tibi opus est ōtiō' inquit 'ut carmina compōnās. velim tē adiuvāre.'
3 eum rogāvit ut posterō diē prīmā hōrā redīret.
4 'eāmus' inquit 'ad collēs Sabīnōs ut fundum īnspiciāmus.'
5 Quīntus, cum fundum vīdisset, tam laetus erat ut vix fārī posset.
6 Quīntus, fundō vīsō, Maecēnātī grātiās reddere cōnātus est.
7 sed Maecēnās dīxit eum omnia illa bene meruisse; nam amīcum fidēlem esse et modestum.
8 nisi multīs negōtiīs occupātus esset, cum Quīntō in fundō mānsisset.
9 posterō diē, Maecēnāte Rōmam profectō, Quīntus vīlicō vocātō dīxit, 'venī mēcum; velim fundum īnspicere.'

10 tōtō fundō īnspectō Quīntus prope fontem sedēns carmen compōnēbat.
11 carmen tam pulchrum composuit ut fōns Bandusia inter fontēs nōbilēs iam numerētur.
12 fundum tantī aestimābat ut ibi semper manēre vellet Rōmamque invītus redīret.

Exercise 46.3

Translate into Latin

When Maecenas said that he would give him a farm, Quintus rejoiced; for he had always wanted to live in the country. Maecenas told him to come early the next day so that they might ride to the Sabine hills and inspect the farm.

Setting out at first light, they arrived there as the sun was setting. Maecenas said, 'If we had ridden quicker, we would have inspected the farm before night. But tomorrow the farm manager will show you everything. Now come in and see the villa.'

The next day Maecenas said that he must return to Rome. 'If I were at leisure,' he said, 'I would stay and inspect the farm with you. But I am so busy that I must return to Rome at once.' Quintus thanked Maecenas again and said goodbye to him. Then he summoned the farm manager and asked him to show him the farm. Quintus was delighted by everything that he saw.

P.S.

The following prepositions/adverbs form comparative and superlative adjectives:

		comparative	*superlative*	
extrā + acc.	outside	**exterior**	**extrēmus**	uttermost, extreme
intrā + acc.	inside	**interior**	**intimus**	innermost, most intimate
post + acc.	after	**posterior**	**postrēmus**	last
prae + acc.	before	**prior**	**prīmus**	first
suprā + acc.	above	**superior**	**suprēmus**	highest, latest
			summus	highest, greatest
ultrā + acc.	beyond	**ulterior**	**ultimus**	furthest, last

Chapter 47

The uses of cum

1 The conjunction **cum** most commonly means 'when'.

In *past* time it is normally followed by the imperfect or pluperfect subjunctive, e.g.

> **cum domum revēnissent, cēnāvērunt.**
> When they had returned home, they dined.
> **cum cēnārent, amīcus quīdam casam intrāvit.**
> When they were dining, a friend entered the house.

But:

(a) As you have seen, if the **cum** clause follows the main clause, the indicative is used, e.g.

cēnābant cum amīcus quīdam casam intrāvit.
They were dining when a friend entered the house.
sōl iam occiderat cum domum revēnērunt.
The sun had already set when they returned home.

(b) If **cum** means 'whenever', the pluperfect indicative is used, e.g.

cum Quīntus ad fundum redierat, semper gaudēbat.
Whenever Quintus had returned to his farm, he always rejoiced.

2   When **cum** meaning 'when' is used in *present* or *future* time it is always followed by the indicative, e.g.

cum Athēnās advēnerō, ad tē scrībam.
When I arrive at Athens I shall write to you.
cum fessī sumus, in hortō quiēscimus.
When we are tired, we rest in the garden.

3   **cum** can also mean 'since'; with this meaning it is always followed by the subjunctive, e.g.

cum fessī sīmus, in hortō quiēscimus.
Since we are tired, we are resting in the garden.
cum fessī essēmus, domum nōn festīnāvimus.
Since we were tired, we did not hurry home.

4   **cum** followed by the subjunctive occasionally means 'although'; this meaning is usually made clear by the insertion of **tamen** at the beginning of the main clause (**tamen** will then be translated 'still', 'even so'), e.g.

cum fessī sīmus, tamen dīligenter labōrāmus.
Although we are tired, we are still working hard.

Exercise 47.1

Translate

1   Quīntus Maecēnāsque, cum prīmā hōrā Rōmā discessissent, in collēs Sabīnōs equitāvērunt.
2   vesper iam aderat cum ad vīllam advēnērunt.
3   cum fessus esset Quīntus, tamen fundum īnspicere volēbat.
4   Maecēnās 'cum nox sit,' inquit, 'pauca vidēre possumus.'
5   Quīntus 'cum primum sōl ortus erit,' inquit, 'omnia īnspiciam.'
6   posterō diē cum Maecēnās Rōmam profectus esset, Quīntus vīlicum arcessīvit.
7   vīlicus, cum negōtiīs occupātus esset, tamen ad Quīntum festīnāvit.
8   omnia īnspexerant cum Quīntus vīlicum dīmīsit.
9   Quīntus, cum quiēscere vellet, prope fontem assēdit.
10   cum sub arbore sedēret, carmen composuit.

11 cum aestās vēnerat, Quīntus in collēs festīnābat.
12 cum Rōmam redierat, fundum semper dēsiderābat (*longed for*).

The uses of dum

1 **dum** most commonly means 'while'; with this meaning it is usually followed by the present indicative, even in past time, e.g.

dum in forō manēmus, amīcum vīdimus ad nōs currentem.
While we were waiting in the forum, we saw a friend running towards us.

But if the action of the **dum** clause goes on throughout the action of the main clause, the imperfect indicative is used, e.g.

dum in forō manēbamus, cum amīcīs colloquēbāmur.
While (= all the time that) we were waiting in the forum, we talked with friends.

2 **dum** can also mean 'until'; like other temporal conjunctions, it usually takes the indicative, e.g.

in forō manēbāmus dum sōl occidit.
We waited in the forum until the sun set.
hostēs secūtī sumus dum in castra fūgērunt.
We followed the enemy until they fled into their camp.

But if the **dum** clause expresses purpose as well as time, it takes the subjunctive, e.g.

in forō manēmus dum pater veniat.
We are waiting in the forum for our father to come (until our father may come).
Antōnius apud Actium morābatur dum mare tranquillum esset.
Antony delayed at Actium until the sea should be calm.

Exercise 47.2

Translate

1 dum Antōnius apud Actium morātur, Octāviānī cōpiae castra haud procul posuērunt.
2 dum Antōnius terrā marīque obsidēbātur, mīlitēs eius et famē et morbō moriēbantur.
3 Agrippa Antōnium obsidēbat dum ille ērumpere coāctus est.
4 Antōnius in castrīs mānsit dum mare tranquillum esset.
5 dum Antōnius classem Agrippae oppugnat, Cleopātra subitō fūgit.
6 dum Antōnius cum Cleopātrā fugiēbat, cōpiae eius fortiter pugnābant.
7 Octāviānus exspectāvit dum omnēs sē dēderent.
8 dum Antōnius ad Aegyptum fugit, Octāviānus captīvōs in exercitum suum accēpit.

The connecting relative

Apollō lyram Quīntō trādidit; quō factō ēvānuit.
Apollo handed his lyre to Quintus; after doing this he vanished (literally: which having been done he vanished).

Antōnius Cleopātram uxōrem suam esse prōnūntiāvit. quae cum cognōvissent senātōrēs, statim bellum Cleopātrae indīxerunt.

Antony proclaimed that Cleopatra was his wife. When the senators learned this (literally: which things when the senators learned), they at once declared war on Cleopatra.

The relative pronoun is often used at the beginning of a sentence instead of a demonstrative. In the first example above, **quō factō = eō factō**, in the second example, **quae cum cognōvissent = cum ea cognōvissent**.

Exercise 47.3

Translate

1 Cleopātra classem suam in fugam dūxit. quae cum vīdisset Antōnius, eam secūtus est.
2 Antōnius Cleopātram vīdit fugientem. quam adeō amāvit ut ipse quoque ē proeliō fūgerit.
3 quibus vīsīs Agrippa Antōniī classem etiam ferōcius oppugnāvit.
4 tandem sē dēdidērunt Antōniī mīlitēs. quōs Octāviānus hūmānē tractātōs in exercitum suum accēpit.
5 quibus cognitīs Antōnius dēspērāvit.

P.S. Alternative verb and noun forms

1 A shortened form of the 3rd person plural of the perfect active is commonly used by the poets: **-ēre** for **-ērunt**, e.g. **parāvēre** for **parāvērunt**. So Horace's spring ode begins **diffūgēre nivēs = diffūgērunt nivēs** (the snows have fled away).

2 In the perfect active of 4th conjugation verbs **v** is often omitted, e.g. **audiit = audīvit, audiērunt = audīvērunt, audierat = audīverat**.
In the perfect infinitive and pluperfect subjunctive, the forms are further shortened by the omission of one **i**: **audīsse = audīvisse** and **audīssem = audīvissem**, etc.
So also from e.g. **petō: petiit** for **petīvit**, and from **eō: iit** for **īvit**; compounds of **eō** always use this form, e.g. **rediit** (never **redīvit**).
So also we find from 1st conjugation verbs **parāvisset** shortened to **parāsset**, and **parāvisse** shortened to **parāsse**.

3 Note carefully the alternative forms of the future infinitive of **esse: futūrus esse, fore**.

4 The active imperatives have alternative forms as follows: **parā/parātō, parāte/parātōte**, but these are found commonly only in the following:

estō, estōte	be!
scītō, scītōte	know! be assured!
mementō, mementōte	remember!

5 The 2nd person singular of the future passive has alternative forms: **parābere** for **parāberis, monēbere** for **monēberis, regēre** for **regēris, capiēre** for **capiēris, audiēre** for **audiēris**.

6 3rd declension nouns with stems in **-i** have an alternative ablative singular in **-ī**, e.g. **nāvī** for **nāve**; and 3rd declension nouns and adjectives have an alternative accusative plural in **-īs**, e.g. **omnīs cīvīs** for **omnēs cīvēs**. (Note that the **i** is long.)

Chapter 48

Clauses of fearing

1 **Antōnius timēbat nē in manūs hostium caderet.**
Antony feared lest/that he might fall into the hands of the enemy.
Cleopātra verēbatur nē Octāviānō prōderētur.
Cleopatra was afraid she would/might be betrayed to Octavian.
timēmus nē hostēs nōs capiant.
We are afraid the enemy may catch us.

Fears for the future are expressed by **nē** + subjunctive: present subjunctive if the leading verb is present or future; imperfect subjunctive if the leading verb is past.
English introduces such clauses by either 'lest', or 'that', or without any connecting conjunction.

2 **timēmus nē puerī domum ante noctem nōn redeant.**
We are afraid the children may not return home before night.

If the clause of fearing is negative **nē nōn** is used.

3 **timēbāmus longius prōgredī.**
We were afraid to advance further.

Latin, like English, uses an infinitive when the meaning is 'I am afraid to do something.' Thus **hoc facere timeō** = I am afraid to do this, but **timeō nē hoc faciat** = I am afraid he may do this.

Exercise 48.1

Translate

1 Maecēnās timēbat nē ad fundum ante noctem nōn advenīrent.
2 'festīnā, Quīnte,' inquit; 'timeō nē sērō adveniāmus.'
3 Quīntus 'equus meus fessus est; timeō celerius equitāre.'
4 puerī, veritī nē magister sibi īrāscerētur, dīligenter labōrābant.
5 timēbant nē magister sē nōn dīmitteret.
6 puellae, veritae nē puerī sē sequantur, domum festīnant.

NB **1** The reflexives **sē** and **suus** refer back to the leading verb (see numbers 4, 5 and 6 above).
(You will notice that **sē** and **suus** refer to the subject of the leading verb not only in indirect statement, question and command, but also to clauses of purpose introduced by **ut** or **nē** (since purpose is a thought in one's head), and to clauses of fearing introduced by **nē** (since the fear is a feeling in one's heart).

2 veritī, veritae (numbers 4 and 6); these are perfect participles, 'having feared', but the English idiom is to use the present, 'fearing'.

Exercise 48.2

Translate the following sentences, in each of which the perfect participle could be translated by an English present (English is less precise in its use of tenses than Latin)

1 ducem secūtī ad urbem mox advēnimus.
2 prīmā lūce profectus domum ante noctem rediī.
3 Cleopātra, verita nē Octāviānō prōderētur, turrem relinquere nōluit.
4 Cleopātra, Antōnium intuita, sciēbat eum moritūrum esse.
5 senex carcerem ingressus custōdēs salūtāvit.

Exercise 48.3

Translate into Latin

1 Let us hurry; I am afraid we may arrive late.
2 Fearing that the master might be angry with them, the boys waited outside the door of the school.
3 The girls were not afraid to enter; for they knew that the master would not be angry with them.
4 Fearing that Antony would be defeated, Cleopatra fled with her ships.
5 Antony was not afraid to fight, but overcome by his love for (= of) Cleopatra he followed her.

P.S. A triumphal arch and a war hero

1 *The following inscription is carved on the triumphal arch in Rome commemorating the emperor Claudius' invasion of Britain (AD 43):*

TIberiō CLAUDiō DRUSI Fīliō CAISARI AUGUSTO
GERMANICO PONTIFICI MAXIMO TRIBūniciā
POTESTATE XI COnsulī V IMPERATORI PATRI PATRIAE
SENATUS POPULUSQUE ROMANUS QUOD REGES
BRITANNIAE XI DEVICTOS SINE ULLA IACTURA IN
DEDITIONEM ACCEPERIT GENTESQUE BARBARAS
TRANS OCEANUM SITAS PRIMUS IN DICIONEM
POPULI ROMANI REDEGERIT.

pontificī maximō high priest
tribūniciā potestāte XI holding tribunician power for the eleventh time (i.e. AD 51–2)
senātus populusque Rōmānus after this subject, supply 'dedicated this arch'; **iactūrā** loss
in dīciōnem . . . redēgerit brought under the power of . . .

The letters in small print are omitted, giving common abbreviations.
The inscription begins with the full names and titles of the emperor in the dative case.

2 *A war hero:*

C. Gaviō L(ūciī) f(īliō) Silvānō, prīmipīlārī leg(iōnis) VIII Aug., tribūnō coh(ortis) II vigilum, tribūnō coh(ortis) XIII urbānae, tribūnō coh(ortis) XII praetōr(iae), dōnīs dōnātō ā dīvō Claud(iō) bellō Britannicō torquibus armillīs phalerīs corōnā aureā, patrōnō colōn(iae), dēcrētō decuriōnum.

(from Turin)

The career of Gavius Silvanus is given in ascending order; he was senior centurion (*prīmipīlāris*) of the Eighth Legion Augusta, which served in Britain in the invasion of Claudius (AD 43). He was promoted to serve in Rome, first as commander of the second cohort of the *vigilēs* (watchmen), then commander of the thirteenth urban cohort (police), lastly as commander of the twelfth cohort of the Praetorian guard (the emperor's bodyguard). For his service in Britain he was highly decorated by Claudius, being awarded *torquēs* (chain), *armillae* (bracelets), *phalerae* (medals) and a golden crown. He became the patron of his colony (Turin), and this memorial was erected by decree of the town councillors (*decuriōnēs*). (In AD 65 he took part in the conspiracy against the emperor Nero and, when it failed, committed suicide: see Tacitus *Annals* 15.50, 60, 71.)

Chapter 49

Impersonal verbs

A small number of verbs in English do not have a personal subject, e.g. 'it rains', 'it snows'; it makes no sense to ask 'Who rains?' 'Who snows?' Such verbs are called 'impersonal', since they have no person as subject. In Latin there is a fair number of such verbs, e.g.

pluit	it rains
ningit	it snows
tonat	it thunders
necesse est	it is necessary
fās est	it is right

Many Latin impersonal verbs are not used impersonally in English, e.g.

with the accusative of the person:

(**mē**) **oportet**	it behoves me = I ought
(**mē**) **pudet**	it shames me = I am ashamed
(**mē**) **iuvat**	it delights me = I like to
(**mē**) **taedet**	it wearies me = I am tired of (+ genitive)

with the dative of the person:

(**mihi**) **licet**	it is allowed to me = I may
(**mihi**) **placet**	it pleases me = I decide

They are often followed by an infinitive, e.g.

hoc facere mē oportet.	I ought to do this.
eī placuit domum redīre.	He decided to return home.
nōbīs licuit lūdōs spectāre.	We were allowed to watch the games.

Exercise 49.1

Translate

1 Octāviānō placuit in Oriente morārī.
2 necesse erat prōvinciās praesidiīs cōnfirmāre.
3 tandem eī licuit Rōmam redīre.
4 omnēs cīvēs bellōrum cīvīlium taeduit.
5 quandō nōbīs licēbit pāce fruī?
6 nōs oportet Octāviānō pārēre, quod pācem populō Rōmānō restituit.
7 Maecēnātem iuvābat poētās fovēre.
8 Quīntum urbis strepitūs taedēbat.
9 Maecēnātī placuit Quīntō fundum dare.
10 Quīntum oportuit Rōmam redīre sed eī placuit in fundō manēre.

Intransitive verbs in the passive

Intransitive verbs must be used impersonally in the passive, e.g.

Antōniō nūntiātum est.   It was announced to Antony.
ferōciter pugnātum est.   It was fought fiercely, i.e. there was a fierce battle.

Sometimes verbs of motion are used impersonally in the passive; in such cases you must translate them in the active, supplying a person from the context, e.g.

prīmā lūce profectī sumus; merīdiē ad montem ventum est.
We set out at dawn; at midday we came (literally: it was come) to the mountain.
undique concurritur.
It is run together from all sides, i.e. men run together from all sides.

Verbs which take the dative are used impersonally in the passive:

captīvīs parsum est.   It was spared to the captives, i.e. the captives were spared.
mihi persuāsum est.   I was persuaded.

Exercise 49.2

Translate

1 Antōniō nūntiātum est Octāviānum omnibus cum cōpiīs in Aegyptum prōgredī.
2 eī placuit prope Alexandrīam proelium committere.
3 terrā marīque ferōciter pugnātum est; tandem tamen Antōniī cōpiae fūgērunt.
4 omnibus captīvīs ab Octāviānō parsum est.
5 Octāviānī cōpiae Alexandrīam prōgressae sunt. ubi in urbem ventum est, nūntium ad Cleopātram mīsit.
6 Cleopātrae imperātum est ut turrem relinqueret.
7 nūntius 'sī tē dēdideris,' inquit, 'tibi ignōscētur.'
8 sed eī nōn persuāsum est ut sē dēderet.

Exercise 49.3

Translate the following sentences into Latin, using impersonal verbs for the phrases in heavy type

1   We set out at the first hour and hurried into the hills; before midday **we reached** the top of the mountain.
2   **We decided** to wait there for two hours.
3   But **we were not allowed** to rest for long.
4   For a shepherd warned us not to delay, and **we were persuaded** to descend at once.
5   It was a long and difficult journey, and before we reached home, **I was tired of** mountains.

P.S. The genders of 3rd declension nouns

These have to be learned in each case, but the following general rules will be some help:

1   Nouns ending **-er** in the nominative are masculine, e.g. **pater**, **imber**, except for:
mulier (woman), **māter** (mother), **linter** (boat), which are feminine
iter (journey), **vēr** (spring), which are neuter

2   All nouns ending **-or/-ōs** in the nominative are masculine, e.g. **honor**, **flōs**, except for:
soror (sister), **uxor** (wife), **arbor** (tree), which are feminine
cor (heart), **aequor** (sea), which are neuter

3   All nouns ending **-iō** in the nominative are feminine, e.g. **īnscrīptiō**, except for **centuriō** (centurion), **decuriō** (town councillor).

4   All nouns ending **-ās** in the nominative, e.g. **aetās** (age), are feminine, with a few rare exceptions, e.g. **gigās** (giant).

5   All nouns ending **-ūdō** in the nominative, e.g. **magnitūdō** (greatness, size), are feminine.

6   All nouns ending **-e, -us, -en** in the nominative, e.g. **mare** (sea), **genus** (race), **flūmen** (river), are neuter.

Chapter 50

Gerunds

ars scrībendī = the art of writing

The gerund is an active verbal noun, declined like **bellum**:

1st	*2nd*	*3rd*	*3rd -iō*	*4th*
para- parandum *preparing*	mone- monendum *warning*	reg- regendum *ruling*	capi- capiendum *taking*	audi- audiendum *hearing*

It is common in the accusative after **ad**, expressing purpose, e.g.

vēnī ad vōbīs succurrendum.   I have come to help you.

It is used in the genitive with **causā** = by reason of, for the sake of, as another way of expressing purpose, e.g.

vēnī vōbīs succurrendī causā.   I have come to help you.
(Notice that **causā** follows the word it governs.)

It is found in the dative with verbs and phrases requiring a dative, e.g.

nōn satis ōtiī habēbō carmina scrībendō.   I shall not have enough leisure for composing poems.

It is common in the ablative expressing cause or means, e.g.

celeriter currendō domum ante noctem advēnī.   By running fast I arrived home before night.

NB **1** the gerund of **eō** is **eundum.**

2 In English the present participle (a verbal adjective) and the gerund (a verbal noun) have the same form, e.g. 'writing'. In Latin the verbal adjective and the verbal noun are clearly distinguished, e.g.

Augustus in tablīnō sedēbat epistolam scrībēns.
Augustus was sitting in the study writing a letter.
(**scrībēns** is a verbal adjective describing Augustus)

Augustus nōn satis ōtiī habēbat ad epistolās scrībendum.
Augustus did not have enough leisure for writing letters.
(**scrībendum** is a verbal noun governed by **ad**)

Exercise 50.1

Translate

1 Quīntus artem dīcendī Rōmae didicit.
2 deinde Athēnās vēnit philosophiae stūdendī causā.
3 dīligenter stūdendō multa ibi didicit.
4 Athēnīs discessit ad mīlitandum cum Brūtō.
5 fortissimum sē praebuit in hostibus resistendō.
6 Brūtō mortuō ad Italiam rediit parentēs quaerendī causā.
7 scrība aerāriī ā Marcō factus, satis ōtiī habēbat carmina scrībendō.
8 Octāviānus inimīcīs ignōscendō omnēs cīvēs sibi conciliāvit.
9 Pompēius Rōmam rediit veniam petendī causā.
10 Quīntus omnēs amīcōs convocāvit ad Pompēiī reditum celebrandum.

Exercise 50.2

Translate into Latin

1 We have come to serve with Brutus (use **ad** + gerund).
2 For he is fighting to defend liberty (use gerund + **causā**).
3 Did you not hear the signal to advance (= of advancing)?
4 Do not try to save yourselves by delaying.
5 By fighting bravely we shall defeat the enemy and save the republic.
6 Quintus was ordered to lead his legion against Antony's forces.
7 There was a fierce battle, but in the end Brutus was defeated.
8 Quintus, throwing away his shield (= his shield having been thrown away), saved himself by running to the camp.
9 There it was announced that Brutus was dead.
10 All saved themselves by fleeing into the woods.

P.S. Funerary inscription for a vestal virgin and an epigram on a British lady in Rome

1 A vestal virgin

Bareius Zoticus and his wife dedicate a memorial to Flavia Publicia, a vestal virgin, who after long years of service guarding the sacred fire, rose to become chief vestal virgin:

Fl(āviae) Pūbliciae, v(irginī) V(estālī) maximae sānctissimae ac rēligiōsissimae, quae per omnēs gradūs sacerdōtiī apud dīvīna altāria omnium deōrum et ad aeternōs ignēs diēbus noctibusque piā mente rīte dēserviēns meritō ad hunc locum cum aetāte pervēnit, Barēius Zōticus cum Flāviā Verēcundā suā ob eximiam eius ergā sē benevolentiam. dēdicāta pr(īdiē) Kal(endīs) Oct(ōbris) dominīs nostrīs Valeriānō Aug(ustō) IIII et Galliēnō Aug(ustō) III cōn(sulibus).

2 A British lady in Rome

Martial writes an epigram on Claudia Rufina, a British lady who married a Roman, taking a Roman name, and became so Romanized that she might have been born a Roman or even an Athenian:

Claudia caeruleīs cum sit Rūfīna Britannīs
   ēdita, quam Latiae pectora gentis habet!
quāle decus fōrmae! Rōmānam crēdere mātrēs
   Italides possunt, Atthides esse suam . . .
sīc placeat superīs ut coniuge gaudeat ūnō
   et semper nātīs gaudeat illa tribus.
                              (Martial 11.53)

maximae chief (vestal virgin)
gradūs sacerdōtiī steps/ranks of the priesthood
rīte duly/according to religious custom
dēserviēns serving diligently
meritō deservedly; **ad hunc locum** i.e. to the post of chief vestal virgin
Bareius Zoticus and his wife (**suā**) (dedicated the memorial to her) because of (**ob**) her outstanding kindness towards them (**ergā sē**) **dēdicāta (est)** . . . (this memorial) was dedicated on 30 September AD 257 (when our lord Valerianus Augustus was consul for the fourth time and Gallienus Augustus for the third)

cum although; **caeruleīs** . . .
   Britannīs ēdita born from the blue (i.e. woad-painted) Britons
quam . . . pectora . . . habet how she has the heart(s) of the Latin race = how Roman she has become at heart
Latiae = **Latīnae**, i.e. **Rōmānae**
quāle decus what beauty
Rōmānam (that she is) a Roman
mātrēs Italides Italian (Roman) mothers
Atthides Athenian (mothers)
superīs the gods above

Chapter 51

Gerundives

cēna paranda est.	Supper is to-be-prepared.
puerī monendī sunt.	The children are to-be-warned.
imperium regendum erat.	The empire was to-be-ruled.
magister audiendus est.	The master is to-be-listened-to.

Besides the *gerund* (an active verbal noun), Latin verbs have a passive verbal adjective called the *gerundive* which looks identical with the gerund:

parandus, -a, -um	to be prepared
monendus, -a, -um	to be warned
regendus, -a, -um	to be ruled
capiendus, -a, -um	to be taken
audiendus, -a, -um	to be heard

The gerundive is commonly used instead of a gerund:

Maecēnās poētās incitābat ad carmina compōnenda.
Maecenas used to encourage poets to compose poems.
Maecēnās amīcōs convocāvit ad recitātiōnem audiendam.
Maecenas called together his friends to hear a recitation.

In these examples the nouns (**carmina, recitātiōnem**) are governed by the preposition **ad,** and the gerundives, being adjectives, agree with the nouns. The literal meaning of the examples is:

1 Maecenas encouraged poets to poems to be composed.
2 Maecenas called together his friends to a recitation to be heard.

But English verbs have no gerundive and the Latin idiom is so alien to English that it is better to grasp the gerundive phrase as a whole than to wrestle with the literal meaning. If you do this, such phrases are not difficult.

NB Deponent verbs besides having a gerund have a gerundive, passive in meaning, e.g.
cōnandus, -a, -um to be tried; **verendus, -a, -um** to be feared; **sequendus, -a -um** to be followed.

Exercise 51.1

Translate

1 Maecēnās amīcōs convocāvit ad poētās audiendōs.
2 inter aliōs Propertius vēnit carminis recitandī causā.
3 carmine optimē recitandō maximum plausum meruit.
4 Tibullus rūs recesserat ad carmina compōnenda.
5 Horātius Tibullum cōnsōlārī cōnātus est epistolā ad eum scribendā.
6 Horātius ad palātium īre solēbat ad Līviam salūtandam.
7 Līvia exemplum praebuit mātrōnae Rōmānae in officiīs perficiendīs.

8   Augustus Horātium rogāvit ut sē adiuvāret in epistolīs scrībendīs.

9   Horātius 'sī prīncipī pāream,' inquit, 'nōn satis ōtiī habeam ad carmina compōnenda.'

10   Maecēnās respondit, 'dīc prīncipī tē nōn satis valēre tantō operī suscipiendō.'

Exercise 51.2

Translate into Latin

One day (**quondam**) the Emperor (**prīnceps**) summoned Quintus to the palace (**palātium**). When he arrived there he found Livia spinning (= making) wool in the tablinum. He asked her why Augustus had summoned him, but she said that she did not know. He hurried to the Emperor, who received him kindly.

'Quintus,' he said, 'I am asking you to help me. I am so busy that I cannot write all my letters. Will you come every day to the palace to help me in writing my letters?'

Quintus was astonished but was not afraid to speak the truth. 'Emperor,' he said, 'I rejoice that you so trust me. I ought to help you. But I am not worthy of so great an honor, and I am afraid that if I were to do this, I would not have enough leisure for composing poems.'

The emperor did not compel Quintus to obey him but accepted his excuse patiently (**aequō animō**).

P.S. Two epigrams

1   *A nightmare doctor:*

> lōtus nōbīscum est, hilaris cēnāvit, et īdem
>   inventus māne est mortuus Andragorās.
> tam subitae mortis causam, Faustīne, requīris?
>   in somnīs medicum vīderat Hermocratem.
>   (Martial 6.53)

lōtus washed, i.e. he took a bath

2   *A noisy schoolmaster:*

> quid tibi nōbīscum est, lūdī scelerāte magister,
>   invīsum puerīs virginibusque caput?
> nōndum cristātī rūpēre silentia gallī:
>   murmure iam saevō verberibusque tonās . . .
> vīcīnī somnum nōn tōtā nocte rogāmus:
>   nam vigilāre leve est, pervigilāre grave est.
> discipulōs dīmitte tuōs. vīs, garrule, quantum
>   accipis ut clāmās, accipere ut taceās?
>   (Martial 9.68)

quid . . . est? What have we to do with you?; **scelerāte** villanous
invīsum . . . caput creature (literally: head) hateful to . . .
cristātī . . . gallī the crested cocks
verberibus tonās you thunder with blows; **vigilāre** to lie awake
pervigilāre to lie awake all night
garrule chatterbox!
vīs . . . accipere will you accept . . .

Chapter 52

Gerundives of obligation

lūdī omnī modō ōrnandī sunt.
The games must be (are to be) embellished in every way.
hoc carmen tibi scrībendum est.
This poem must be written by you, i.e. You must write this poem.

The gerundive is commonly used with **esse** expressing obligation (must/ought/have to). The person concerned is in the dative.

In English we often prefer to make such sentences active in form with the person concerned as the subject, e.g.

templum nōbīs aedificandum est.
We must build a temple.
multae recitātiōnēs mihi audiendae erant.
I had to listen to many recitations.
ad palātium vōbīs festīnandum erit.
You will have to hurry to the palace.

The gerundive of intransitive verbs is used impersonally in such expressions, literally 'it will have to be hurried by you'.

Exercise 52.1

Translate

1 lūdī summā rēligiōne celebrandī sunt.
2 tōtī populō fēriae agendae sunt.
3 sacrificia Augustō in monte Capitōlīnō facienda erant.
4 tertiō diē omnibus cīvibus ad Palātium conveniendum erat.
5 carmen Horātiī chorō puerōrum puellārumque cantandum erit.
6 festīnāte, amīcī; statim proficīscendum est.
7 nox adest. sī morābimur, in montibus tōtam noctem manendum erit.
8 nōn poterimus domum hodiē pervenīre; hīc manendum est dum sōl oriātur.
9 pāstor quaerendus est quī nōs in casam suam accipiet.
10 sī pāstōrem nōn invēnerimus, in silvīs dormiendum erit; sīc tūtī erimus.

The gerundive is sometimes found agreeing with the object of verbs such as **cūrō, mittō, dō** in phrases expressing purpose or intent:

Augustus corpus Vergiliī cūrāvit Neāpolī sepeliendum.
Augustus arranged for (cared for) Virgil's body to be buried at Naples.

Exercise 52.2

Translate

1 Maecēnās epistolam cursōrī (*his runner*) trādidit ad Quīntum ferendam.
2 Maecēnās multōs amīcōs convocandōs cūrāvit ad recitātiōnem audiendam.
3 omnibus bellīs cōnfectīs Augustus lūdōs saeculārēs celebrandōs cūrāvit.
4 Quīntus carmen composuit Apollinī Diānaeque cantandum.

Exercise 52.3

Translate into Latin

1 Since all wars are finished, the doors of the temple of Janus must be shut.
2 The peace which we now enjoy must be preserved for ever.
3 We must celebrate the new age with games (= the new age is to be celebrated by us).
4 Horace has written an excellent poem to be sung by a chorus.
5 All the citizens must hurry to the Palatine mount (= it is to be hurried by all the citizens).
6 There we shall have to listen to the song which Horace has written.

Exercise 52.4

Translate into Latin

Quintus said that on his farm he could enjoy leisure for composing poems. He liked to read the books of the ancients and lie idle in the shade. But in fact whenever he returned to his farm, he always had to work hard. He called his farm manager and arranged for the fields to be plowed; he sent out boys to guard the sheep; he himself with his own hands used to move stones from the fields. The grapes had to be picked and the wine had to be made. When evening came, he often used to ask his neighbors to dinner; after they had dined modestly, they sat in the garden drinking wine and talking about philosophy. You could scarcely say that Quintus was an idle (**ignāvus, -a, -um**) man, but he was content with his life and was always sad when he had to return to Rome.

P.S. Memorābilia: famous lines from Virgil

1 omnia vincit Amor: et nōs cēdāmus Amōrī. (*Ecl.* 10.69)

2 fēlīx quī potuit rērum cognōscere causās. (*Geo.* 2.490)
(of Lucretius, poet, philosopher and scientist)

3 fortūnātus et ille deōs quī nōvit agrestēs. (*Geo.* 2.493)   **deōs agrestēs** the gods of the country

4 tantae mōlis erat Rōmānam condere gentem. (*Aen.* 1.33)   **tantae mōlis erat** so great a task it was

5   equō nē crēdite, Teucrī.
quidquid id est, timeō Danaōs et dōna ferentēs. (*Aen.* 2.47–8)   **et** even

6   revocāte animōs maestumque timōrem
mittite; forsan et haec ōlim meminisse iuvābit. (*Aen.* 1.202–3)   **forsan . . . iuvābit** perhaps you will
(Aeneas encourages his followers when they are wrecked in   delight
Libya)

7   vīxī et quem dederat cursum Fortūna perēgī.   (*Aen.* 4.652)
(Dido speaks, just before her suicide)

8   Trōs Anchīsiadēs, facilis dēscēnsus Avernō:
noctēs atque diēs patet ātrī iānua Dītis;   **patet** is open
sed revocāre gradūs superāsque ēvadere ad aurās,   **ātrī . . . Dītis** of black Death
hoc opus, hic labor est.   (*Aen.* 6.126–9)
(The Sibyl warns Aeneas of the dangers of attempting to go
down to the underworld)

9   stābant ōrantēs prīmī trānsmittere cursum   **trānsmittere** to cross
tendēbantque manūs rīpae ulteriōris amōre. (*Aen.* 6.313–14)
(Aeneas sees the souls of the dead waiting to cross the river
Styx into the underworld)

Chapter 53

The predicative dative (dative of purpose)

vīlicus Quīntō magnō auxiliō erat.
His farm manager was a great help to Quintus.
fūmus strepitusque urbis Quīntō odiō erant.
The smoke and racket of the city were hateful to Quintus.

In certain phrases Latin uses a noun in the dative after the verb **esse** instead of a complement in the
nominative; thus the first example above means literally: 'The farm manager was *for a great help* to
Quintus.' The second means literally: 'The smoke and racket of the city were *for a hatred* to Quintus.'

The commonest of such phrases are:

auxiliō esse	to be a help to
cordī esse	to be dear to (**cor, cordis**, n. heart)
cūrae esse	to be a care to, a cause of anxiety to
exemplō esse	to be an example to
exitiō esse	to be a cause of destruction to
odiō esse	to be hateful to
salūtī esse	to be a cause of safety to
ūsuī esse	to be useful to

Exercise 53.1

Translate

1 segetēs Quīntō magnae cūrae erant.
2 grandinēs (*hailstones*) nōnnumquam ūvīs exitiō fuērunt.
3 fundus Quīntō semper cordī erat.
4 Līvia exemplō erat mātrōnīs Rōmānīs.
5 fēminae dissolūtae (*licentious*) eī odiō erant.
6 Līvia Augustō magnō auxiliō fuit.
7 'nōnne vīs hunc canem emere? magnō ūsuī tibi erit.'
8 'canem iam habeō quī mihi cordī est ovēsque bene custōdit.'
9 'sed tuus canis īnfirmus est; sine dubiō hic canis auxiliō tibi erit.'
10 'ille canis saevus esse mihi vidētur; timeō nē exitiō ovibus sit.'

Exercise 53.2

Translate and identify the following parts of the verbs **dīcō** *and* **loquor**

1	dīcēns	6	dīcendus	11	locūtus	16	loquerētur
2	dīxistī	7	dīc	12	loquī	17	loquere
3	dictus	8	dīxisse	13	loquendum	18	locūtī essent
4	dīcendum	9	dīcēmus	14	loquēns	19	loquāmur
5	dictūrus	10	dīcāmus	15	locūtūrus esse	20	loquēbāris

The relative with the subjunctive

> **Quīntus servōs ēmīsit <u>quī</u> segetēs <u>meterent</u>, puerōs dēsignāvit <u>quī</u> ovēs <u>custōdīrent</u>.**
> Quintus sent out slaves <u>to reap</u> the corn, he appointed boys <u>to guard</u> the sheep.

The relative with the subjunctive can be used to express purpose; in the example above, **quī . . . meterent** means literally 'who might reap'; **quī . . . custōdīrent** means 'who might guard'.

> **prīmā lūce profectī sumus quō celerius domum advenīrēmus.**
> We set out at first light to reach (so that we might reach) home more quickly.

quō celerius literally means 'by which the more quickly'; purpose clauses containing a comparative are usually introduced by **quō**, not **ut**.

Exercise 53.3

Translate

1 Augustus quīnque legiōnēs in Oriente relīquit quae fīnēs prōvinciārum custōdīrent.
2 quattuor classēs īnstrūxit quae praedōnibus (*pirates*) exitiō essent mercātōribusque salūtī.
3 in urbe Rōmā vigiliās (*watches*) īnstituit quae cīvēs ā latrōnibus (*robbers*) incendiīsque tuerentur.
4 viās pūblicās per Italiam custōdīvit quō tūtius viātōrēs iter facerent.
5 Quīntus nūntium ad Maecēnātem mīsit, quī eī dīceret sē mox Rōmam reditūrum esse.

Exercise 53.4

Translate into Latin

1 This dog was a great help to the shepherd.
2 For he was very useful in defending the sheep.
3 And so he was dear to the heart of the shepherd.
4 When he was wounded by a wolf, the shepherd was very concerned for him (= he was a great care to the shepherd).
5 The shepherd's wife looked after the dog with the greatest care but did no good (= achieved nothing).
6 The shepherd summoned the doctor to cure him (= the dog) but he could not save him.
7 The shepherd's wife said that he must buy another dog.
8 But the new dog was no use to the shepherd in guarding the sheep.
9 The shepherd asked his master to give him a good dog to guard his sheep.
10 The master sent a messenger to say that he would soon give him an excellent dog.

Exercise 53.5

Translate into Latin

Dear Maecenas,

When I left Rome, I promised to return in five days. But I am still here on my farm. I ask you to forgive me. I cannot bear the heat (**calor, calōris,** m.) of summer in the city; I must stay in the hills until autumn comes. If I returned to Rome now, I would without doubt be ill, and you would be sad if you heard that I had died of fever (**febris, febris,** f.).

Besides, I am very busy. I am writing a poem about the art of poetry (**ars poētica**), which is very long and difficult. When summer is over, I shall go down to Naples and spend the winter there. But as soon as spring returns and I see the first swallow (**hirundō, hirundinis,** f.), I shall hurry to Rome and hope to see you there.

Your loving friend, Quintus.

P.S. Memorābilia: famous lines from Horace

1 nātūram expellās furcā, tamen usque recurret.
                              (*Epistles* 1.10.24)

furcā with a pitchfork
usque always

2 caelum nōn animum mūtant quī trāns mare currunt.
                              (*Epistles* 1.11.27)

3   dum loquimur, fūgerit invida
   aetās: carpe diem, quam minimum crēdula posterō.
                              (*Odes* 1.11.7)

invida aetās jealous time
quam minimum crēdula posterō
   trusting as little as possible in
   tomorrow

4 multīs ille bonīs flēbilis occidit.   (*Odes* 1.24.9)

5 aequam mementō rēbus in arduīs
   servāre mentem.   (*Odes* 2.3.1)

rēbus in arduīs in difficult things/in a
   crisis

6 omnēs eōdem cōgimur   (*Odes* 2.3.25)   **eōdem** the same way, i.e. to death

7 sī frāctus illābātur orbis,   **illābātur** were to fall on (him)
     impavidum ferient ruīnae.   (*Odes* 3.3.7)   **orbis** the globe, the sky
                                                            impavidum fearless; supply 'him' =
                                                               'the good man'

Chapter 54

Summary of the uses of ut

ut + the indicative means either 'as' or 'when', e.g.

Horātius est vir ingeniōsus, ut dīcunt.	Horace is a clever man, as they say.
magister īrātus est, ut vidētur.	The master is angry, as it seems.
ego ita erō ut mē esse oportet.	I shall be such as I should be.
haec rēs sīc est ut nārrō.	This situation is such as I say.
ut vēnī cōram tē, pauca locūtus sum.	When I came into your presence, I said little.
ut domum rediimus, laetī cēnāvimus.	When we returned home, we dined happily.

ut + the subjunctive is used:

(a) in purpose clauses (see chapter 34)
(b) in indirect commands (see chapter 35)
(c) in result clauses (see chapter 43)

Other uses of **ut** will be met when you read Latin texts.

Exercise 54.1

Translate the following sentences and explain the constructions in bold type

1 Augustus, **bellīs cīvīlibus cōnfectīs**, pācem populō Rōmānō reddidit.
2 sed imperium Rōmānum numquam tūtum **fuisset, nisi** fīnēs ad flūmina Rhēnum Dānuviumque **prōtulisset**.
3 **ut haec efficeret**, multōs annōs aut ipse aut ducēs eius mīlitābant multāsque gentēs externās imperiō adiēcērunt.
4 poētae canēbant **eum** cōpiās in Parthōs **ductūrum esse, nē** clādem ā Crassō acceptam **relinqueret** inultam.
5 nesciēbant tamen **quae** Augustus in animō **habēret**; ille enim nūllum bellum **suscēpit, nisi** pugnāre necesse **erat**.
6 ūnam clādem accēpit quā Vārus cum tribus legiōnibus in Germāniā dēlētus est. **cuius clādis** Augustus numquam oblītus est.
7 tandem, **pāce** tōtum per imperium **restitūtā**, lūdōs saeculārēs celebrāre **eī placuit**.
8 **Quīntō carmen scrībendum erat, quod** chorus puerōrum puellārumque in lūdīs **cantāvit**.
9 **cum** Maecēnās **periisset**, Quīntum vītae taeduit.
10 nam verēbātur **nē** omnibus amīcīs mortuīs sōlus **relinquerētur**.

Exercise 54.2

Write short sentences in Latin to illustrate the following constructions and translate them

1 indirect statement
2 indirect command
3 indirect question
4 purpose clause
5 result clause
6 ablative absolute
7 impersonal verb
8 predicative dative (dative of purpose)
9 gerund
10 gerundive of obligation

P.S. Augustī testāmentum

Augustus survived Horace by twenty-two years, dying at the age of seventy-seven in AD 14. By the time of his death he had established the imperial system so firmly that he was able to hand over power to his stepson, Tiberius, and leave behind him a dynasty which was to rule the Roman world for the next fifty years. He had given the Roman world peace and order, but at a heavy cost; liberty had been replaced by monarchy, which was to degenerate into tyranny under emperors such as Nero.

Below are six extracts from the *Rēs Gestae Dīvī Augustī* (The Achievements of the Divine Augustus – Augustus was declared divine after his death; hence he is called *Dīvus*). This was the testament which Augustus wrote shortly before his death, in which he outlined his career and all that he claimed to have achieved for Rome. It was read out in the senate after his death; it was then engraved on two bronze pillars set up in Rome. These have been lost, but copies were made in various parts of the empire and some of these have been partially preserved. The most complete copy is from Ancyra in southern Turkey, engraved on the wall of a mosque, which had previously been the temple of Rome and Augustus (see illustration, p. 183).

Translate the following extracts and write a short historical commentary on each (most of the events to which Augustus refers have been described in our narrative, but to explain some you may need the help of a book on Roman history)

1 eōs quī parentem meum trucīdāvērunt in exsilium expulī et posteā, cum bellum īnferrent reīpūblicae, vīcī bis aciē.
(Here explain whom Augustus means by **parentem meum**. Who were **eōs quī . . . trucīdāvērunt**? What battles is he referring to? How true is his account of these events?)

trucīdāvērunt murdered
bis twice

2 bella terrā et marī cīvīlia externaque tōtō in orbe terrārum saepe gessī, victorque omnibus veniam petentibus cīvibus pepercī. externās gentēs, quibus tūtō ignōscere potuī, cōnservāre quam dēlēre māluī.

3 templum Iānī, quod clausum esse maiōrēs nostrī voluērunt cum per tōtum imperium Rōmānum terrā marīque esset parta pāx, ter mē prīncipe senātus claudendum esse cēnsuit.

esset parta had been won
cēnsuit voted

4 omnium prōvinciārum populī Rōmānī, quibus fīnitimae fuērunt gentēs quae nōn pārērent imperiō nostrō, fīnēs auxī. Aegyptum imperiō populī Rōmānī adiēcī. prō quō meritō senātūs cōnsultō Augustus appellātus sum.

omnium prōvinciārum is governed by **fīnēs**; **fīnitimae** bordering
prō quō meritō for this service, achievement; **senātūs cōnsultō** by decree of the senate

5 in cōnsulātū sextō et septimō postquam bella cīvīlia exstīnxeram, per cōnsēnsum ūniversōrum potītus omnium rērum, rempūblicam ex meā potestāte in senātūs populīque Rōmānī arbitrium trānstulī.

in cōnsulātū . . . septimō i.e. 28 and 27 BC
potītus (+ gen.) having control of
arbitrium the rule

6 post id tempus auctōritāte omnibus praestitī, potestātis autem nihil amplius habuī quam cēterī quī in magistrātū quōque conlēgae fuērunt.

praestitī (+ dat.) I excelled
nihil amplius no more
in magistrātū quōque in each magistracy/office

7 cum scrīpsī haec annum agēbam septuāgēsimum sextum.

septuāgēsimum seventieth

Posterity saw Augustus' rule in a different light, looking back on the tyranny of some of his successors. A hundred years later, Tacitus, the greatest of the Roman historians, began his *Annals*, which described events from the death of Augustus, with an attack on the changes in the Roman state and character for which Augustus was responsible.

Read the following and summarize Tacitus' account in your own words

ubi mīlitēs dōnīs, populum annōnā, cūnctōs dulcēdine ōtiī pellexit, īnsurgēbat paulātim, mūnia senātūs, magistrātuum, lēgum in sē trahēbat, nūllō adversante, cum ferōcissimī aut per bellum aut per prōscrīptiōnem cecidissent, cēterī nōbilium quantō quis servitiō prōmptior erat, tantō magis opibus et honōribus extollerentur et, novīs ex rēbus auctī, tūta et praesentia quam vetera et perīculōsa māllent . . . igitur versō cīvitātis statū nihil usquam erat prīscī et integrī mōris: omnēs iussa prīncipis aspectābant.

(*Annals* 1.2)

annōnā by free grain, the dole
dulcēdine the sweetness, the attractions;
pellexit he coaxed, seduced
īnsurgēbat he increased his powers
mūnia the functions
quantō quis servitiō prōmptior erat the readier any was for slavery
tantō magis so much the more
extollerentur they were raised
tūta et praesentia things safe and present, i.e. their present safety
usquam anywhere
nihil . . . prīscī et integrī mōris none of the old upright behavior

P.P.S. The death of the centurion Lucilius

You encountered Lucilius as the centurion who was responsible for training Quintus and Pompeius when they joined the army of Brutus in chapter 35. He was a historical character who died in AD 14 serving in the army on the eastern frontier of the empire.

When Augustus died, the legions stationed on the eastern frontier of the empire mutinied. The commanding officer, Blaesus, succeeded in quelling this mutiny and arrested and imprisoned the ringleaders. But it soon broke out again and the soldiers freed those who had been imprisoned. In the ensuing riot, stirred up by a soldier called Vibulenus, the centurion Lucilius was killed, as Tacitus describes:

flagrantior inde vīs, plūrēs sēditiōnī ducēs. et Vibulēnus quīdam gregārius mīles, ante tribūnal Blaesī adlevātus circumstantium umerīs, 'vōs' inquit 'hīs innocentibus et miserrimīs lūcem et spīritum reddidistis: sed quis frātrī meō vītam, quis frātrem mihi reddit? quem nocte proximā Blaesus iugulāvit per gladiātōrēs suōs, quōs in exitium mīlitum habet atque armat. respondē, Blaese; ubi cadāver abiēcistī? nē hostēs quidem sepultūrā invident. cum ōsculīs, cum lacrimīs dolōrem meum implēverō, mē quoque trucīdārī iubē.'

incendēbat haec flētū et pectus atque ōs manibus verberāns. sīc tantum tumultum excīvit ut mīlitēs haud multum ab exitiō lēgātī abessent. tribūnōs tamen et praefectum castrōrum extrūsērunt, sarcinae fugientium dīreptae sunt, et centuriō Lūcīlius interficitur, cui vocābulum 'cēdō alteram' dederant, quia frāctā vīte in tergō mīlitis alteram clārā vōce et rūrsus aliam poscēbat.

(Annals 1.23)

flagrantior (erat) vīs the violence was (even) fiercer

gregārius mīles a common soldier

adlevātus lifted up

vōs i.e. Blaesus' fellow soldiers who had freed the arrested mutineers (**hīs innocentibus et miserrimīs**)

iugulāvit murdered; **cadāver** corpse

sepultūrā invident begrudge burial

implēverō I have satisfied

trucīdārī to be murdered

ōs his face; **excīvit** he stirred up

haud multum abessent were not far from

extrūsērunt they drove out

sarcinae the packs

dīreptae sunt were plundered

vocābulum the nickname

'cēdō alteram' give (me) another

vīte vine-staff

tū regere imperiō populōs, Rōmāne, mementō
(hae tibi erunt artēs) pācīque impōnere mōrem,
parcere subiectīs et dēbellāre superbōs.

(*Aeneid* 6.851–3)

1 **mementō** remember to! (an old imperative form)
2 **pācīque impōnere mōrem** and to impose custom on peace = to make peace customary
3 **subiectīs** the conquered
dēbellāre to war down, overcome by war

The Res Gestae Divi Augusti, Ancyra

1 Augustus

This is Augustus' account of his conquests (see map, p. 110 above):

mare pācāvī ā praedōnibus . . . omnium prōvinciārum
populī Rōmānī quibus fīnitimae fuērunt gentēs quae nōn
pārērent imperiō nostrō fīnēs auxī. Galliās et Hispāniās
prōvinciās, item Germāniam, quā inclūdit Oceanus ā
5   Gādibus ad ōstium Albis flūminis, pācāvī. Alpēs ē regiōne
eā quae proxima est Hadriānō marī ad Tuscum pācāvī nūllī
gentī bellō per iniūriam inlātō . . . Aegyptum imperiō
Rōmānō adiēcī . . . Pannoniōrum gentēs, quās ante mē
prīncipem populī Rōmānī exercitus numquam adiit,
10   dēvictas . . . imperiō populī Rōmānī subiēcī, prōtulīque
fīnēs Illyricī ad rīpam flūminis Dānuī.

(*Res Gestae Divi Augusti* 25–30)

1 **pācāvī** I pacified, made peaceful
ā praedōnibus from pirates
omnium prōvinciārum is governed by
fīnēs (line 3)
2 **fīnitimae** bordering
4 **item** likewise
quā inclūdit Oceanus where the Ocean forms the boundary
5 **ad ōstium Albis** to the mouth of the Elbe
6 **Hadriānō marī** the Adriatic sea
7 **per iniūriam** unjustly
10 **flūminis Dānuī** of the river Danube

2 Virgil

In the following two passages Virgil gives his view of Rome's imperial mission. In the first Jupiter prophesies the future of the descendants of Aeneas:

Rōmulus excipiet gentem et Māvortia condet
moenia Rōmānōsque suō de nōmine dīcet.
hīs ego nec mētās rērum nec tempora pōnō:
imperium sine fīne dedī. quīn aspera Iūnō
cōnsilia in melius referet, mēcumque fovēbit   5
Rōmānōs, rērum dominōs gentemque togātam . . .
nāscētur pulchrā Trōiānus orīgine Caesar,
imperium Oceanō, fāmam quī terminet astrīs . . .
aspera tum positīs mītēscent saecula bellīs:
cāna Fidēs et Vesta, Remō cum frātre Quirīnus   10
iūra dabunt; dīrae ferrō et compāgibus artīs
claudentur Bellī portae; Furor impius intus
saeva sedēns super arma et centum vīnctus aēnīs
post tergum nōdīs fremet horridus ōre cruentō.

(Aeneid 1.276–96)

1 **excipiet gentem** will take over the race; Jupiter has already foretold events from the Trojans' arrival in Latium up to the foundation of Rome by Romulus, son of Mars

1–2 **Māvortia . . . moenia** the walls of Mars

2 **dīcet** will call them

3 **mētās rērum** bounds of power

4 **quīn aspera Iūnō** even fierce Juno; Juno had always been the enemy of the Trojans and tried to prevent Aeneas reaching Italy

7 **Caesar** Augustus; his full name owing to his adoption by Julius Caesar was: C. Iulius Caesar Octavianus Augustus. The Julian *gēns* claimed descent from Iulus, Aeneas' son; hence he is **Trōiānus.** Virgil makes the reign of Augustus and the establishment of the Pax Romana the culmination of Roman history

8 **imperium . . . astrīs = quī imperium Oceanō terminet . . .** to bound his empire with the Ocean, his glory with the stars

9 **aspera . . . saecula** the fierce generations **mītēscent** will grow gentle

10 **cāna Fidēs** grey-haired Faith; Fides represents the old-fashioned Roman virtues of loyalty and good faith: Vesta, goddess of the hearth and home, represents traditional family ties

Remō . . . Quirīnus Quirinus is another name for Romulus; the killing of Remus by his brother is the epitome of civil war. Now they will be united

11 **dīrae ferrō et compāgibus artīs** grim with iron and close-knit fastenings, i.e. (gates) grim with close-knit fastenings of iron

12 **Bellī portae** the gates of War; the gates of the temple of Janus were closed when there was peace throughout the Roman empire **Furor impius** wicked Madness; throughout the *Aeneid* Furor is opposed to Pietas; now at last Pietas will triumph and Furor – mad strife, the cause of a hundred years of civil war – will be confined

13–14 **centum aēnis . . . nōdīs** bound by a hundred bronze knots behind its back

14 **fremet** shall growl; **cruentō** bloodstained

In Book 6 of the Aeneid, *Aeneas goes down into the underworld to consult his dead father. Anchises shows him the souls of his descendants waiting to be born and foretells their imperial mission. In this pageant of Roman history, Aeneas first sees the souls of the kings descended from him who will rule over Alba Longa, ending with Romulus, the founder of Rome. From Romulus he jumps to Augustus, the second founder of Rome:*

hūc geminās nunc flecte aciēs, hanc aspice gentem
Rōmānōsque tuōs. hīc Caesar et omnis Iūlī
prōgeniēs magnum caelī ventūra sub axem.
hic vir, hic est, tibi quem prōmittī saepius audīs,
Augustus Caesar, dīvī genus, aurea condet
5   saecula quī rūrsus Latiō regnāta per arva
Sāturnō quondam, super et Garamantas et Indōs
prōferet imperium; iacet extrā sīdera tellūs,
extrā annī sōlisque viās, ubi caelifer Atlās
10 axem umerō torquet stellīs ardentibus aptum . . .

After Augustus Anchises shows Aeneas the souls of heroes of earlier times – the kings of Rome, then the great men of the republic, ending with the two Scipios who had defeated the Carthaginians and Quintus Fabius Maximus who had saved Italy from Hannibal. He breaks off this pageant to prophesy Rome's mission; others (the Greeks) will excel in the arts and sciences, but Rome will bring peace to the world:

excūdent aliī spīrantia mollius aera
(crēdō equidem), vīvōs dūcent de marmore vultūs,
ōrābunt causās melius, caelīque meātūs
dēscrībent radiō et surgentia sīdera dīcent:
15 tū regere imperiō populōs, Rōmāne, mementō,
(hae tibi erunt artēs), pācīque impōnere mōrem,
parcere subiectīs et dēbellāre superbōs.

(*Aeneid* 6.788–853)

1   **hūc . . . aciēs** now turn your two eyes this way

2–3 **Iūlī prōgeniēs** the descendants of Iulus (Aeneas' son)

3   **caelī ventūra sub axem** about to/destined to come beneath the vault of heaven

5   **dīvī genus** the son of a god; Julius Caesar was deified by decree of the senate after his death

5–6 **aurea condet saecula quī** = **quī aurea saecula condet**

6–7 **Latiō . . . Sāturnō quondam** throughout the fields in Latium once ruled by Saturn; the god Saturn, according to legend, ruled over Latium in the Golden Age

7   **Garamantas et Indōs** the Garamantes were a tribe in North Africa, conquered by the Romans in 19 BC. Augustus had received an embassy from India the same year. These two peoples represent the ends of the world

8–9 **iacet . . . viās** the land lies beyond the stars, beyond the paths of the year and the sun, i.e. beyond the Zodiac and the annual path of the sun. Virgil means that the land beyond the Garamantes and the Indians, to which Augustus will extend the empire, lies beyond all known geographical limits

9   **caelifer Atlās** heaven-bearing Atlas, i.e. Atlas who holds up the heavens. The giant Atlas supports the heavens on his shoulders and turns (**torquet**) the axle-tree (**axem**) of the bowl of heaven, studded with shining stars (**stellīs ardentibus aptum**)

11 **excūdent** will beat out
spīrantia mollius aera bronzes (bronze statues) that breath more softly (i.e. more lifelike)

12 **equidem** I (emphatic)
dē marmore from marble

13 **ōrābunt causās melius** i.e. they will excel in rhetoric
caelī meātūs the wanderings (of the stars) of heaven

14 **radiō** with the (astronomer's) rod

15–17 see p. 183 above

3 Tacitus

The Romans invaded Britain in AD *43 and quickly brought the lowlands under their control, consolidating on a line from the Severn to the Trent. After that their advance into the highland zones was slower and more uncertain and they nearly lost out altogether when their harsh rule resulted in the rebellion of Boudicca (= Boadicea) in* AD *60–61. In* AD *77 Agricola was appointed governor; he first consolidated earlier conquests, finally subduing Wales and the central highlands of Britain. He then embarked on a series of campaigns which carried him into the highlands of Scotland. In his last campaign in* AD *84 he advanced as far as the region of Aberdeen and defeated the Caledonians, who made a last stand at the Mons Graupius (probably in the Grampian hills).*

The historian Tacitus married Agricola's daughter; he wrote a life of his father-in-law in which he describes in detail the battle of the Mons Graupius, the last and greatest of Agricola's victories. By a long tradition ancient historians attributed speeches to generals before key battles. In the speech made by Calgacus, the leader of the Caledonian forces, Tacitus gives us a picture of the Roman imperial mission as seen by the conquered.

Britannī nihil frāctī pugnae priōris ēventū et ultiōnem aut servitium expectantēs, tandemque doctī commūne perīculum concordiā prōpulsandum, lēgātiōnibus et foederibus omnium cīvitātium vīrēs excīverant. iamque
5 super trīgintā mīlia armātōrum aspiciēbantur, et adhūc adfluēbat omnis iuventūs, cum Calgacus apud contractam multitūdinem proelium poscentem in hunc modum locūtus fertur:

'quotiēns causās bellī et necessitātem nostram intueor,
10 magnus mihi animus est hodiernum diem cōnsēnsumque vestrum initium lībertātis tōtī Britanniae fore: nam et

1 **nihil frāctī** quite unbroken; **nihil** is used adverbially; **pugnae priōris** the previous year Agricola had defeated the Britons when they made a sudden attack on the ninth legion; **ultiōnem** vengeance
3 **prōpulsandum (esse)** must be repulsed
4–5 **vīrēs** the strength, the powers; **excīverant** had roused; **super** above = more than
6 **iuventūs** the youth
6–7 **apud contractam multitūdinem** before a crowd assembled
7 **in hunc modum** as follows (in this way)
8 **fertur** is said
9 **quotiēns** as often as, whenever
10 **magnus mihi animus est** (+ acc. and inf.) I have great confidence that
11 **fore = futūrum esse**
11–12 **et ūniversī coīstis** you are both all united (you have all come together)
12 **et servitūtis expertēs (estis)** and you are untouched by (having no part in) slavery
14 **quae . . . honesta** supply **sunt**
16 **īnfestiōrēs (sunt)** are more hostile (than the waves and rocks)
17 **per obsequium** by obedience
18 **raptōrēs orbis** plunderers of the world **postquam . . . terrae** after the land(s) has failed them plundering everything, i.e. when there is no more land left for them to plunder
19 **scrūtantur** they fix their eyes on; **locuplēs** wealthy; **avārī (sunt)** they are greedy
20 **ambitiōsī** ambitious = eager for glory **satiāverit** will satisfy (will have satisfied)
21 **opēs atque inopiam** wealth and want **parī adfectū** with equal eagerness
22 **auferre trucīdāre rapere** the infinitives are used as nouns which are the object of **appellant** (they call plundering, murdering, raping empire)
23 **sōlitūdinem** a desert
24 **līberōs . . . ac propinquōs suōs** his own children and relatives
24–5 **nātūra . . . voluit** nature has willed that . . .
25 **per dīlectūs** by levies, by conscription
26 **libīdinem** lust

ūniversī coīstis et servitūtis expertēs, et nūllae ultrā terrae
ac nē mare quidem sēcūrum, imminente nōbīs classe
Rōmānā. ita proelium atque arma, quae fortibus honesta,
15   eadem etiam ignāvīs tūtissima sunt . . . nūlla iam ultrā gēns,
nihil nisi fluctūs et saxa, et īnfestiōrēs Rōmānī, quōrum
superbiam frūstrā per obsequium ac modestiam effugiās.
raptōrēs orbis, postquam cūncta vastantibus dēfuēre terrae,
mare scrūtantur: sī locuplēs hostis est, avārī, sī pauper,
20   ambitiōsī, quōs nōn Oriēns, nōn Occidēns satiāverit: sōlī
omnium opēs atque inopiam parī adfectū concupīscunt.
auferre trucīdāre rapere falsīs nōminibus imperium atque
ubi sōlitūdinem faciunt, pācem appellant.

'līberōs cuique ac propinquōs suōs nātūra cārissimōs
25   esse voluit: hī per dīlectūs alibī servītūrī auferuntur;
coniugēs sorōrēsque etiam sī hostīlem libīdinem effūgērunt,
nōmine amīcōrum atque hospitum polluuntur. bona
fortūnaeque in tribūtum, ager atque annus in frūmentum,
corpora ipsa ac manūs silvīs ac palūdibus ēmūniendīs inter
30   verbera et contumēliās conteruntur. nāta servitūtī mancipia
semel vēneunt, atque ultrō ā dominīs aluntur: Britannia
servitūtem suam cotīdiē emit, cotīdiē pāscit . . . ita sublātā
spē veniae tandem sūmite animum . . . Brigantēs fēminā
duce exūrere colōniam, expugnāre castra . . . exuere iugum
35   potuēre: nōs integrī et indomitī et in lībertātem ēdūcātī,
prīmō statim congressū ostendāmus, quōs sibi Calēdonia
virōs sēposuerit.

'hīc dux, hīc exercitus: ibi tribūta et metalla et cēterae
servientium poenae, quās in aeternum perferre aut statim
40   ulcīscī in hōc campō est. proinde itūrī in aciem et maiōrēs
vestrōs et posterōs cōgitāte.'

(Agricola 29–33)

The Caledonians were defeated in a hard fought battle,
but shortly afterwards Agricola was recalled and his
successors made no attempt to follow up this victory.
Consequently the Caledonians remained free.

27   **polluuntur** are polluted, raped

27–9   **bona . . . ager . . . corpora** these are all
     subjects of **conteruntur** = are wasted away

28   **ager atque annus** our land and its yearly
     produce; **in frūmentum** on the grain tax

29   **silvīs . . . ēmūniendīs** in making roads
     through forests and marshes

29–30   **inter verbera et contumēliās** to the
     accompaniment of blows and insults

30   **nāta servitūtī mancipia** slaves born for
     (into) servitude

31   **semel vēneunt** are sold once (and for all)
     ultrō . . . aluntur are even fed
     Britannia = Britannī

32   **pāscit** feeds; the Britons buy their slavery by
     paying tribute and feed it by paying grain tax

33   **Brigantēs** Tacitus refers to the great revolt
     of AD 60–61 led by Boudicca, who was
     queen of the Iceni (not the Brigantes;
     Tacitus seems to have made an error here)

34   **exūrere** (to burn) and **expugnāre** (to
     storm) all depend on **potuēre** (=
     potuērunt). Boudicca's army burnt down
     the Roman colony of Camulodunum
     (Colchester), defeated the ninth legion in
     battle and destroyed several Roman forts.
     The province was only saved after a
     tremendous battle in which nearly 80,000
     Britons fell according to Tacitus

35   **integrī et indomitī** untouched and
     unsubdued
     in lībertātem ēdūcātī trained/brought up
     for liberty

36   **prīmō . . . congressū** at the first clash

36–7   **quōs sibi Calēdonia virōs sēposuerit**
     what sort of men Caledonia has kept for
     herself in reserve

38   **hīc dux** supply **est**; **hīc** (here) = on this
     side, **ibi** (there) = on the Roman side, i.e. if
     you are defeated by the Romans
     metalla the mines

39   **poenae** penalties

39–40   **perferre . . . ulcīscī** to endure . . . to
     avenge; the infinitives depend on **in hōc**
     campō est: it depends on this field (of
     battle) whether you endure . . . or avenge
     proinde and so; **in aciem** into battle

41   **posterōs** your descendants

Indirect statements are expressed by the accusative and infinitive; if there is more than one indirect statement, the subject of the second and subsequent infinitives is often omitted, if it is the same as that of the first:

Horātius ad fundum suum Rōmā discessūrus Maecēnātī <u>dīxit sē</u> quīnque diēbus tantum <u>mānsūrum esse</u>; deinde Rōmam <u>regressum eum revīsūrum esse</u>.

When Horace was about to leave Rome for his farm, <u>he said</u> to Maecenas that <u>he would stay</u> for only five days; then <u>he would return</u> to Rome and <u>revisit</u> him.

The reflexives **sē** and **suus** always refer to the subject of the introductory verb:

Horātius ad Maecēnātem scrīpsit sē cōnstituisse rūre manēre; <u>veniam sibi daret</u>; reditūrum esse cum vēr vēnisset. sī anteā in urbem redīret, sine dubiō aegrōtātūrum esse.

Horace wrote to Maecenas that he had decided to stay in the country; <u>he (Maecenas) must forgive him</u>; he would return when spring came. If he returned to the city before that, he would undoubtedly be ill.

Indirect commands (or requests) are in the subjunctive *without* **ut**; if negative, they are introduced by **nē**.

All subordinate clauses are in the subjunctive, following the sequence of tenses, i.e. present or perfect subjunctive if the introductory verb is present, future or perfect with have; imperfect or pluperfect subjunctive if the introductory verb is past.

Indirect questions are introduced by an interrogative word and have verbs in the subjunctive, following the sequence of tenses.

Maecēnās ad Horātium rescrīpsit sē eum valdē dēsīderāre. nē diūtius rūre morārētur. quandō Rōmam reditūrus esset?

Maecenas wrote back to Horace that he missed him a lot. He must not (let him not) delay any longer in the country. When would he come back to Rome?

Appendix 3 — Uses of the indicative and subjunctive

The *indicative* is used in statements and questions in main clauses.

In subordinate clauses, the verb is in the indicative in:

1 definite relative clauses
2 causal clauses when the cause is stated as a fact*
3 temporal clauses*
4 open and future more vivid conditional clauses
5 concessive clauses introduced by **quamquam** (= although)

*for the uses of **cum** with subjunctive, see below

The *subjunctive* is used in all types of clause which are not expressing facts:

1 in main clauses

(a) jussive subjunctive (negative **nē**):

domum redeāmus.	Let us return home.
nē domum redeat.	Let him not return home.
nē hoc fēcerīs/nē hoc faciās.	Do not do this.

(b) deliberative subjunctive:

utrum domum redeāmus an hīc maneāmus?
Are we to return home or stay here?

(c) wishes (negative **nē**):

deī nōs servent.	May the gods preserve us.
utinam nē domī mānsissem.	I wish I had not stayed at home.

(d) potential subjunctive (negative **nōn**), e.g. **velim** (I should like to), **nōlim**, **mālim, ausim** (I should dare to):

nōn ausim hoc facere.	I should not dare to do this.

(e) in contrary to fact and future less vivid conditional clauses:

sī domī mānsissēs, incolumis fuissēs.
If you had stayed at home, you would have been safe.
sī domī iam essēs, incolumis essēs.
If you were now at home, you would be safe.
sī domum maneās, in perīculum nōn cadās.
If you were to stay at home, you would not fall into danger.

2 in subordinate clauses

(a) clauses of purpose, introduced by **ut/nē**

(b) indirect commands, introduced by **ut/nē**

(c) indirect questions

(d) clauses of fearing, introduced by **nē/nē nōn**

(e) (i) causal clauses introduced by **cum** = since

(ii) causal clauses where the cause is not stated as a fact:

condemnātus est quod senem occīdisset.
He was condemned for killing the old man/on the grounds that he had killed the old man.

(f) (i) temporal clauses introduced by **cum** (= when) in past time (see chapter 47)

(ii) temporal clauses expressing purpose as well as time:

in forō manēbat dum pater redīret.
He was waiting in the forum for his father to return.
(Compare: **in forō manēbat dum pater rediit**. He waited in the forum until his father returned.)

in Italiam redī antequam ā mīlitibus capiāris.
Return to Italy before you are caught by the soldiers.
(Here the **antequam** clause expresses both time and purpose, which we cannot do in English.)

(g) concessive clauses introduced by **cum** (= although) and **quamvīs** (= however much):

quamvīs dīves esset, nihil pauperibus dabat.
Although he was rich, he gave nothing to the poor.

(h) relative clauses expressing purpose or consequence:

nūntium mīsit quī patrī omnia dīceret.
He sent a messenger to tell his father everything.
servus dignus est quī praemium accipiat.
The slave is worthy to receive a reward.

(i) all subordinate clauses in indirect speech (see Appendix 2 above)

In all the types of clause listed above, except for those introduced by **cum**, the subjunctive is used because they are not expressing facts (e.g. a purpose is an idea in someone's head; indirect speech is not an expression of fact but a report by someone who may be wrong or lying).

(j) clauses of result or consequence introduced by **ut/ut nōn** have their verbs in the subjunctive although they often express facts:

tam fessus erat ut diū dormīret.
He was so tired that he slept a long time.

Reference grammar

NOUNS

	1st declension	2nd declension		3rd declension	
	stems in **-a**	stems in **-o**		stems in consonants	
	feminine	*masculine*	*neuter*	*masc. & fem.*	*neuter*
singular					
nom.	puell-a	colōn-us	bell-um	rēx	lītus
gen.	puell-ae	colōn-ī	bell-ī	rēg-is	lītor-is
dat.	puell-ae	colōn-ō	bell-ō	rēg-ī	lītor-ī
acc.	puell-am	colōn-um	bell-um	rēg-em	lītus
abl.	puell-ā	colōn-ō	bell-ō	rēg-e	lītor-e
plural					
nom.	puell-ae	colōn-ī	bell-a	rēg-ēs	lītor-a
gen.	puell-ārum	colōn-ōrum	bell-ōrum	rēg-um	lītor-um
dat.	puell-īs	colōn-īs	bell-īs	rēg-ibus	lītor-ibus
acc.	puell-ās	colōn-ōs	bell-a	rēg-ēs	lītor-a
abl.	puell-īs	colōn-īs	bell-īs	rēg-ibus	lītor-ibus

	3rd declension		4th declension		5th declension
	stems in **-i**		stems in **-u**		stems in **-e**
	masc. & fem.	*neuter*	*masc.*	*neuter*	*feminine*
singular					
nom.	nāvis	mare	grad-us	corn-ū	r-ēs
gen.	nāv-is	mar-is	grad-ūs	corn-ūs	r-eī
dat.	nāv-ī	mar-ī	grad-uī	corn-uī	r-eī
acc.	nāv-em	mare	grad-um	corn-ū	r-em
abl.	nāv-e	mar-ī	grad-ū	corn-ū	r-ē
plural					
nom.	nāv-ēs	mar-ia	grad-ūs	corn-ua	r-ēs
gen.	nāv-ium	mar-ium	grad-uum	corn-uum	r-ērum
dat.	nāv-ibus	mar-ibus	grad-ibus	corn-ibus	r-ēbus
acc.	nāv-ēs	mar-ia	grad-ūs	corn-ua	r-ēs
abl.	nāv-ibus	mar-ibus	grad-ibus	corn-ibus	r-ēbus

Notes

1 The vocative is the same as the nominative for all nouns of all declensions except for 2nd declension masculine nouns in **-us**, e.g. **colōn-us**, which form vocative singular **-e**, e.g. **colōn-e**, and in **-ius**, e.g. **fīli-us**, which form vocative singular **-ī**, e.g. **fīl-ī**.

2 All nouns of the 1st declension are feminine except for a few which are masculine by meaning, e.g. **nauta** a sailor, **agricola** a farmer.

3 2nd declension masculine nouns with nominative singular **-er**, e.g. **puer**, **ager**: some keep **-e-** in the other cases, e.g. **puer**, **puer-ī**; others drop it, e.g. **ager**, **agr-ī**.

The genitive singular of masculine nouns ending **-ius** and neuter nouns ending **-ium** in nominative is often contracted from **-iī** to **-ī**, e.g. **fīlī**, **ingenī**.

4 The following 2nd declension nouns have minor irregularities: **deus** a god has nominative plural **deī** or **dī**, genitive plural **deōrum** or **deum**, ablative plural **deīs** or **dīs**; **vir**, **virī** man has genitive plural **virōrum** or **virum**.

5 3rd declension. The gender of all 3rd declension nouns has to be learned.

Genitive plural: the general rule is that nouns with stems in **-i** have genitive plural **-ium**, those with stems in consonants have genitive plural **-um**. All nouns with nominative **-is**, e.g. **nāvis**, have stems in **-i**. And so do nouns the nominative of which ends in two consonants, e.g. **fōns**, **urbs**, genitive plural **fontium**, **urbium** (their original nominative was, e.g. **urbis**).

Nouns with stems in **-i** have alternative forms for ablative singular, e.g. **nāve** or **nāvī**, and for accusative plural, e.g. **nāvēs** or **nāvīs**.

6 Most 4th declension nouns are masculine; **manus** is the only common noun which is feminine. There are very few neuter nouns; the only common one is **cornū** horn or the wing of an army.

7 All 5th declension nouns are feminine except for **diēs**, which is masculine.

ADJECTIVES

Masculine & neuter 2nd declension; feminine 1st declension

singular	m.	f.	n.
nom.	bon-us	bon-a	bon-um
gen.	bon-ī	bon-ae	bon-ī
dat.	bon-ō	bon-ae	bon-ō
acc.	bon-um	bon-am	bon-um
abl.	bon-ō	bon-ā	bon-ō

plural			
nom.	bon-ī	bon-ae	bon-a
gen.	bon-ōrum	bon-ārum	bon-ōrum
dat.	bon-īs	bon-īs	bon-īs
acc.	bon-ōs	bon-ās	bon-a
abl.	bon-īs	bon-īs	bon-īs

Note

Similarly, **miser, misera, miserum** (keeping -e- like **puer**) and **pulcher, pulchra, pulchrum** (dropping the -e-, like **ager**).

3rd declension

	consonant stems		stems in -i	
singular	m. & f.	n.	m. & f.	n.
nom.	pauper	pauper	omnis	omn-e
gen.	pauper-is	pauper-is	omn-is	omn-is
dat.	pauper-ī	pauper-ī	omn-ī	omn-ī
acc.	pauper-em	pauper	omn-em	omn-e
abl.	pauper-e	pauper-e	omn-ī	omn-ī

	consonant stems		stems in -i	
plural	m. & f.	n.	m. & f.	n.
nom.	pauper-ēs	pauper-a	omn-ēs	omn-ia
gen.	pauper-um	pauper-um	omn-ium	omn-ium
dat.	pauper-ibus	pauper-ibus	omn-ibus	omn-ibus
acc.	pauper-ēs	pauper-a	omn-ēs	omn-ia
abl.	pauper-ibus	pauper-ibus	omn-ibus	omn-ibus

Notes

1 Most 3rd declension adjectives have stems in **-i**. Other types of adjective with stems in **-i** are: **ingēns** (neuter **ingēns**), genitive **ingent-is**; **ferōx** (neuter **ferōx**), genitive **ferōc-is**; **celer** (f. **celere**, n. **celere**), genitive **celer-is**.
2 3rd declension adjectives with stems in consonants are few, eg. **dīves, dīvit-is**; **pauper, pauper-is**; **vetus, veter-is**; and the comparative adjective, eg. **fortior** (n. **fortius**), genitive **fortiōr-is**.

	alter (one or the other of two)			**uter** (which of two?)		
	m.	f.	n.	m.	f.	n.
nom.	alter	altera	alterum	uter	utra	utrum
gen.	alterīus	alterīus	alterīus	utrīus	utrīus	utrīus
dat.	alterī	alterī	alterī	utrī	utrī	utrī
acc.	alterum	alteram	alterum	utrum	utram	utrum
abl.	alterō	alterā	alterō	utrō	utrā	utrō

Plural like that of **bon-ī, bon-ae, bon-a**. Similarly: **uterque, utraque, utrumque** (each of two).

The following adjectives have the same characteristic, i.e. gen. sing. **-īus**, dat. sing. **-ī**:

alius, alia, aliud	other	*gen. sing.*	**alīus**	*dat. sing.*	**aliī**
nūllus, nūlla, nūllum	no		**nūllīus**		**nūllī**
ūllus, ūlla, ūllum	any		**ūllīus**		**ūllī**
sōlus, sōla, sōlum	only		**sōlīus**		**sōlī**
tōtus, tōta, tōtum	whole		**tōtīus**		**tōtī**
ūnus, ūna, ūnum	one		**ūnīus**		**ūnī**

Comparison of adjectives

Most adjectives add **-ior** to the stem to form the comparative and **-issimus** to form the superlative:

positive	*comparative*	*superlative*
longus	**longior**	**longissimus**
long	longer	longest, very long
trīstis	**trīstior**	**trīstissimus**
sad	sadder	saddest, very sad

The comparative declines as a 3rd declension adjective (consonant stem):

	singular		*plural*	
	m. & f.	*n.*	*m. & f.*	*n.*
nom.	longior	longius	longiōrēs	longiōra
gen.	longiōris	longiōris	longiōrum	longiōrum
dat.	longiōrī	longiōrī	longiōribus	longiōribus
acc.	longiōrem	longius	longiōrēs	longiōra
abl.	longiōre	longiōre	longiōribus	longiōribus

The superlative declines like **bonus, bona, bonum**.

The following common adjectives have irregular comparison:

positive	*comparative*	*superlative*
bonus	melior	optimus
malus	peior	pessimus
magnus	maior	maximus
multus	plūs*	plūrimus
parvus	minor	minimus

* **plūs** in the singular is a neuter noun, declining: **plūs, plūs, plūris, plūrī, plūre**. So **plūs cibī** = more (of) food.
In the plural it is an adjective: **plūrēs, plūra** etc. So **plūrēs puellae** = more girls.

Adjectives ending -**er** in the nominative double the -**r**- in the superlative, e.g.

> **miser, miserior, miserrimus**
> **pulcher, pulchrior, pulcherrimus**
> **celer, celerior, celerrimus**

Six adjectives with nominative -**ilis** double the -**l**- in the superlative:

> **facilis** (easy), **facilior, facillimus**
> **difficilis** (difficult), **difficilior, difficillimus**
> **gracilis** (slender), **gracilior, gracillimus**
> **humilis** (low), **humilior, humillimus**
> **similis** (like), **similior, simillimus**
> **dissimilis** (unlike), **dissimilior, dissimillimus**

Other adjectives with nominative -**ilis** form regular superlatives, e.g. **amābilis** (loveable), **amābilior, amābilissimus**.

ADVERBS

1   From **bonus** type adjectives, adverbs are usually formed by adding -**ē** to the stem, e.g. **lent-us** slow: **lent-ē** slowly; **miser** miserable: **miser-ē** miserably. A few add -**ō**, e.g. **subit-us** sudden: **subit-ō** suddenly.

2   From 3rd declension adjectives, adverbs are usually formed by adding -**ter** to the stem, e.g. **fēlīx** fortunate: **fēlīci-ter** fortunately; **celer** quick: **celeri-ter** quickly. A few 3rd declension adjectives use the accusative neuter singular as an adverb, e.g. **facilis** easy, **facile** easily; so also comparative adverbs, e.g. **fortior** braver, **fortius** more bravely.

3   There are many adverbs which have no corresponding adjectival form, e.g. **diū, quandō? iam, semper**.

4   Comparison of adverbs. The comparative adverb is the same as the neuter accusative of the comparative adjective; the superlative adverb is formed by changing the nominative ending -**us** to -**ē**, e.g.

adjective	adverb	comparative adverb	superlative adverb
longus	longē	longius	longissimē
fortis	fortiter	fortius	fortissimē

Note the following irregular adverbs:

adjective	adverb	comparative adverb	superlative adverb
bonus	bene	melius	optimē
malus	male	peius	pessimē
facilis	facile	facilius	facillimē
magnus	magnopere	maius	maximē
multus	multum	plūs	plūrimum
parvus	paulum	minus	minimē
prīmus	prīmum	–	–

NUMERALS

cardinals

1	ūnus	I	16	sēdecim	XVI
2	duo	II	17	septendecim	XVII
3	trēs	III	18	duodēvīgintī	XVIII
4	quattuor	IV	19	ūndēvīgintī	XIX
5	quīnque	V	20	vīgintī	XX
6	sex	VI	30	trīgintā	XXX
7	septem	VII	40	quadrāgintā	XL
8	octō	VIII	50	quīnquāgintā	L
9	novem	IX	100	centum	C
10	decem	X	200	ducentī, -ae, -a	CC
11	ūndecim	XI	300	trecentī, -ae, -a	CCC
12	duodecim	XII	400	quadringentī, -ae, -a	CCCC
13	tredecim	XIII	1,000	mīlle	M
14	quattuordecim	XIV	2,000	duo mīlia	
15	quīndecim	XV			

Notes

1 The numbers 4–100 do not decline; 200–900 decline like **bonī, -ae, -a**.

2 **mīlle** does not decline; **mīlia** is a 3rd declension noun, so:

mīlle passūs = 1,000 paces (a mile)

duo mīlia passuum = 2,000 (of) paces (2 miles)

3 Adverbial numbers: **semel, bis, ter** (once, twice, three times etc.); **centiēs/centiēns** 100 times, **mīliēs/mīliēns** 1,000 times.

ordinals

1st	prīmus, -a, -um	6th	sextus, -a, -um	20th	vīcēsimus, -a, -um
2nd	secundus, -a, -um/alter, -a, -um	7th	septimus, -a, -um	100th	centēsimus, -a, -um
3rd	tertius, -a, -um	8th	octāvus, -a, -um	1,000th	mīllēsimus, -a, -um
4th	quārtus, -a, -um	9th	nōnus, -a, -um		
5th	quīntus, -a, -um	10th	decimus, -a, -um		

Declension of **ūnus**, **duo**, **trēs**

	m.	*f.*	*n.*	*m.*	*f.*	*n.*	*m.*	*f.*	*n.*
nom.	ūnus	ūna	ūnum	duo	duae	duo	trēs	trēs	tria
gen.	ūnīus	ūnīus	ūnīus	duōrum	duārum	duōrum	trium	trium	trium
dat.	ūnī	ūnī	ūnī	duōbus	duābus	duōbus	tribus	tribus	tribus
acc.	ūnum	ūnam	ūnum	duōs	duās	duo	trēs	trēs	tria
abl.	ūnō	ūnā	ūnō	duōbus	duābus	duōbus	tribus	tribus	tribus

PRONOUNS

singular personal pronouns

nom.	ego (I)	tū (you)		
gen.	meī	tuī	suī	
dat.	mihi	tibi	sibi	
acc.	mē	tē	sē (himself, herself)	
abl.	mē	tē	sē	

Possessive adjectives:

meus, -a, -um (my)

tuus, -a, -um (your)

suus, -a, -um (his own)

plural

nom.	nōs (we)	vōs (you)		
gen.	nostrum, nostrī	vestrum, vestrī	suī	
dat.	nōbīs	vōbīs	sibi	
acc.	nōs	vōs	sē (themselves)	
abl.	nōbīs	vōbīs	sē	

noster, nostra, nostrum (our)

vester, vestra, vestrum (your)

suus, -a, -um (their own)

All decline like **bonus, -a, -um**, but the vocative of **meus** is **mī**

they/those

	demonstrative pronouns			this / that			ne him she/her it/it		
	m.	*f.*	*n.*	*m.*	*f.*	*n.*	*m.*	*f.*	*n.*
nom.	hic	haec	hoc (this)	ille	illa	illud (that)	is	ea	id (he, she, it;
gen.	huius	huius	huius	illīus	illīus	illīus	eius	eius	eius that)
dat.	huic	huic	huic	illī	illī	illī	eī	eī	eī
acc.	hunc	hanc	hoc	illum	illam	illud	eum	eam	id
abl.	hōc	hāc	hōc	illō	illā	illō	eō	eā	eō

plural

	m.	*f.*	*n.*	*m.*	*f.*	*n.*	*m.*	*f.*	*n.*
nom.	hī	hae	haec	illī	illae	illa	eī	eae	ea
gen.	hōrum	hārum	hōrum	illōrum	illārum	illōrum	eōrum	eārum	eōrum
dat.	hīs	hīs	hīs	illīs	illīs	illīs	eīs	eīs	eīs
acc.	hōs	hās	haec	illōs	illās	illa	eōs	eās	ea
abl.	hīs	hīs	hīs	illīs	illīs	illīs	eīs	eīs	eīs

singular | | | | | | | relative pronoun | |

	m.	*f.*	*n.*	*m.*	*f.*	*n.*	*m.*	*f.*	*n.*
nom.	ipse	ipsa	ipsum (self)	īdem	eadem	idem (same)	quī	quae	quod (who, which)
gen.	ipsīus	ipsīus	ipsīus	eiusdem	eiusdem	eiusdem	cuius	cuius	cuius
dat.	ipsī	ipsī	ipsī	eīdem	eīdem	eīdem	cui	cui	cui
acc.	ipsum	ipsam	ipsum	eundem	eandem	idem	quem	quam	quod
abl.	ipsō	ipsā	ipsō	eōdem	eādem	eōdem	quō	quā	quō

plural

	m.	*f.*	*n.*	*m.*	*f.*	*n.*	*m.*	*f.*	*n.*
nom.	ipsī	ipsae	ipsa	eīdem	eaedem	eadem	quī	quae	quae
gen.	ipsōrum	ipsārum	ipsōrum	eōrundem	eārundem	eōrundem	quōrum	quārum	quōrum
dat.	ipsīs	ipsīs	ipsīs	eīsdem	eīsdem	eīsdem	quibus	quibus	quibus
acc.	ipsōs	ipsās	ipsa	eōsdem	eāsdem	eadem	quōs	quās	quae
abl.	ipsīs	ipsīs	ipsīs	eīsdem	eīsdem	eīsdem	quibus	quibus	quibus

quīdam (a certain, a) declines like the relative pronoun with the suffix **-dam**:

nom.	quīdam	quaedam	quoddam
acc.	quendam	quandam	quoddam etc.

The interrogative pronoun **quis**? (who? what?):

nom.	quis?	quis?	quid?
acc.	quem?	quam?	quid? (the rest exactly like the relative pronoun)

The interrogative adjective **quī**? (which? what?):

nom.	quī?	quae?	quod? (exactly like the relative pronoun)

The indefinite pronoun **aliquis** (someone, something) declines like **quis**? with the prefix **ali-**:

nom.	aliquis	aliquis	aliquid etc.

quisquam, **quicquam** (anyone, anything, after a negative) declines like **quis** with the suffix **-quam**:

nom.	quisquam	quisquam	quicquam

Interrogatives and demonstratives

quis? quī?	who? which?	**is, ille, iste** that		**quō?**	where to?	**eō, illō** to there
uter?	which of two?	**alter** one or the other of two		**quā?**	by what way?	**eā** by that way
quālis?	of what kind?	**tālis** of such kind, such		**quam?**	how?	**tam** so
quantus?	how great?	**tantus** so great		**quandō?**	when?	**tum** then
ubi?	where?	**ibi, illīc, istīc** there		**quotiēns?**	how often?	**totiēns** so often
unde?	from where?	**inde** from there				

VERBS

Active

Indicative

		1st conjugation	2nd conjugation	3rd conjugation	3rd -*iō* conjugation	4th conjugation
		stems in **-a**	stems in **-e**	stems in consonants		stems in **-i**
present						
singular	1	par-ō	mone-ō	reg-ō	capi-ō	audi-ō
	2	parā-s	monē-s	reg-is	capi-s	audī-s
	3	para-t	mone-t	reg-it	capi-t	audi-t
plural	1	parā-mus	monē-mus	reg-imus	capi-mus	audī-mus
	2	parā-tis	monē-tis	reg-itis	capi-tis	audī-tis
	3	para-nt	mone-nt	reg-unt	capi-unt	audi-unt
future						
singular	1	parā-bō	monē-bō	reg-am	capi-am	audi-am
	2	parā-bis	monē-bis	reg-ēs	capi-ēs	audi-ēs
	3	parā-bit	monē-bit	reg-et	capi-et	audi-et
plural	1	parā-bimus	monē-bimus	reg-ēmus	capi-ēmus	audi-ēmus
	2	parā-bitis	monē-bitis	reg-ētis	capi-ētis	audi-ētis
	3	parā-bunt	monē-bunt	reg-ent	capi-ent	audi-ent
imperfect						
singular	1	parā-bam	monē-bam	regē-bam	capiē-bam	audiē-bam
	2	parā-bās	monē-bās	regē-bās	capiē-bās	audiē-bās
	3	parā-bat	monē-bat	regē-bat	capiē-bat	audiē-bat
plural	1	parā-bamus	monē-bāmus	regē-bāmus	capiē-bāmus	audiē-bāmus
	2	parā-bātis	monē-bātis	regē-bātis	capiē-bātis	audiē-bātis
	3	parā-bant	monē-bant	regē-bant	capiē-bant	audiē-bant
perfect						
singular	1	parāv-ī	monu-ī	rēx-ī	cēp-ī	audīv-ī
	2	parāv-istī	monu-istī	rēx-istī	cēp-istī	audīv-istī
	3	parāv-it	monu-it	rēx-it	cēp-it	audīv-it
plural	1	parāv-imus	monu-imus	rēx-imus	cēp-imus	audīv-imus
	2	parāv-istis	monu-istis	rēx-istis	cēp-istis	audīv-istis
	3	parāv-ērunt	monu-ērunt	rēx-ērunt	cēp-ērunt	audīv-ērunt
future perfect						
singular	1	parāv-erō	monu-erō	rēx-erō	cēp-erō	audīv-erō
	2	parāv-eris	monu-eris	rēx-eris	cēp-eris	audīv-eris
	3	parāv-erit	monu-erit	rēx-erit	cēp-erit	audīv-erit
plural	1	parāv-erimus	monu-erimus	rēx-erimus	cēp-erimus	audīv-erimus
	2	parāv-eritis	monu-eritis	rēx-eritis	cēp-eritis	audīv-eritis
	3	parāv-erint	monu-erint	rēx-erint	cēp-erint	audīv-erint
pluperfect						
singular	1	parāv-eram	monu-eram	rēx-eram	cēp-eram	audīv-eram
	2	parāv-erās	monu-erās	rēx-erās	cēp-erās	audīv-erās
	3	parāv-erat	monu-erat	rēx-erat	cēp-erat	audīv-erat
plural	1	parāv-erāmus	monu-erāmus	rēx-erāmus	cēp-erāmus	audīv-erāmus
	2	parāv-erātis	monu-erātis	rēx-erātis	cēp-erātis	audīv-erātis
	3	parāv-erant	monu-erant	rēx-erant	cēp-erant	audīv-erant

[handwritten: 1stpp part ☑]

Subjunctive

	1st conjugation	2nd conjugation	3rd conjugation	3rd -iō conjugation	4th conjugation
	[handwritten: par☑]	*[handwritten: mone☑]*	*[handwritten: reg☑]*	*[handwritten: capi☑]*	*[handwritten: audi☑]*
present					
singular	1 par-em	mone-am	reg-am	capi-am	audi-am
	2 par-ēs	mone-ās	reg-ās	capi-ās	audi-ās
	3 par-et	mone-at	reg-at	capi-at	audi-at
plural	1 par-ēmus	mone-āmus	reg-āmus	capi-āmus	audi-āmus
	2 par-ētis	mone-ātis	reg-ātis	capi-ātis	audi-ātis
	3 par-ent	mone-ant	reg-ant	capi-ant	audi-ant

[handwritten left margin: ciem steums clame; +em]
[handwritten: remove off]

	[handwritten: parare ☑]	*[handwritten: moner☑]*	*[handwritten: regere☑]*	*[handwritten: capere☑]*	*[handwritten: audire☑]*
imperfect					
singular	1 parār-em	monēr-em	reger-em	caper-em	audīr-em
	2 parār-ēs	monēr-ēs	reger-ēs	caper-ēs	audīr-ēs
	3 parār-et	monēr-et	reger-et	caper-et	audīr-et
plural	1 parār-ēmus	monēr-ēmus	reger-ēmus	caper-ēmus	audīr-ēmus
	2 parār-ētis	monēr-ētis	reger-ētis	caper-ētis	audīr-ētis
	3 parār-ent	monēr-ent	reger-ent	caper-ent	audīr-ent

[handwritten left margin: 3rd pp part +enm; parav☑]

	[handwritten: 3rd pp part☑]	*[handwritten: monu☑]*	*[handwritten: rex☑]*	*[handwritten: cep☑]*	*[handwritten: audiv☑]*
perfect					
singular	1 parāv-erim	monu-erim	rēx-erim	cēp-erim	audīv-erim
	2 parāv-erīs	monu-erīs	rēx-erīs	cēp-erīs	audīv-erīs
	3 parāv-erit	monu-erit	rēx-erit	cēp-erit	audīv-erit
plural	1 parāv-erīmus	monu-erīmus	rēx-erīmus	cēp-erīmus	audīv-erīmus
	2 parāv-erītis	monu-erītis	rēx-erītis	cēp-erītis	audīv-erītis
	3 parāv-erint	monu-erint	rēx-erint	cēp-erint	audīv-erint

[handwritten left margin: parav☑]

	[handwritten: 3rd part +issem, monu☑]		*[handwritten: rex☑]*	*[handwritten: cep☑]*	*[handwritten: audiv☑]*
pluperfect					
singular	1 parāv-issem	monu-issem	rēx-issem	cēp-issem	audīv-issem
	2 parāv-issēs	monu-issēs	rēx-issēs	cēp-issēs	audīv-issēs
	3 parāv-isset	monu-isset	rēx-isset	cēp-isset	audīv-isset
plural	1 parāv-issēmus	monu-issēmus	rēx-issēmus	cēp-issēmus	audīv-issēmus
	2 parāv-issētis	monu-issētis	rēx-issētis	cēp-issētis	audīv-issētis
	3 parāv-issent	monu-issent	rēx-issent	cēp-issent	audīv-issent

Imperative

singular	parā	monē	rege	cape	audī
plural	parāte	monēte	regite	capite	audīte

Infinitives

present	parāre	monēre	regere	capere	audīre
perfect	parāvisse	monuisse	rēxisse	cēpisse	audīvisse
future	parātūrus esse	monitūrus esse	rēctūrus esse	captūrus esse	audītūrus esse

Participles

present	parāns *[handwritten: -loving]*	monēns	regēns	capiēns	audiēns
future	parātūrus *[handwritten: to be loved / about to —]*	monitūrus	rēctūrus	captūrus	audītūrus

Gerund

	parandum	monendum	regendum	capiendum	audiendum

Supine

	parātum	monitum	rēctum	captum	audītum

Passive

Indicative

	1st conjugation	2nd conjugation	3rd conjugation	3rd **-iō** conjugation	4th conjugation
	stems in **-a**	stems in **-e**	stems in consonants		stems in **-i**
present					
singular 1	par-or	mone-or	reg-or	capi-or	audi-or
2	parā-ris	monē-ris	reg-eris	cap-eris	audī-ris
3	parā-tur	monē-tur	reg-itur	cap-itur	audī-tur
plural 1	parā-mur	monē-mur	reg-imur	cap-imur	audī-mur
2	parā-minī	monē-minī	reg-iminī	cap-iminī	audī-minī
3	para-ntur	mone-ntur	reg-untur	capi-untur	audi-untur
future					
singular 1	parā-bor	monē-bor	reg-ar	capi-ar	audi-ar
2	parā-beris	monē-beris	reg-ēris	capi-ēris	audi-ēris
3	parā-bitur	monē-bitur	reg-ētur	capi-ētur	audi-ētur
plural 1	parā-bimur	monē-bimur	reg-ēmur	capi-ēmur	audi-ēmur
2	parā-biminī	monē-biminī	reg-ēminī	capi-ēminī	audi-ēminī
3	parā-buntur	monē-buntur	reg-entur	capi-entur	audi-entur
imperfect					
singular 1	parā-bar	monē-bar	reg-ēbar	capi-ēbar	audi-ēbar
2	parā-bāris	monē-bāris	reg-ēbāris	capi-ēbāris	audi-ēbāris
3	parā-bātur	monē-bātur	reg-ēbātur	capi-ēbātur	audi-ēbātur
plural 1	parā-bāmur	monē-bāmur	reg-ēbāmur	capi-ēbāmur	audi-ēbāmur
2	parā-bāminī	monē-bāminī	reg-ēbāminī	capi-ēbāminī	audi-ēbāminī
3	parā-bantur	monē-bantur	reg-ēbantur	capi-ēbantur	audi-ēbantur
perfect					
singular 1	parātus sum	monitus sum	rēctus sum	captus sum	audītus sum
2	parātus es	etc.	etc.	etc.	etc.
3	parātus est				
plural 1	parātī sumus				
2	parātī estis				
3	parātī sunt				
future perfect					
singular 1	parātus erō	monitus erō	rēctus erō	captus erō	audītus erō
2	parātus eris	etc.	etc.	etc.	etc.
3	parātus erit				
plural 1	parātī erimus				
2	parātī eritis				
3	parātī erunt				
pluperfect					
singular 1	parātus eram	monitus eram	rēctus eram	captus eram	audītus eram
2	parātus erās	etc.	etc.	etc.	etc.
3	parātus erat				
plural 1	parātī erāmus				
2	parātī erātis				
3	parātī erant				

Subjunctive

		1st conjugation	*2nd conjugation*	*3rd conjugation*	*3rd* ***-iō*** *conjugation*	*4th conjugation*
singular	1	par-er	mone-ar	reg-ar	capi-ar	audi-ar
	2	par-ēris	mone-āris	reg-āris	capi-āris	audi-āris
	3	par-ētur	mone-ātur	reg-ātur	capi-ātur	audi-ātur
plural	1	par-ēmur	mone-āmur	reg-āmur	capi-āmur	audi-āmur
	2	par-ēminī	mone-āminī	reg-āminī	capi-āminī	audi-āminī
	3	par-entur	mone-antur	reg-antur	capi-antur	audi-antur
imperfect						
singular	1	parār-er	monēr-er	reger-er	caper-er	audīr-er
	2	parār-ēris	monēr-ēris	reger-ēris	caper-ēris	audīr-ēris
	3	parār-ētur	monēr-ētur	reger-ētur	caper-ētur	audīr-ētur
plural	1	parār-ēmur	monēr-ēmur	reger-ēmur	caper-ēmur	audīr-ēmur
	2	parār-ēminī	monēr-ēminī	reger-ēminī	caper-ēminī	audīr-ēminī
	3	parār-entur	monēr-entur	reger-entur	caper-entur	audīr-entur
perfect						
singular	1	parātus sim	monitus sim	rēctus sim	captus sim	audītus sim
	2	parātus sīs	etc.	etc.	etc.	etc.
	3	parātus sit				
plural	1	parātī sīmus				
	2	parātī sītis				
	3	parātī sint				
pluperfect						
singular	1	parātus essem	monitus essem	rēctus essem	captus essem	audītus essem
	2	parātus essēs	etc.	etc.	etc.	etc.
	3	parātus esset				
plural	1	parātī essēmus				
	2	parātī essētis				
	3	parātī essent				
Imperative						
singular		parāre	monēre	regere	capere	audīre
plural		parāminī	monēminī	regiminī	capiminī	audīminī
Infinitives						
present		parārī	monērī	regī	capī	audīrī
perfect		parātus esse	monitus esse	rēctus esse	captus esse	audītus esse
future		parātum īrī	monitum īrī	rēctum īrī	captum īrī	audītum īrī
Participle						
perfect		parātus, having been loved	monitus	rēctus	captus	audītus
Gerundive		parandus	monendus	regendus	capiendus	audiendus

fut passive
amanda: to be about to ___
dative of [purpose]
amando – doing it for loving
faciendus – to be made

Deponent verbs

	indicative	subjunctive
present	cōnor	cōner
future	cōnābor	–
imperfect	cōnābar	cōnārer
perfect	cōnātus sum	cōnātus sim
future perfect	cōnātus erō	–
pluperfect	cōnātus eram	cōnātus essem

Imperative

	singular cōnāre	*plural* cōnāminī

Infinitives

	present cōnārī	*perfect* cōnātus esse	*future* cōnātūrus esse

Participles

	present cōnāns	*perfect* cōnātus	*future* cōnātūrus

Gerund

cōnandum

Gerundive

cōnandus

Irregular verbs

	sum: I am	**possum**: I am able	**eō**: I go
present			
singular	1 sum	possum	eō
	2 es	potes	īs
	3 est	potest	it
plural	1 sumus	possumus	īmus
	2 estis	potestis	ītis
	3 sunt	possunt	eunt
future			
singular	1 erō	pot-erō	ī-bō
	2 eris	pot-eris	ī-bis
	3 erit	pot-erit	ī-bit
plural	1 erimus	pot-erimus	ī-bimus
	2 eritis	pot-eritis	ī-bitis
	3 erunt	pot-erunt	ī-bunt
imperfect			
singular	1 eram	pot-eram	ī-bam
	2 erās	pot-erās	ī-bās
	3 erat	pot-erat	ī-bat
plural	1 erāmus	pot-erāmus	ī-bāmus
	2 erātis	pot-erātis	ī-bātis
	3 erant	pot-erant	ī-bant
perfect stem	**fu-**	**potu-**	**i-**
singular	1 fu-ī	potu-ī	i-ī
	2 fu-istī	potu-istī	īstī
	3 fu-it	potu-it	i-it
plural	1 fu-imus	potu-imus	i-imus
	2 fu-istis	potu-istis	īstis
	3 fu-ērunt	potu-ērunt	i-ērunt

future perfect	fu-erō etc.	potu-erō etc.	i-erō etc.	
pluperfect	fu-eram etc.	potu-eram etc.	i-eram etc.	

Imperative				
singular	es, estō	–	ī	
plural	este	–	īte	

Infinitives				
present	esse	posse	īre	
perfect	fuisse	potuisse	īsse	
future	futūrus esse, fore	–	itūrus esse	

Participles				
present	–	(potēns)	iēns, euntis	
future	futūrus	–	itūrus	

Gerund	–	–	eundum	

volō, velle, voluī   I wish, I am willing
nōlō, nōlle, nōluī   I am unwilling, I refuse
mālō, mālle, māluī   I prefer
ferō, ferre, tulī, lātum   I carry, bear

present				*active*	*passive*
singular	1 volō	nōlō	mālō	ferō	feror
	2 vīs	nōn vīs	māvīs	fers	ferris
	3 vult	nōn vult	māvult	fert	fertur
plural	1 volumus	nōlumus	mālumus	ferimus	ferimur
	2 vultis	nōn vultis	māvultis	fertis	feriminī
	3 volunt	nōlunt	mālunt	ferunt	feruntur

future					
singular	1 volam	nōlam	mālam	feram	ferar
	2 volēs	nōlēs	mālēs	ferēs	ferēris
	3 volet etc.	nōlet etc.	mālet etc.	feret etc.	ferētur etc.

imperfect	volēbam etc.	nōlēbam etc.	mālēbam etc.	ferēbam etc.	ferēbar etc.
perfect	voluī etc.	nōluī etc.	māluī etc.	tulī etc.	lātus sum etc.
future perfect	voluerō etc.	nōluerō etc.	māluerō etc.	tulerō etc.	lātus erō etc.
pluperfect	volueram etc.	nōlueram etc.	mālueram etc.	tuleram etc.	lātus eram etc.

Imperative	–	nōlī	–	fer	ferre
	–	nōlīte	–	ferte	feriminī

Infinitives					
present	velle	nōlle	mālle	ferre	ferrī
perfect	voluisse	nōluisse	māluisse	tulisse	lātus esse
future	–	–	–	lātūrus esse	lātum īrī

Participles					
present	volēns	nōlēns	–	ferēns	–
perfect	–	–	–	–	lātus
future	–	–	–	lātūrus	–

Gerund	–	–	–	ferendum	–
Gerundive	–	–	–	–	ferendus

Principal parts of verbs

Regular verbs of 1st, 2nd and 4th conjugations

	present	*infinitive*	*perfect*	*supine*
1st	parō	parāre	parāvī	parātum
2nd	moneō	monēre	monuī	monitum
4th	audiō	audīre	audīvī	audītum

The following are irregular:

1st conjugation

1 Perfect **-uī**

cubō, cubāre, cubuī, cubitum	I lie down
vetō, vetāre, vetuī, vetitum	I forbid

2 Perfect with lengthened vowel

iuvō, iuvāre, iūvī, iūtum	I help
lavō, lavāre, lāvī, lautum	I wash

3 Reduplicated perfect

dō, dare, dedī, datum	I give
stō, stāre, stetī, statum	I stand

2nd conjugation

1 Perfect **-uī**, supine **-tum**

doceō, docēre, docuī, doctum	I teach
teneō, tenēre, tenuī, tentum	I hold

2 Perfect **-vī**

dēleō, dēlēre, dēlēvī, dēlētum	I destroy
fleō, flēre, flēvī, flētum	I weep

3 Perfect **-sī**

augeō, augēre, auxī, auctum	I increase
ardeō, ardēre, arsī, arsum	I burn, am on fire
iubeō, iubēre, iussī, iussum	I order
maneō, manēre, mānsī, mānsum	I stay, remain
rīdeō, rīdēre, rīsī, rīsum	I laugh
suādeō, suādēre, suāsī, suāsum + dat.	I persuade

4 Perfect with lengthened vowel

caveō, cavēre, cāvī, cautum	I beware
faveō, favēre, fāvī, fautum + dat.	I favor
foveō, fovēre, fōvī, fōtum	I cherish, look after
moveō, movēre, mōvī, mōtum	I move
sedeō, sedēre, sēdī, sessum	I sit
videō, vidēre, vīdī, vīsum	I see

5 Perfect with no change

respondeō, respondēre, respondī, respōnsum	I answer

4th conjugation

1 Perfect in **-uī**

aperiō, aperīre, aperuī, apertum I open

2 Perfect with lengthened vowel

sentiō, sentīre, sēnsī, sēnsum I feel
veniō, venīre, vēnī, ventum I come

3rd conjugation

1a Perfect **-sī**, supine **-tum**

carpō, carpere, carpsī, carptum	I pick
dīcō, dīcere, dīxī, dictum	I say, tell
dūcō, ducere, dūxī, ductum	I lead
gerō, gerere, gessī, gestum	I carry, wear
nūbō, nūbere, nūpsī, nūptum	I marry
regō, regere, rēxī, rēctum	I rule
scrībō, scrībere, scrīpsī, scrīptum	I write
sūmō, sūmere, sūmpsī, sūmptum	I take
surgō*, surgere, surrēxī, surrēctum	I rise, get up (**surrigō**)
tegō, tegere, tēxī, tēctum	I cover
trahō*, trahere, trāxī, tractum	I drag (**traghō**)
vehō*, vehere, vēxī, vectum	I carry (**veghō**)
vīvō*, vīvere, vīxī, vīctum	I live (**vigvō**)

Note

1 verbs marked *: the forms in parentheses are the original form of the verb.
2 **regō, surgō, mittō** lengthen the vowel of the stem in the perfect.
3 Compound verbs usually form the perfect in the same way as the simple verb, e.g. **prōcēdō, prōcēdere, prōcessī, prōcessum** **remittō, remittere, remīsī, remissum**

1b Perfect **-sī**, supine **-sum**

cēdō, cēdere, cessī, cessum	I yield ('go' in compounds)
claudō, claudere, clausī, clausum	I shut
ēvādō, ēvādere, ēvāsī, ēvāsum	I escape
lūdō, lūdere, lūsī, lūsum	I play
mittō, mittere, mīsī, missum	I send
plaudō, plaudere, plausī, plausum	I clap, applaud

2a Perfect stem the same as the present, supine **-tum**

cōnstituō, cōnstituere, cōnstituī, cōnstitūtum	I decide
contendō, contendere, contendī, contentum	I march, hasten
induō, induere, induī, indūtum	I put on
solvō, solvere, solvī, solūtum	I loosen

2b Perfect stem the same as the present, supine **-sum**

accendō, accendere, accendī, accēnsum	I light (a fire)
ascendō, ascendere, ascendī, ascēnsum	I climb
dēscendō, dēscendere, dēscendī, dēscēnsum	I climb down
dēfendō, dēfendere, dēfendī, dēfēnsum	I defend
vertō, vertere, vertī, versum	I turn
vīsō, vīsere, vīsī, vīsum	I visit

2c Perfect stem the same as the present but no supine

bibō, bibere, bibī	I drink
metuō, metuere, metuī	I fear
vīsō, vīsere, vīsī	I go to see

3 Verbs lengthening stem vowel in the perfect, supine **-tum**

agō, agere, ēgī, āctum	I do, I drive
cōgō, cōgere, coēgī, coāctum	I drive together, I compel
emō, emere, ēmī, ēmptum	I buy
legō, legere, lēgī, lēctum	I read, I gather
frangō*, frangere, frēgī, frāctum	I break
relinquō*, relinquere, relīquī, relictum	I leave
rumpō*, rumpere, rūpī, ruptum	I burst open
vincō*, vincere, vīcī, victum	I conquer

Note

Verbs marked * insert **n** (**m** before **p**) in the present, which is dropped in perfect and supine, e.g. **fra-n-gō**, original stem **fragō**, hence **frēgī, frāctum**.

4a Verbs with reduplicated perfect, supine **-tum**

addō, addere, addidī, additum	I add (so all compounds of **dō**)
canō, canere, cecinī, cantum	I sing
(cōn)sistō, (cōn)sistere, (cōn)stitī, (cōn)stitum	I stand
tangō, tangere, tetigī, tāctum	I touch

4b Verbs with reduplicated perfect, supine **-sum**

cadō, cadere, cecidī, casum	I fall
caedō, caedere, cecīdī, caesum	I beat, kill
currō, currere, cucurrī, cursum	I run
discō, discere, didicī	I learn
parcō, parcere, pepercī, parsum + dat.	I spare
pellō, pellere, pepulī, pulsum	I drive
poscō, poscere, poposcī	I demand

NB Compounds of **cadō**, **caedō**, **currō** and **pellō** do not have reduplicated perfects, e.g.

occidō, occidere, occidī, occasum	I fall down, die
occīdō, occīdere, occīdī, occīsum	I kill
occurrō, occurrere, occurrī, occursum	I run to meet, meet
expellō, expellere, expulī, expulsum	I drive out

5 Verbs forming perfect **-vī/-uī**

arcessō, arcessere, arcessīvī, arcessītum	I summon
colō, colere, coluī, cultum	I cultivate
petō, petere, petīvī, petītum	I seek
pōnō, pōnere, posuī, positum	I place
quaerō, quaerere, quaesīvī, quaesītum	I ask, seek
sinō, sinere, sīvī, situm	I allow
dēsinō, dēsinere, dēsiī, dēsitum	I cease

6 Inceptive verbs

cognōscō, cognōscere, cognōvī, cognitum	I get to know, learn
crēscō, crēscere, crēvī, crētum	I grow
nōscō, nōscere, nōvī, nōtum	I get to know
quiēscō, quiēscere, quiēvī, quiētum	I rest

7 3rd **-iō** conjugation

capiō, capere, cēpī, captum	I take
cupiō, cupere, cupīvī, cupītum	I desire
faciō, facere, fēcī, factum	I make, do
fugiō, fugere, fūgī, fugitum	I flee

iaciō, iacere, iēcī, iactum	I throw
rapiō, rapere, rapuī, raptum	I seize
(īn)spiciō, (īn)spicere, (īn)spexī, (īn)spectum	I look at

Deponent verbs

1st conjugation (all regular)

cōnor, cōnārī, cōnātus sum	I try

2nd conjugation

cōnfiteor, cōnfitērī, cōnfessus sum	I confess
vereor, verērī, veritus sum	I fear

3rd conjugation

fruor, fruī, (frūctus sum) + abl.	I enjoy
loquor, loquī, locūtus sum	I speak
queror, querī, questus sum	I complain
sequor, sequī, secūtus sum	I follow
īrāscor, īrāscī, īrātus sum + dat.	I am angry
nancīscor, nancīscī, nactus sum	I obtain
nāscor, nāscī, nātus sum	I am born
oblīvīscor, oblīvīscī, oblītus sum + gen.	I forget
proficīscor, proficīscī, profectus sum	I set out
amplector, amplectī, amplexus sum	I embrace
lābor, lābī, lāpsus sum	I slip
revertor, revertī, reversus sum	I return
ūtor, ūtī, ūsus sum + abl.	I use

4th conjugation

experior, experīrī, expertus sum	I try
orior, orīrī, ortus sum	I arise

Mixed conjugation

gradior, gradī, gressus sum	I walk
morior, morī, mortuus sum (fut. part. moritūrus)	I die
patior, patī, passus sum	I suffer
prōgredior, prōgredī, prōgressus sum	I advance

Semi-deponent verbs

2nd conjugation

audeō, audēre, ausus sum	I dare
gaudeō, gaudēre, gāvīsus sum	I rejoice
soleō, solēre, solitus sum	I am accustomed

3rd conjugation

cōnfīdō, cōnfīdere, cōnfīsus sum + dat.	I trust

Irregular

fīō, fierī, factus sum	I am made, I become

PREPOSITIONS

The following take the accusative:

ad	to, towards
ante	before
apud	at
circum	around
contrā	against
extrā	outside
in	into, onto, to, against
inter	among
per	through
post	after, behind
prope	near
propter	on account of
secundum	along
sub	up to; towards (of time)
super	above
trāns	across
ultrā	beyond

The following take the ablative:

ā/ab	from, by
cum	with
dē	down from; about
ē/ex	out of
in	in, on
prō	in front of, on behalf of
sine	without
sub	under

CONJUNCTIONS

Coordinating

atque	and
aut	or
aut . . . aut	either . . . or
enim*	for
ergō	and so
et	and
et . . . et	both . . . and
igitur*	therefore, and so
itaque	and so
nam	for
nec/neque	and not, nor
nec/neque . . . nec/neque	neither . . . nor
-que	and
sed	but
tamen*	but, however

Subordinating

antequam	before
cum	when, since, although
dōnec	until
dum	while, until
nē	lest, that not
nisi	unless
priusquam	before
postquam	after
quamquam	although
quod	because
sī	if
ubi	when
ut + indicative	as, when
ut + subjunctive	1 that (purpose, command) 2 that (result)

*these come second word in their sentence

Vocabulary

Latin – English

The numbers after the words indicate the chapter vocabularies in which the words occur; those with no number have not been learned.
Principal parts of all verbs are given except for regular verbs of the 1st conjugation, which are listed with infinitive only.

ā/ab + abl. (7) from; by
abhinc ago
abiciō, abicere, abiēcī, abiectum (38) I throw away
absēns, absentis (44) absent
absum, abesse, āfuī + abl. (18) I am away from, I am absent
ac/atque and
accūsō, accūsāre (47) I accuse
accēdō, accēdere, accessī, accessum (4) I approach
accendō, accendere, accendī, accēnsum (27) I set fire to
accidit, accidere, accidit (26) it happens
accipiō, accipere, accēpī, acceptum (9) I receive
accurrō, accurrere, accurrī, accursum I run to
aciēs, aciēī, *f.* (54) line of battle, battle
acūtus, -a, -um sharp, acute
ad + acc. (3) towards, to
addō, addere, addidī, additum I add
addūcō, addūcere, addūxī, adductum I lead to; I influence
adeō (adv.) (43) so, to such an extent
adfluō, adfluere, adflūxī, adfluctum I flow to, flock in
adhūc (18) still
adiciō, adicere, adiēcī, adiectum (49) I add to
adimō, adimere, adēmī, adēmptum (39) I take away
adiuvō, adiuvāre, adiūvī, adiūtum (33) I help
administrō, administrāre (33) I manage, administer
admīrātiō, admīrātiōnis, *f.* (16) wonder
admīror, admīrārī (41) I admire, wonder at
admittō, admittere, admīsī, admissum I let in, admit; I commit
adsistō, adsistere, adstitī + dat. I stand by
adsum, adesse, adfuī (4) I am present
adulēscēns, adulēscentis, *m.* (48) young man
adversor, adversārī + dat. I oppose
adoptō, adoptāre I adopt
adveniō, advenīre, advēnī, adventum (5) I arrive
adventus, adventūs, *m.* (29) arrival
adversus, -a, -um (32) facing, contrary, against
aedēs, aedium, *f. pl.* (21) house
aedificium, -ī, *n.* (19) building
aedificō, aedificāre (11) I build
aeger, aegra, aegrum (23) sick, ill
aegrē with difficulty
aegrōtō, aegrōtāre (54) I am ill
aequus, -a, -um (30) equal, fair
aerārium, -ī, *n.* (40) treasury
aestās, aestātis, *f.* (45) summer
aestimō, aestimāre (40) I value
aetās, aetātis, *f.* (49) age
afficiō, afficere, affēcī, affectum I affect
affīgō, affīgere, affīxī, affīxum I affix
age, agite (34) come on!

ager, agrī, *m.* (3) field
agnōscō, agnōscere, agnōvī, agnitum (38) I recognize
agō, agere, ēgī, āctum (19) I drive; I do, manage
agora, -ae, *f.* agora, city center
āiō (imperfect **āiēbam**) (45) I say
alibī elsewhere
aliquamdiū (46) for some time
aliquandō (38) sometimes
aliquis, aliquid (21) someone, something
alius, alia, aliud (5) other, another
  aliī . . . aliī some . . . others
alter, altera, alterum (29) one or the other (of two); second
altus, -a, -um (19) high, deep
amātor, amātōris, *m.* lover
amātōrius, -a , -um of love
ambitiō, ambitiōnis, *f.* ambition
ambō, ambae, ambō (53) both
ambulō, ambulāre (1) I walk
amīcitia, -ae, *f.* (41) friendship
amīcus, -ī, *m.* (4) friend
amīcus, -a, -um friendly
amō, amāre (12) I love
amoenus, -a, -um pleasant, lovely
amor, amōris, *m.* (12) love
amplus, -a, -um (46) large
an? (29) or?
anima, -ae, *f.* soul
animus, -ī, *m.* (12) mind
  in animō habeō I have in mind, intend
annus, -ī, *m.* (18) year
ante + acc. (12) before
anteā (adv.) (34) before
antequam (conj.) (34) before
antīquus, -a, -um (30) old, ancient
ānxietās, ānxietātis, *f.* (23) anxiety
ānxius, -a, -um (3) anxious
aperiō, aperīre, aperuī, apertum (19) I open
apertus, -a, -um (19) open
appāreō, appārēre, appāruī, appāritum (52) I appear, am seen
appellō, appellāre (20) I call (by name)
apud + acc. (47) at the house of, with
aqua, -ae, *f.* (2) water
āra, -ae, *f.* (52) altar
arbor, arboris, *f.* (13) tree
arcessō, arcessere, arcessīvī, arcessītum (30) I summon
ardeō, ardēre, arsī, arsum (26) I am on fire
argentum, -ī, *n.* (28) silver, money
arithmētica, -ae, f. arithmetic
arma, armōrum, *n. pl.* (11) arms, weapons
armātus, -a, -um (26) armed
arrīdeō, arrīdēre, arrīsī, arrīsum + dat. I smile at
arripiō, arripere, arripuī, arreptum (45) I snatch up
arrogāns, arrogantis arrogant
ars, artis, *f.* (43) art, skill
ascendō, ascendere, ascendī, ascēnsum (3) I climb

asinus, -ī, *m.* ass
aspectō, aspectāre I look at
assequor, assequī, assecūtus sum (49) I pursue, catch up, attain
astō, astāre, astitī + dat. I stand by, help
at (45) but
atque (32) and
ātrium, -ī, *n.* (21) hall
attendō, attendere, attendī, attentum I attend
attentē attentively
attonitus, -a, -um astonished
auctōritās, auctōritātis, *f.* (44) influence, authority
audāx, audācis daring, rash
audeō, audēre, ausus sum (40) I dare
audiō, audīre, audīvī, audītum (3) I hear
audītor, audītōris, *m.* listener, audience
auferō, auferre, abstulī, ablātum I carry away
augeō, augēre, auxī, auctum (27) I increase
aula, -ae, *f.* courtyard
aura, -ae, *f.* (13) breeze, air
aureus, -a, -um (52) golden
auris, auris, *f.* (45) ear
aurum, -ī, *n.* (41) gold
aut . . . aut (12) either . . . or
autem (47) but
auxilium, -ī, *n.* (15) help
āvertō, āvertere, āvertī, āversum (44) I turn away
avis, avis, *f.* (41) bird

balnea, -ōrum, *n. pl.* (23) baths
barbarus, -a, -um (49) barbarian
beātus, -a, -um (41) blessed, happy
bellum, -ī, *n.* (11) war
bene (8) well
benignus, -a, -um (27) kind
bibō, bibere, bibī (9) I drink
bis (51) twice
bona, -ōrum, *n. pl.* (32) goods
bonus, -a, -um (5) good
brevis, breve (25) short

cadō, cadere, cecidī, cāsum (3) I fall
caelum, -ī, *n.* (10) sky, heaven
campus, -ī, *m.* (25) field, plain
candidātus, -ī, *m.* (17) candidate
candidus, -a, -um (17) white
canis, canis, *c.* (7) dog
canō, canere, cecinī, cantum (14) I sing
cantō, cantāre (44) I sing (of)
capiō, capere, cēpī, captum (7) I take
capsula, -ae, *f.* box, satchel
captīvus, -a, -um (48) captive
caput, capitis, *n.* (26) head
carcer, carceris, *m.* (48) prison
careō, carēre, caruī + abl. I lack, am without
carmen, carminis, *n.* (14) song
carpō, carpere, carpsī, carptum (42) I pluck, pick
cārus, -a, -um (7) dear
casa, -ae, *f.* (1) house, cottage
castra, castrōrum, *n. pl.* (11) camp
castus, -a, -um chaste, pure
cāsus, -ūs, *m.* (22) mishap, misfortune

caupōna, -ae, *f.* inn
causa, -ae, *f.* (26) cause, reason
  causā + gen. (50) for the sake of
cautus, -a, -um (33) cautious
caveō, cavēre, cāvī, cautum (24) I beware
cēdō, cēdere, cessī, cessum (49) I yield, give way to
celebrō, celebrāre (52) I celebrate
celer, celeris quick
celeritās, celeritātis, *f.* (23) speed
celeriter (6) quickly
cēlō, cēlāre (36) I hide
cēna, -ae, *f.* (1) dinner
cēnō, cēnāre (1) I dine
centum a hundred
centuriō, centuriōnis, *m.* (14) centurion
certē certainly
certus, -a, -um (33) certain; resolved
  aliquem certiōrem faciō (32) I inform someone
  prō certō habeō I am certain
cessō, cessāre (35) I idle, linger
cēterī, cēterae, cētera (6) the others, the rest
chorus, -ī, *m.* (30) chorus
cibus, -ī, *m.* (3) food
circā + acc. (46) around; about (of time)
circum + acc. (8) around
circumdō, -dare, -dedī, -datum I surround
circumspectō, circumspectāre I look around
circumstō, -stāre, -stetī, -statum I stand around
circumveniō, -venīre, -vēnī, -ventum (15) I surround
circumvolō, circumvolāre I fly around
cīvīlis, cīvīle (27) of citizens, civil
cīvis, cīvis, *c.* (15) citizen
clādēs, clādis, *f.* (37) disaster
clam (32) secretly
clāmō, clāmāre (5) I shout
clāmor, clāmōris, *m.* (10) shout
clārus, -a, -um (21) clear, bright, famous
classis, classis, *f.* (47) fleet
claudō, claudere, clausī, clausum (19) I shut
clēmentia, -ae, *f.* (47) mercy
cliēns, clientis, *m.* (24) client, dependant
coepī, coepisse (54) I began
cōgitō, cōgitāre (37) I think, reflect
cognōscō, cognōscere, cognōvī, cognitum (11) I get to know, learn
cōgō, cōgere, coēgī, coāctum (32) I compel
cohors, cohortis, *f.* cohort
colligō, colligere, collēgī, collēctum (27) I gather, collect
collis, collis, *m.* (11) hill
collocō, collocāre (47) I place, position
colloquium, -ī, *n.* (41) conversation, talk
colloquor, colloquī, collocūtus sum (41) I talk with
collum, -ī, *n.* neck
colō, colere, coluī, cultum (13) I till; I worship
colōnus, -ī, *m.* (3) farmer
comes, comitis, *c.* (7) companion
cōmis, cōme friendly
comitia, -ōrum, *n. pl.* elections
comitor, comitārī, comitātus sum (44) I accompany
commendō, commendāre I introduce, commend
committō, committere, commīsī, commissum (33) I entrust

commōtus, -a, -um (12) moved

commoveō, commovēre, commōvī, commōtum I move deeply

cōmoedia, -ae, f. comedy

comparō, comparāre (32) I acquire, get

complector, complectī, complexus sum (38) I embrace

compōnō, compōnere, composuī, compositum I put together, compose

comprehendō, comprehendere, comprehendī, comprehēnsum (48) I seize

conciliō, conciliāre I unite, conciliate

conclāmō, conclāmāre I shout aloud

concordia, -ae, f. harmony

concurrō, concurrere, concurrī, concursum I run together

condō, condere, condidī, conditum (29, 41) I store; I found

condūcō, condūcere, condūxī, conductum I hire

cōnfectus, -a, -um (19) finished

cōnficiō, cōnficere, cōnfēcī, cōnfectum (21) I finish

cōnfidō, cōnfidere, cōnfīsus sum + dat. (29) I trust

cōnfirmō, cōnfirmāre (49) I strengthen, encourage

cōnfugiō, cōnfugere, cōnfūgī (47) I flee for refuge

coniciō, conicere, coniēcī, coniectum (8) I hurl

coniungō, coniungere, coniūnxī, coniūnctum (36) I join together

coniūrātus, -ī, m. conspirator

conlēga, -ae, m. colleague

cōnor, cōnārī, cōnātus sum (36) I try

cōnscendō, cōnscendere, cōnscendī, cōnscēnsum (9) I board (a ship)

cōnsecrō, cōnsecrāre I consecrate

cōnsēnsus, -ūs, m. (49) agreement, consensus

cōnservō, cōnservāre I preserve, save

cōnsilium, -ī, n. (11) plan

cōnsistō, cōnsistere, cōnstitī, cōnstitum (32) I halt, stand still

cōnsōlātiō, cōnsōlātiōnis, f. consōlation, comfort

cōnsōlor, cōnsōlārī, cōnsōlātus sum (36) I comfort, console

cōnspectus, cōnspectūs, m. (24) sight, view

cōnspiciō, cōnspicere, cōnspexī, cōnspectum (18) I catch sight of

cōnstituō, cōnstituere, cōnstituī, cōnstitūtum (6) I decide

cōnstruō, cōnstruere, cōnstrūxī, cōnstructum I construct, build

cōnsul, cōnsulis, m. (15) consul

cōnsulō, cōnsulere, cōnsuluī, cōnsultum I consult

cōnsūmō, cōnsūmere, cōnsūmpsī, cōnsūmptum I consume, eat

contemnō, contemnere, contempsī, contemptum (40) I despise

contendō, contendere, contendī, contentum (14) I walk, march

contentus, -a, -um (22) content

conterō, conterere, contrīvī, contrītum I wear out

continuō (19) immediately

continuus, -a, -um continuous, on end

contrā + acc. against, opposite

conveniō, convenīre, convēnī, conventum (9) I come together, meet

conventus, -ūs, m. meeting

convīva, -ae, c. (42) guest

convīvium, -ī, n. (42) dinner party

convocō, convocāre (7) I call together

cōpia, -ae, f. plenty

    cōpiae, -ārum, f. pl. (32) forces

cor, cordis, n. (53) heart

cornū, -ūs, n. (37) horn; wing of an army

corōna, -ae, f. (42) crown, garland

corpus, corporis, n. body

corripiō, corripere, corripuī, correptum (32) I seize, steal

cotīdiē (21) every day

crās (27) tomorrow

crēdō, crēdere, crēdidī, crēditum + dat. (17) I believe, trust

creō, creāre I elect, appoint

crēscō, crēscere, crēvī, crētum (28) I grow, increase

crūdēlis, crūdēle (24) cruel

cubō, cubāre, cubuī, cubitum (38) I lie down, recline

cum + abl. (5) with

cum (conjunction) (17) when, since, although

    cum prīmum (28) as soon as

cūnctus, -a, -um (54) all

cupiō, cupere, cupīvī, cupītum (6) I desire, want

cūr? (4) why

cūra, -ae, f. care

cūrō, cūrāre (4) I care for, look after

currō, currere, cucurrī, cursum (3) I run

currus, -ūs, m. (22) chariot

cursus, -ūs, m. (22) running; a course

custōdiō, custōdīre, custōdīvī, custōdītum (16) I guard

custōs, custōdis, m. (16) guard

dē + abl. (10) down from

dē + abl. (15) about

dea, -ae, f. (12) goddess

dēbeō, dēbēre, dēbuī, dēbitum (7) I ought, must

dēcidō, dēcidere, dēcidī I fall down

decimus, -a, -um tenth

dēcrētum, -ī, n. decree

dēdecus, dēdecoris, n. (48) disgrace

dēditiō, dēditiōnis, f. surrender

dēdō, dēdere, dēdidī, dēditum (15) I give up, surrender

dēfendō, dēfendere, dēfendī, dēfēnsum (7) I defend

dēfēnsor, dēfēnsōris, defender, protector

deinde (17) then, next

dēlectō, dēlectāre (30) I please, delight

dēleō, dēlēre, dēlēvī, dēlētum (49) I destroy

dēmittō, dēmittere, dēmīsī, dēmissum (48) I send down, let down

dēnārius, -ī, m. a penny

dēnique (24) finally, lastly

dēpōnō, dēpōnere, dēposuī, dēpositum (13) I put down

dēscendō, dēscendere, dēscendī, dēscēnsum I descend, come down

dēscrībō, dēscrībere, dēscrīpsī, dēscrīptum I write down, describe

dēserō, dēserere, dēseruī, dēsertum I desert

dēsertus, -a, -um deserted

dēsīderium, -ī, n. (50) longing

dēsīderō, dēsīderāre (50) I long for, miss

dēsiliō, dēsilīre, dēsiluī I jump down

dēsinō, dēsinere, dēsiī, dēsitum (36) I cease

dēsistō, dēsistere, dēstitī, destitum I cease from

dēspērātiō, dēspērātiōnis, f. despair

dēspērō, dēspērāre (12) I despair

dēspiciō, dēspicere, dēspexī, dēspectum (34) I look down on

dēsum, dēesse, dēfuī + dat. (43) I fail

deus, -ī, *m.* (12) god

dēvincō, dēvincere, dēvīcī, dēvictum I conquer, subdue

dēvōrō, dēvōrāre I swallow down, devour

dexter, dextra, dextrum (28) right

   dextrā (manū) (28) on the right (hand)

dī immortālēs! immortal gods!

dīcō, dīcere, dīxī, dictum (5) I say

dictātor, dictātōris, *m.* (15) dictator

dictō, dictāre I dictate

diēs, diēī, *m.* (18) day

   in diēs daily

difficilis, difficile (19) difficult

difficultās, difficultātis, *f.* (38) difficulty

diffugiō, diffugere, diffūgī I flee away

dignus, -a, -um + abl. (16) worthy (of)

dīligenter (6) carefully, hard

dīligentia, -ae, *f.* (25) care, diligence

dīligō, dīligere, dīlēxī, dīlēctum (43) I esteem, love

dīmittō, dīmittere, dīmīsī, dīmissum (6) I send away, dismiss

dīrus, -a, -um (38) terrible, dire

discēdō, discēdere, discessī, discessum (17) I go away, depart

disciplīna, -ae, *f.* (35) training, discipline, learning

discipulus, -ī, *m.* (20) pupil

discō, discere, didicī (18) I learn

discurrō, discurrere, discurrī, discursum (44) I run about

dispōnō, dispōnere, disposuī, dispositum I arrange, dispose

disserō, disserere, disseruī, dissertum (31) I discuss

diū (4) for a long time

diūtius for a longer time, longer

dīves, dīvitis (30) rich

dīvidō, dīvidere, dīvīsī, dīvīsum (32) I divide

dīvīnus, -a, -um (13) divine

dīvitiae, -ārum, *f. pl.* (17) riches

dō, dare, dedī, datum (5) I give

doceō, docēre, docuī, doctum (6) I teach

doctor, doctōris, *m.* teacher

doctrīna, -ae, *f.* (51) teaching, doctrine

doctus, -a, -um (29) learned

doleō, dolēre, doluī (51) I feel pain, I grieve for

dolor, dolōris, *m.* (33) pain, grief

dolus, -ī, *m.* (48) trick

domicilium, -ī, *n.* lodging

domina, -ae, *f.* (13) mistress

dominor, dominārī, dominātus sum + dat. (47) I control, dominate

dominus, -ī, *m.* (21) master

domum (6) (to) home

dōnec (35) until

dōnō, dōnāre (42a) I give

domus, domūs, *f.* home

dōnum, -ī, *n.* (30) gift

dormiō, dormīre, dormīvī, dormītum (4) I sleep

dubitō, dubitāre (34) I doubt, hesitate

dubius, -a, -um (30) doubtful

   sine dubiō (30) without doubt

dūcō, dūcere, dūxī, ductum (3) I lead; I draw (water)

dulcis, dulce (29) sweet ·

dum (11) while

duo, duae, duo (5) two

dux, ducis, *c.* leader

ē/ex + abl. (8) out of, from

eam, eum (3) her, him

eās, eōs (4) them

ēbrius, -a, -um drunk

ecce! look!

ēdō, ēdere, ēdidī, ēditum I give out, utter, publish

edō, ēsse, ēdī, ēsum (28) I eat

efficiō, efficere, effēcī, effectum (17) I effect, do

effugiō, effugere, effūgī, effugitum I flee away, escape

effundō, effundere, effūdī, effūsum I pour out

ego (6) I (acc. mē)

ēgredior, ēgredī, ēgressus sum (36) I go out of

ēlābor, ēlābī, ēlāpsus sum (42) I slip out of

ēloquentia, -ae, *f.* eloquence

emō, emere, ēmī, ēmptum (5) I buy

enim (17) for

eō, īre , iī, itum (6) I go

eō (adv.) (14) thither, (to) there

epistola, -ae, *f.* (21) letter

eques, equitis, *m.* (31) horseman

equidem = ego quidem I (emphatic)

equitēs, equitum, *m. pl.* (31) cavalry

equitō, equitāre (47) I ride (a horse)

equus, -ī, *m.* horse

ergō (27) and so

ēripiō, ēripere, eripuī, ēreptum (45) I snatch away, rescue

errō, errāre (11) I wander; I err, am wrong

et (1) and

et ... et (15) both ... and

etiam (12) also, even

euge! good!

ēvādō, ēvādere, ēvāsī, ēvāsum (16) I escape

ēventus, -ūs, *m.* outcome

ēvertō, ēvertere, ēvertī, ēversum (32) I overturn

ēvigilō, ēvigilāre I wake up

ēvolō, ēvolāre I fly out

excitō, excitāre (13) I rouse, wake up

excūsātiō, excūsātiōnis, *f.* excuse

exemplum, -ī, *n.* (16) example

exeō, exīre, exiī, exitum (6) I go out

exerceō, exercēre, exercuī, exercitum (14) I exercise, train

exercitus, -ūs, *m.* army

exitium, -ī, *n.* (27) destruction

expellō, expellere, expulī, expulsum (31) I drive out

explōrō, explōrāre I explore

expōnō, expōnere, exposuī, expositum I put out; I explain

exsilium, -ī, *n.* (49) exile

exspectō, exspectāre (8) I wait for

exstinguō, exstinguere, exstīnxī, exstīnctum I put out, quench, destroy

externus, -a, -um external, foreign

extrā + acc. (19) outside

exuō, exuere, exuī, exūtum I take off, throw off

fābula, -ae, *f.* (2) story, play

fābulōsus, -a, -um fabulous, from a story

facile (20) easily

facilis, facile (20) easy

facilitās, facilitātis, *f.* (25) ease, facility

faciō, facere, fēcī, factum (5) I do; I make

falsus, -a, -um false

fāma, -ae, *f.* (11) fame, reputation, report

famēs, famis, *f.* (47) hunger
familia, -ae, *f.* (14) family, household
fānum, -ī, *n.* shrine
fās (indecl.) (49) right
fātum, -ī, *n.* (40) fate, destiny
faveō, favēre, fāvī, fautum + dat. (22) I favor, support
fēmina, -ae, *f.* (1) woman
feriō, ferīre (26) I strike
ferō, ferre, tulī, lātum (11) I carry, bear
ferōx, ferōcis (24) fierce
ferrum, -ī, *n.* (32) iron; sword
ferula, -ae, *f.* cane
ferus, -a, -um wild
fessus, -a, -um (1) tired
festīnō, festīnāre (1) I hurry
fēstus, -a, -um festal, feast
fidēlis, fidēle (46) faithful, loyal
fīlia, -ae, *f.* (2) daughter
fīliolus, -ī, *m.* (33) little son
fīlius, -ī, *m.* (3) son
fīnis, fīnis, *m.* (31) end
    fīnēs, fīnium *m. pl.* (31) boundaries, territory
fīnitimus, -a, -um on the boundaries, neighboring
fīō, fierī, factus (24) I am made, I become
flamma, -ae, *f.* flame
flēbilis, flēbile to be wept for, lamentable
fleō, flēre, flēvī, flētum (18) I weep
flētus, -ūs, *m.* weeping
flōs, flōris, *m.* (14) flower
fluctus, -ūs, *m.* (47) wave
flūmen, flūminis, *n.* (16) river
fluō, fluere, fluxī, fluxum (46) I flow
foedus, foederis, *n.* (16) treaty
fōns, fontis, *m.* spring, fountain
for, fārī, fātus sum (43) I speak, say
fōrma, -ae, *f.* (13) shape, beauty
forsitan (39) perhaps
forte (35) by chance
fortis, forte (7) brave
fortiter (7) bravely
forum, -ī, *n.* forum, city center
foveō, fovēre, fōvī, fōtum I cherish, support, assist
frāctus, -a, -um (22) broken
frangō, frangere, frēgī, frāctum (22) I break
frāter, frātris, *m.* (7) brother
frīgidus, -a, -um (54) cold
frīgus, frīgoris, *n.* (46) cold
frūmentum, -ī, *n.* (16) grain
fruor, fruī, frūctus sum + abl. (41) I enjoy
frūstrā in vain
fugiō, fugere, fūgī, fugitum (7) I flee
fūmus, -ī, *m.* smoke
fundus, -ī, *m.* (46) farm
fūnus, fūneris, *n.* funeral
furor, furōris, *m.* madness
futūra, -ōrum, *n. pl.* (38) the future

gaudeō, gaudēre, gāvīsus sum (9) I rejoice;
    + abl. I rejoice in
gaudium, -ī, *n.* joy
gēns, gentis, *f.* (49) race, people
genus, generis, *n.* (24) sort, kind, race

gerō, gerere, gessī, gestum (14) I carry, wear
    mē gerō (30) I behave myself
    rem gerō (30) I conduct a matter
gladius, -ī, *m.* (26) sword
glōria, -ae, *f.* (14) glory
gradus, -ūs, *m.* (20) step
grāmen, grāminis, *n.* grass
grātiae, -ārum, *f. pl.* (20) thanks
    grātiās agō + dat. (20) I give thanks
grātulātiō, grātulātiōnis, *f.* congratulations
grātus, -a, -um (29) pleasing; grateful
gravis, grave (17) heavy, grave, serious

habeō, habēre, habuī, habitum (9) I have
    prō certō habeō (42) I am sure that
habitō, habitāre (10) I inhabit, live
hasta, -ae, *f.* (8) spear
haud (15) not
herī (30) yesterday
hērōs, hērōis, *m.* hero
hīc (8) here
hic, haec, hoc (15) this
hiems, hiemis, *f.* (12) winter
hilaris, hilare (31) cheerful
hodiē (14) today
hodiernus, -a, -um (51) of today, today's
homō, hominis, *c.* (10) human being, man
honestus, -a, -um (33) honorable
honor, honōris, *m.* (43) honor, office
hōra, -ae, *f.* (17) hour
horreō, horrēre, horruī (41) I tremble, shudder at
horribilis, horribile horrible
horridus, -a, -um rough, savage
hortus, -ī, *m.* (5) garden
hospes, hospitis, *c.* (53) host, guest
hostis, hostis, *m.* (11) enemy
hūc (8) hither, this way
hūc...illūc (19) this way and that
hūmānus, -a, -um (29) human; humane, kind

iaceō, iacēre, iacuī (5) I lie (down)
iaciō, iacere, iēcī, iactum (7) I throw
iam (4) now, already
iamdūdum (45) long ago
iānua, -ae, *f.* (6) door
ibi (12) there
īdem, eadem, idem (31) the same
igitur (17) therefore, and so
ignāvus, -a, -um lazy, cowardly
ignis, ignis, *m.* (18) fire
ignōscō, ignōscere, ignōvī, ignōtum + dat. (40) I pardon, forgive
ignōtus, -a, -um (11) unknown
ille, illa, illud (4) that; he, she, it
illīc there
illūminō, illūmināre I light up, illuminate
illūstrō, illūstrāre I light up, illustrate
imber, imbris, *m.* (44) rain
immemor, immemōris + gen. (38) forgetful of
immineō, imminēre, + dat. (33) I hang over, threaten
immortālis, immortāle (31) immortal
imperātor, imperātōris, *m.* (14) general

imperium, -ī, *n.* (12) order
  imperium Rōmānum (26) the Roman empire
imperō, imperāre + dat. (11) I order
impius, -a, um (36) impious, wicked
improbus, -a, -um (45) immoral, bad
imprūdēns, imprūdentis imprudent, foolish
impudēns, impudentis impudent, shameless
in + acc. (2) into, to
in + abl. (5) in, on
incendium, -ī, *n.* fire
incendō, incendere, incendī, incēnsum I set on fire
incertus, -a, -um uncertain
incidō, incidere, incidī, incāsum I fall into
incipiō, incipere, incēpī, inceptum I begin
incitō, incitāre (51) I urge on, incite
inclūdō, inclūdere, inclūsī, inclūsum I shut in
incolumis, incolume (8) safe
inde (28) thence, from there
indignus, -a, -um + abl. (43) unworthy (of)
induō, induere, induī, indūtum (20) I put on (clothes)
ineō, inīre, iniī, initum (18) I enter, begin
īnfāns, īnfantis, *c.* (33) infant, baby
īnfēlīx, īnfēlīcis (12) unhappy, unlucky
īnferō, īnferre, intulī, illātum I bring into, bring against
īnfirmus, -a, -um (41) weak
ingēns, ingentis (9) huge
ingeniōsus, -a, -um (21) clever, talented
ingenium, -ī, *n.* (21) character, talents
ingredior, ingredī, ingressus sum (36) I go into, enter
inimīcus, -ī, *m.* (24) enemy
initium, -ī, *n.* (52) beginning
innocēns, innocentis innocent, harmless
inquit (3) he/she says
  inquiunt they say
īnscrīptiō, īnscrīptiōnis, *f.* inscription
īnsidiae, -ārum, *f. pl.* ambush, trap
īnsignis, īnsigne (25) outstanding, distinguished
īnspiciō, īnspicere, īnspexī, īnspectum I look at
īnstituō, īnstituere, īnstituī, īnstitūtum I establish, train
īnstruō, īnstruere, īnstrūxī, īnstructum I set up, establish, teach, train
īnsula, -ae, *f.* (9) island
īnsum, inesse, īnfuī (23) I am in, I am among
integer, integra, integrum whole, fresh, upright, honest
intellegō, intellegere, intellēxī, intellēctum (20) I understand
intentē intently
inter + acc. (9) between, among
interdum (39) from time to time
interficiō, interficere, interfēcī, interfectum (37) I kill
intersum, interesse, interfuī + dat. (21) I am among, I take part in
intereā (12) meanwhile
intimus, -a, -um (45) innermost, most intimate
intrō, intrāre (1) I go into, enter
intueor, intuērī, intuitus sum (38) I gaze at
intus (adv.) inside
inultus, -a, -um unavenged
inveniō, invenīre, invēnī, inventum (11) I find
invideō, invidēre, invīdī, invīsum + dat. (13) I envy
invidia, -ae, *f.* (45) envy, spite
invīsus, -a, -um (54) hated

invītō, invītāre I invite
invītus, -a, -um (19) unwilling
invocō, invocāre I call on, invoke
iocus, -ī, *m.* joke
ipse, ipsa, ipsum (15) himself, herself, itself
īra, -ae, *f.* (7) anger
īrāscor, īrāscī, īrātus sum + dat. (48) I become angry
īrātus, -a, -um (2) angry
irrīdeō, irrīdere, irrīsī, irrīsum I laugh at
irrumpō, irrumpere, irrūpī, irruptum I burst in
is, ea, id (14) he, she, it; that
ita (43) so, thus
itaque (6) and so, therefore
iter, itineris, *n.* (18) journey
iterum (6) again
iubeō, iubēre, iussī, iussum (6) I order
  valēre iubeō (18) I bid goodbye
iūcundus, -a, -um (29) pleasant, delightful
iūdicium, -ī, *n.* (45) judgement, law-court
iugum, -ī, *n.* yoke
Iuppiter, Iovis, *m.* (19) Jupiter
iūs, iūris, *n.* (25) right, justice
iussum, -ī, *n.* order
iuvenis, iuvenis, *m.* (14) young man
iuvō, iuvāre, iūvī, iūtum (2) I help
  (me) iuvat, iuvāre, iūvit (49) it pleases, delights (me)

lābor, lābī, lāpsus sum (36) I slip, slide
labor, labōris, *m.* (9) work, suffering
labōriōsus, -a, -um laborious, toilsome
labōrō, labōrāre (1) I work
lacerō, lacerāre I tear to pieces
lacrima, -ae, *f.* (18) tear
laetus, -a, -um (1) happy, joyful
lāna, -ae, *f.* wool
lapis, lapidis, *m.* stone
lateō, latēre, latuī (48) I lie hidden
lātus, -a, -um (21) wide, broad
latus, lateris, *n.* (34) side, lung
laudō, laudāre (2) I praise
lavō, lavāre, lāvī, lautum (14) I wash
lectus, -ī, *m.* bed, couch
lēgātiō, lēgātiōnis, *f.* embassy
lēgātus, -ī, *m.* (32) deputy, officer, envoy
legiō, legiōnis, *f.* (14) legion
legō, legere, lēgī, lēctum (17) I read
lēnis, lēne (46) gentle
lentē (4) slowly
levis, leve (41) light
lēx, lēgis, *f.* (25) law
libēns, libentis willing
libenter (29) gladly
liber, librī, *m.* (20) book
līber, lībera, līberum (16) free
līberālis, līberāle (54) generous, liberal
līberō, līberāre (16) I free
lībertās, lībertātis, *f.* (31) freedom
lībertīnus, -a, -um of a freedman; a freedman
lībertus, -ī, *m.* freedman
mihi licet, licēre, licuit (49) it is permitted for me, I am allowed, I may
līmen, līminis, *n.* (30) threshold

littera, litterae, *f.* (6) a letter
    litterae, -ārum, *f. pl.* (25) literature
lītus, lītoris, *n.* (10) shore
locus, locī, *m.* (**loca, locōrum,** *n. pl.*) (14) a place
longē (18) far
longus, -a, -um (18) long
loquor, loquī, locūtus sum (36) I speak
lūceō, lūcēre, lūxī (25) I shine
lūdō, lūdere, lūsī, lūsum (6) I play
lūdus, lūdī, *m.* (4) school, game
    lūdī, -ōrum, *m. pl.* (22) the games
lūgeō, lūgēre, lūxī, luctum I mourn
lūmen, lūminis, *n.* (30) light
lūna, -ae, *f.* (28) moon
lupus, -ī, *m.* wolf
lūx, lūcis, *f.* (13) light
lyra, -ae, *f.* (40) lyre

maestus, -a, -um (50) sad
magister, magistrī, *m.* (6) master
magnificē magnificently
magnitūdō, magnitūdinis, *f.* great size
magnopere (24) greatly
magnus, -a, -um (4) great, big
maiestās, maiestātis, *f.* majesty
maiōrēs, maiōrum, *m. pl.* (54) ancestors
mala, -ōrum, *n. pl.* (36) evils, troubles
malignus, -a, -um malignant, spiteful
mālō, mālle, māluī (23) I prefer
malus, -a, -um (5) bad
māne (27) early (in the morning)
maneō, manēre, mānsī, mānsum (3) I stay, remain, await
manus, manūs, *f.* (20) hand; band (of people)
marītus, -ī, *m.* (13) husband
māter, mātris, *f.* (8) mother
mātrimōnium, -ī, *n.* marriage
mātrōna, -ae, *f.* married woman
maximus, -a, -um (22) very great, greatest
mē (acc.) (6) me
medicus, -ī, *m.* doctor
meditor, meditārī, meditātus sum (45) I think over, meditate
medius, -a, -um (19) middle
meminī, meminisse + gen. or acc. (50) I remember
memor, memoris + gen. (38) mindful of, remembering
memoria, -ae, *f.* memory
mēns, mentis, *f.* (44) mind
mēnsa, -ae, *f.* table
mēnsis, mēnsis, *m.* (33) month
mercātor, mercātōris, *m.* merchant
mereō, merēre, meruī, meritum (46) I deserve, earn
merīdiēs, merīdiēī, *m.* (21) midday
meritum, -ī, *n.* deserts, reward
meus, -a, -um (6) my
mīles, mīlitis, *m.* (14) soldier
mīlitāris, mīlitāre (35) of soldiers, military
mīlitia, -ae, *f.* (42a) warfare, military service
mīlitō, mīlitāre (31) I serve (as a soldier), I campaign
mīlle a thousand
    mīlle passūs a mile
    mīlia, mīlium, *n. pl.* thousands; **mīlia passuum** miles
minor, minārī, minātus sum + dat. (49) I threaten
mīror, mīrārī, mīrātus sum (50) I wonder at, admire

mīrus, -a, -um (40) wonderful
miser, misera, miserum (4) miserable
mittō, mittere, mīsī, missum (3) I send
modestus, -a, -um (50) modest, moderate
modicus, -a, -um (53) moderate, modest, small
modo only; lately
modo . . . modo (41) now . . . now
modus, -ī, *m.* (52) way; kind, sort
moenia, moenium, *n. pl.* (15) walls, fortifications
mollis, molle (51) soft
moneō, monēre, monuī, monitum (9) I warn, advise
mōns, montis, *m.* (10) mountain
monumentum, -ī, *n.* monument
mora, -ae, *f.* (23) delay
morbus, -ī, *m.* (47) disease
morior, morī, mortuus sum (36) I die
moror, morārī, morātus sum (36) I delay
mors, mortis, *f.* (8) death
mortālis, mortāle (41) mortal
mortuus, -a, um (8) dead
mōs, mōris, *m.* (30) custom
    mōs maiōrum (30) the custom of our ancestors
mox (1) soon
mulier, mulieris, *f.* (47) woman
multitūdō, multitūdinis, *f.* (25) multitude, crowd
multus, -a, -um (4) much, many
mūnus, mūneris, *n.* (46) gift, duty; (gladiatorial) show
murmur, murmuris, *n.* murmur
murmurō, murmurāre I murmur
mūrus, -ī, *m.* (8) wall
mūtō, mūtāre (50) I change

nam (3), **namque** (44) for
nārrō, nārrāre (2) I tell, narrate
nāscor, nāscī, nātus sum (43) I am born
nātus, -ī, *m.* son
nauta, -ae, *m.* (10) sailor
nāvigō, nāvigāre (7) I sail
nāvis, nāvis, *f.* (7) ship
nē (34) lest, in order not to
nē . . . quidem not even
nec/neque (5) nor, and not
nec/neque . . . nec/neque (6) neither . . . nor
necesse est (41) it is necessary
necessitās, necessitātis, *f.* necessity
nefās (indecl.) (49) wrong
neglegō, neglegere, neglēxī, neglēctum I neglect
negō, negāre (41) I deny, say that . . . not
negōtium, -ī, *n.* (29) business
nēmō, nēminis, *c.* (13) no one
nesciō, nescīre, nescīvī, nescītum (39) I do not know
nescioquis, nescioquid (45) someone/something or other
niger, nigra, nigrum black
nihil/nīl (44) nothing
nimis too much
nimium, -ī, *n.* + gen. (23) too much
nisi (29) unless; except
nōbilis, nōbile (22) famous, noble
noctū (38) by night
nocturnus, -a, -um (53) of the night, nocturnal
nōlō, nōlle, nōluī (15) I am unwilling, I refuse
nōmen, nōminis, *n.* (11) name

nōmine by name, called
nōn (1) not
nōndum not yet
nōnnūllī, -ae, -a (31) some
nōnnumquam (51) sometimes
nōtus, -a, -um (11) known
novus, -a, -um (9) new
nox, noctis, *f.* (9) night
nūbēs, nūbis, *f.* (28) cloud
nūbō, nūbere, nūpsī, nūptum + dat. (30) I marry
nūgae, -ārum *f. pl.* trifles, nonsense
nūllus, -a, -um (13) no
num? (26) surely not?
num (39) whether (in indirect questions)
numerō, numerāre (24) I count
numerus, -ī, *m.* (17) number
numquam (13) never
nunc (12) now
nūndinae, -ārum, *f. pl.* market day
nūntius, -ī, *m.* (12) message; messenger
nūper (30) lately
nūptiae, -ārum, *f. pl.* (30) wedding
nūptiālis, nūptiāle (30) of a wedding, nuptial

obeō, obīre, obiī, obitum I go to meet, meet; I die
oblīvīscor, oblīvīscī, oblītus sum + gen. or acc. (54) I forget
obscūrō, obscūrāre I darken
obses, obsidis, *c.* (16) hostage
obsideō, obsidēre, obsēdī, obsessum (47) I besiege
obviam eō + dat. I come to meet
Occidēns, Occidentis, *m.* the West
occidō, occidere, occidī, occāsum (34) I fall, die; I set (of sun)
occīdō, occīdere, occīdī, occīsum (7) I kill
occupātus, -a, -um occupied, busy
occupō, occupāre (32) I seize, occupy
occurrō, occurrere, occurrī, occursum + dat. (11) I meet
Oceanus, -ī, *m.* Ocean
oculus, -ī, *m.* (12) eye
ōdī, ōdisse (54) I hate
odium, -ī, *n.* (47) hatred
offerō, offerre, obtulī, oblātum (46) I offer
officium, -ī, *n.* (31) duty
ōlim (47) once (in past), some time (in future)
olīva, -ae, *f.* olive; olive tree
ōmen, ōminis, *n.* omen
ōmittō, ōmittere, ōmīsī, ōmissum (45) I let go, neglect
omnīnō (35) altogether, completely
omnipotēns, omnipotentis all powerful
omnis, omne (7) all
onus, oneris, *n.* (45) burden
opēs, opum, *f. pl.* (54) wealth
mē oportet, oportēre, oportuit (49) I ought
opprimō, opprimere, oppressī, oppressum (31) I oppress
oppugnō, oppugnāre (7) I attack
optimus, -a, -um (17) very good, best
optō, optāre (46) I wish for, pray for
opus, operis, *n.* (35) work; fortification
  opus est mihi + abl. (36) I have need of
ōra, -ae, *f.* shore
ōrāculum, -ī, *n.* (34) oracle
ōrātiō, ōrātiōnis, *f.* (17) speech

ōrātor, ōrātōris, *m.* (21) speaker, orator
orbis, orbis, *m.* (27) circle, globe
  orbis terrārum (27) the world
ōrdō, ōrdinis, *m.* (24) rank, line, order
Oriēns, Orientis, *m.* (44) the East
orīgo, orīginis, *f.* origin
orior, orīrī, ortus sum (36) I arise, rise
ōrnō, ōrnāre (52) I adorn
ōrō, ōrāre (10) I beg, pray
ōs, ōris, *n.* mouth, face
ōsculum, -ī, *n.* kiss
ostendō, ostendere, ostendī, ostentum (11) I show
ōtiōsus, -a, -um (33) at leisure, idle
ōtium, -ī, *n.* (27) leisure, idleness
ovis, ovis, *f.* (41) sheep

paene (19) nearly
pānis, pānis, *m.* bread
parātus, -a, -um (1) prepared, ready
parcō, parcere, pepercī, parsum + dat. (42a) I spare
parēns, parentis, *c.* (14) parent
pāreō, pārēre, pāruī, pāritum + dat. (22) I obey
parō, parāre (2) I prepare
pars, partis, *f.* (26) part
partēs, partium, *f. pl.* (32) political party
parvus, -a, -um (9) small
pāstor, pāstōris, *m.* shepherd
pater, patris, *m.* (7) father
patior, patī, passus sum (36) I suffer
patria, -ae, *f.* (11) fatherland
patrius, -a, -um (42a) of one's father
paucī, -ae, -a (9) few
paulātim (41) little by little
paulīsper (23) for a little (time)
paulum (38) a little
pauper, pauperis (15) poor
paupertās, paupertātis, *f.* (39) poverty
pāx, pācis, *f.* (16) peace
pectus, pectoris, *n.* (43) heart, breast
pecūnia, -ae, *f.* (17) money
pecus, pecoris, *n.* (46) herd, flock
pellō, pellere, pepulī, pulsum I drive
penātēs, penātium, *m. pl.* household gods
penitus deeply
per + acc. (5) through, throughout
peragō, peragere, perēgī, perāctum (53) I complete, accomplish, pass (of time)
perdō, perdere, perdidī, perditum (22) I lose, waste, destroy
perdūcō, perdūcere, perdūxī, perductum I lead, conduct
pereō, perīre, periī, peritum (30) I perish, die
pererrō, pererrāre I wander through
perficiō, perficere, perfēcī, perfectum (12) I carry out, complete
perīculum, -ī, *n.* (10) danger
perītus, -a, -um + gen. (35) skilled in
perlegō, perlegere, perlēgī, perlēctum I read through
perpetuus, -a, -um everlasting, perpetual
perrumpō, perrumpere, perrūpī, perruptum I break through
persequor, persequī, persecūtus sum (45) I follow after, pursue
persōna, -ae, *f.* character

persuādeō, persuādēre, persuāsī, persuāsum + dat. I persuade

perveniō, pervenīre, pervēnī, perventum (26) I reach

pēs, pedis, *m.* (36) foot

pessimus, -a, -um (17) very bad, worst

petō, petere, petīvī, petītum (12) I ask, seek, pursue

philosophia, -ae, *f.* (27) philosophy

philosophus, -ī, *m.* philosopher

pictūra, -ae, *f.* picture

pictor, pictōris, *m.* painter

pietās, pietātis, *f.* (54) piety, goodness, loyalty

pius, -a, -um (36) pious, good, loyal

placeō, placēre, placuī, placitum + dat. (12) I please
  mihi placet (12) it pleases me to; I decide

plānē clearly, extremely

plaudō, plaudere, plausī, plausum I clap, applaud

plausus, -ūs, *m.* (51) applause

plēnus, -a, -um (+ abl.) (27) full (of)

plērīque, plēraeque, plēraque (37) several

plērumque often, usually

plūrimus, -a, -um (22) very many, most

plūs, plūris, *n.* more

poēma, poēmatis, *n.* poem

poēta, -ae, *m.* (20) poet

polliceor, pollicērī, pollicitus sum (53) I promise

pompa, -ae, *f.* procession

pōnō, pōnere, posuī, positum (5) I put, place

populus, -ī, *m.* (14) people

porta, -ae, *f.* (8) gate

portō, portāre (2) I carry

portus, portūs, *m.* (27) port

poscō, poscere, poposcī (16) I demand

possideō, possidēre, possēdī, possessum (46) I possess

possum, posse, potuī (8) I am able, I can

post + acc. (12) after

posteā (14) afterwards

posterus, -a, -um the next

posthāc (40) after this, hereafter

postquam (conj.) after

postrīdiē (15) the next day

postulō, postulāre (35) I demand

potēns, potentis (30) powerful

potestās, potestātis, *f.* (27) power

pōtō, pōtāre (53) I drink

praebeō, praebēre, praebuī, praebitum I offer, give, show

praeceptum, -ī, *n.* (51) precept, advice

praedīcō, praedīcere, praedīxī, praedictum I predict, foretell

praeficiō, -ficere, -fēcī, -fectum (32) I put x (acc.) in command of y (dat.)

praemittō, praemittere, praemīsī, praemissum I send ahead

praemium, -ī, *n.* (24) reward, prize

praesēns, praesentis (50) present

praesidium, -ī, *n.* (16) garrison

praesum, praeesse, praefuī + dat. (32) I am in command of

praetereā (21) moreover

praetereō, praeterīre, praeterii, praeteritum (24) I pass, go past

praetor, praetōris, *m.* praetor

precēs, precum *f. pl.* (51) prayers

precor, precārī, precātus sum (52) I pray

prīmum (adv.) (10) first
  quam prīmum (38) as soon as possible

prīmus, -a, -um (6) first

prīnceps, prīncipis, *m.* (7) prince

prīncipia, -ōrum, *n. pl.* headquarters

prīscus, -a, -um (52) old, old-fashioned

prīvātus, -a, -um (43) private

prō + abl. (26) in front of; on behalf of, for

probō, probāre (41) I approve of

prōcēdō, prōcēdere, prōcessī, prōcessum (4) I go forward, proceed

procul (15) far from, far off

prōdō, prōdere, prōdidī, prōditum (38) I betray

proelium, -ī, *n.* (15) battle

prōferō, prōferre, prōtulī, prōlātum I bring forward, bring out

prōficiō, prōficere, prōfēcī, prōfectum (40) I make progress, accomplish

proficīscor, proficīscī, profectus sum (36) I set out

prōgredior, prōgredī, prōgressus sum (36) I advance

prohibeō, prohibēre, prohibuī, prohibitum (36) I prevent

prōmittō, prōmittere, prōmīsī, prōmissum (17) I promise

prōnūntiō, prōnūntiāre I proclaim

prope + acc. (6) near

prōpōnō, prōpōnere, prōposuī, prōpositum (53) I put out, explain

prōpositum, -ī, *n.* intention, plan

propter + acc. (29) because of, on account of

prōspectō, prōspectāre (41) I look out at

prōspiciō, prōspicere, prōspexī, prōspectum (34) I look out at

prōvideō, prōvidēre, prōvīdī, prōvīsum (24) I foresee

prōvincia, -ae, *f.* (49) province

proximus, -a, -um nearest, next

prūdēns, prūdentis (27) sensible, wise

prūdentia, -ae, *f.* prudence, good sense

pūblicus, -a, -um public

pudor, pudōris, *m.* (43) shame, modesty

puella, puellae, *f.* (1) girl

puer, puerī, *c.* (3) boy; child

puerīlis, puerīle (25) of boys, childish

pugna, -ae, *f.* (7) fight

pugnō, pugnāre (7) I fight

pulcher, pulchra, pulchrum (13) pretty, beautiful

pulchritūdō, pulchritūdinis, *f.* beauty

pulsō, pulsāre I hit, knock

pulvis, pulveris, *m.* (54) dust

pūniō, pūnīre, pūnīvī, pūnītum (35) I punish

pupa, -ae, *f.* doll

puppis, puppis, *f.* stern

pūrus, -a, -um pure

putō, putāre (47) I think

pyra, -ae, *f.* pyre

quadrīga, -ae, *f.* four-horsed chariot

quaerō, quaerere, quaesīvī, quaesītum (10) I ask; I look for

quālis, quāle? of what kind?

quam how (in exclamations); than (24);
  quam + superlative, e.g. **quam celerrimē** = as quickly as possible (25)

quamquam (24) although

quandō? (29) when?

quantus, -a, -um? (26) how great?
quasi (49) as if, like
-que (8) and
queror, querī, questus sum (39) I complain
quī, quae, quod (13) who, which
quia (43) because
quid? (53) why?
quīdam, quaedam, quoddam (14) a certain, a
quidem (44) indeed
quiēs, quiētis, *f.* (54) rest
quiēscō, quiēscere, quiēvī, quiētum (10) I rest
quis, quid? (5) who, what?
quis, quid (40) anyone, anything
quisquam, quicquam (29) anyone, anything (after a negative)
quisquis, quicquid (51) whoever, whatever
quō? (22) whither? where to?
quōcumque (45) (to) wherever
quod (4) because
quōmodo? (15) how?
quondam once, some time
quoque (16) also
quot? (34) how many?

rapiō, rapere, rapuī, raptum (22) I snatch, seize, steal
rārō (adv.) rarely
recēdō, recēdere, recessī, recessum (51) I go back, retire
recipiō, recipere, recēpī, receptum (32) I take back
    mē recipiō (32) I retreat
recitō, recitāre (20) I read aloud, recite
rēctē (20) straight, rightly
rēctus, -a, -um (20) straight, right
recurrō, recurrere, recurrī, recursum I run back
reddō, reddere, reddidī, redditum (8) I give back, return
redeō, redīre, rediī, reditum (3) I go back, return
reditus, -ūs, *m.* (42) return
referō, referre, rettulī, relātum (23) I bring back; I report
rēgia, -ae, *f.* palace
rēgīna, -ae, *f.* (11) queen
regō, regere, rēxī, rēctum I rule
regredior, regredī, regressus sum (36) I go back
rēligiō, rēligiōnis, *f.* (52) reverence, piety
relinquō, relinquere, relīquī, relictum (8) I leave behind
reliquus, -a, -um (28) remaining
removeō, removēre, remōvī, remōtum I move back, remove
rēmus, -ī, *m.* oar
renovō, renovāre (42) I renew
repellō, repellere, reppulī, repulsum (15) I drive back
reportō, reportāre I carry back; I win (a victory)
requīrō, requīrere, requīsīvī, requīsītum I seek for, ask
rēs, reī, *f.* (21) thing, matter
    rē vērā (21) in truth, really, in fact
resistō, resistere, restitī + dat. (7) I resist
respiciō, respicere, respexī, respectum I look back (at)
respondeō, respondēre, respondī, respōnsum (5) I answer
respōnsum, -ī, *n.* (40) answer, reply
rēspūblica, reīpūblicae, *f.* (21) public affairs; the republic
restituō, restituere, restituī, restitūtum (49) I restore
retineō, retinēre, retinuī, retentum (23) I hold back
reverentia, -ae, *f.* reverence
revertō, revertere, revertī, reversum (44) I turn back
revertor, revertī, reversus sum (44) I turn back, return
revīsō, revīsere, revīsī I revisit

revocō, revocāre I call back
rēx, rēgis, *m.* (7) king
rīdeō, rīdere, rīsī, rīsum (20) I laugh
rīpa, -ae, *f.* bank
rīsus, -us, *m.* laughter, smile
rogō, rogāre (5) I ask, I ask for
rūmor, rūmōris, *m.* rumor, report
rumpō, rumpere, rūpī, ruptum (16) I burst, break
ruō, ruere, ruī, rutum (27) I rush
rūrsus (35) again
rūs, rūris, *n.* (38) the country; *pl.* estates
    rūre (38) in the country
rūsticus, -a, um rustic, country

sacer, sacra, sacrum (19) sacred, holy
sacerdōs, sacerdōtis, *m.* (34) priest
sacrificium, -ī, *n.* (52) sacrifice
saeculum, -ī, *n.* (49) generation, age
saepe (4) often
saeviō, saevīre I rage
saevus, -a, -um (35) savage
saliō, salīre, saluī, saltum I jump
saltus, -ūs, *m.* dancing
salūs, salūtis, *f.* (53) safety; greetings
salūtō, salūtāre (2) I greet
salvē, salvēte! (21) greetings!
sānctitās, sānctitātis, *f.* sanctity, holiness
sānctus, -a, - um (52) holy
sanguis, sanguinis, *m.* blood
sapiēns, sapientis (52) wise
satis + gen. (26) enough
saxum, -ī, *n.* (10) rock
scelestus, -a, -um (27) wicked, criminal
scelus, sceleris, *n.* (47) crime
schola, -ae, *f.* (20) school, schoolroom; lecture
    scholam habeō (29) I give a lecture
sciō, scīre, scīvī, scītum (34) I know
scrība, -ae, *m.* (50) scribe, secretary
scrībō, scrībere, scrīpsī, scrīptum (6) I write, I draw
sculptor, sculptōris, *m.* sculptor
scūtum, -ī, *n.* (35) shield
sēcūrus, -a, um free from care, safe
secundus, -a, -um (35) second; favorable
sedeō, sedēre, sēdī, sessum (3) I sit
sēditiō, sēditiōnis, *f.* mutiny, sedition
seges, segetis, *f.* (46) grain crop
semel (51) once
semper (11) always
senātor, senātōris, *m.* senator
senātus, -ūs, *m.* (15) senate
senecta, -ae, *f.* (54) old age
senēscō, senēscere, senuī I grow old
senex, senis, *m.* (14) old man
senior, seniōris (31) older, senior
sentiō, sentīre, sēnsī, sēnsum (30) I feel, realize
sepeliō, sepelīre, sepelīvī, sepultum I bury
sepulcrum, -ī, *n.* tomb
sequor, sequī, secūtus sum (36) I follow
serēnus, -a, -um clear, serene
sērō late
serpēns, serpentis, *m.* (48) serpent
serviō, servīre, serviī, servītum + dat. (40) I serve

217

servitium, -ī, *n.* slavery
servō, servāre (8) I save
servus, -ī, *m.* slave
sevērus, -a, -um (20) severe
sī (13) if
sīc (9) thus, like that
sīcut (29) just as, like
signum, -ī, *n.* (22) sign, signal, seal
silentium, -ī, *n.* (42) silence
silva, -ae, *f.* (18) wood, forest
similis, simile (50) like
simul (46) together, at the same time
simul ac/atque (54) as soon as
simulō, simulāre (45) I pretend
sine + abl. (18) without
sinister, sinistra, sinistrum (28) left
　　sinistrā (manū) (28) on the left (hand)
sinō, sinere, sīvī, situm (21) I allow
situs, -a -um (34) sited, positioned
socius, -ī, *m.* companion, ally
sōl, sōlis, *m.* (30) sun
sōlācium, -ī, *n.* (51) comfort
soleō, solēre, solitus sum (40) I am accustomed to
sōlitūdō, sōlitūdinis, *f.* loneliness; desert
sollicitus, -a, -um (33) anxious
sōlus, -a, -um (8) alone
　　nōn sōlum . . . sed etiam (16) not only . . . but also
solvō, solvere, solvī, solūtum (28) I loosen, cast off
somnium, -ī, *n.* (40) dream
somnus, -ī, *m.* (11) sleep
sonus, -ī, *m.* (13) sound
sordidus, -a, -um dirty
soror, sorōris, *f.* (21) sister
sors, sortis, *f.* (53) lot, fate
spectāculum, -ī, *n.* (24) sight, show
spectātor, spectātōris, *m.* (24) spectator
spectō, spectāre (5) I look at
spērō, spērāre (22) I hope
spīritus, -ūs, *m.* breath
spēs, speī, *f.* (21) hope
squālidus, -a, -um filthy
statim (5) at once
statua, -ae, *f.* (16) statue
status, -ūs, *m.* state
　　status rērum state of affairs
stō, stāre, stetī, statum (11) I stand
strēnuus, -a, -um energetic
strepitus, -ūs, *m.* noise, din
studeō, studēre, studuī + dat. (18) I study
studium, -ī, *n.* (21) study
stultus, -a, -um foolish
sub + abl. (10) under
sub + acc. (35) up to (of place); towards (of time)
subitō (2) suddenly
subitus, -a, -um sudden
sublātus, -a, -um past participle passive of **tollō**
succurrō, succurrere, succurrī, succursum + dat. (11) I (run to) help
sum, esse, fuī (17) I am
sūmō, sūmere, sūmpsī, sūmptum (25) I take (up); I put on
summus, -a, -um (16) highest; greatest

super + acc. (29) above, over
superbus, -a, -um (24) proud
superō, superāre (17) I overcome
superus, -a, -um above
supplex, supplicis, *c.* suppliant
supplicō, supplicāre + dat. (30) I beg, supplicate, pray to
supprimō, supprimere, suppressī, suppressum I suppress
suprēmus, -a, -um (51) highest, last
surgō, surgere, surrēxī, surrēctum (4) I rise, get up
suscipiō, suscipere, suscēpī, susceptum (40) I undertake
suspicor, suspicārī, suspicātus sum (48) I suspect
sustulī perfect of **tollō**
suus, -a, -um (14) his, her, their (own)

tabellārius, -ī, *m.* postman
taberna, -ae, *f.* stall, shop, pub
tablīnum, -ī, *n.* (21) study (the room)
tabula, -ae, *f.* writing tablet
taceō, tacēre, tacuī, tacitum (9) I am silent
tacitus, -a, -um (9) silent
mē taedet, taedēre, taeduit + gen. (49) I am tired of
tālis, tāle (22) such
tam (18) so
tamen (17) but, however
tandem (4) at last
tangō, tangere, tetigī, tāctum (42a) I touch
tantum (45) only
tantus, -a, -um (12) so great
tardus, -a, -um (44) late
taurus, -ī, *m.* (46) bull, ox
tegō, tegere, tēxī, tēctum I cover
tēlum, -ī, *n.* (35) missile, javelin
tellūs, tellūris, *f.* (54) earth
tempestās, tempestātis, *f.* storm
templum, -ī, *n.* (11) temple
temptō, temptāre (15) I try, attempt
tempus, temporis, *n.* (18) time
tendō, tendere, tetendī, tēnsum I stretch
teneō, tenēre, tenuī, tentum (13) I hold
tepidus, -a, -um warm
ter (51) three times
tergum, -ī, *n.* (35) back
terra, terrae, *f.* (3) earth, land
terreō, terrēre, terruī, territum I terrify
territus, -a, -um (8) terrified, frightened
terror, terrōris, *m.* (36) terror, fear
testāmentum, -ī, *n.* will
theātrum, -ī, *n.* (26) theatre
timeō, timēre, timuī (8) I fear, I am afraid
timidus, -a, -um timid
timor, timōris, *m.* (26) fear
toga, -ae, *f.* (15) toga
togātus, -a, -um wearing a toga
tollō, tollere, sustulī, sublātum (10, 30) I raise, lift
tot (indecl.) (32) so many
totiēns (32) so often
tōtus, -a, -um (9) whole
tractō, tractāre I treat, handle
trādō, trādere, trādidī, trāditum (5) I hand over
trahō, trahere, trāxī, tractum I drag
trāiciō, trāicere, trāiēcī, trāiectum (47) I throw across
tranquillitās, tranquillitātis, *f.* calm

tranquillus, -a, -um calm
trāns + acc. (15) across
trānseō, trānsīre, trānsiī, trānsitum (18) I cross
trānsferō, trānsferre, trānstulī, trānslātum I carry
    across, transfer
trēs, tria (5) three
tribūnal, tribūnālis, n. platform
tribūnus mīlitum (35) tribune of the soldiers
trīstis, trīste (12) sad
trīstitia, -ae, f. sadness
triumphus, -ī, m. (48) triumph
trucīdō, trucīdāre I slaughter, murder
tū (6) you (sing.)
tueor, tuērī, tuitus sum (53) I protect
tum then
tumultus, -ūs, m. (25) uproar, riot
tumulus, -ī, m. (54) mound, tomb
tunica, -ae, f. tunic
turba, -ae, f. (22) a crowd
turpis, turpe (40) ugly, disgraceful
turris, turris, f. (48) tower
tūtus, -a, -um (51) safe
tuus, -a, -um (6) your
tyrannus, -ī, m. (26) tyrant

ubi (19) where
ubi (conj.) (4) when
ubīque (19) everywhere
ulcīscor, ulcīscī, ultus sum I avenge
ūllus, -a, -um (27) any
ultimus, -a, -um (26) furthest, last
ultiō, ultiōnis, f. vengeance
ultrā + acc. (49) beyond
umbra, -ae, f. shadow
umerus, -ī, m. shoulder
umquam (13) ever
unda, -ae, f. (10) wave
unde? (23) whence? from where?
undēvīgintī nineteen
undique (23) from all sides
ūniversī, -ae, -a (49) all
ūnus, -a, -um (5) one
urbs, urbis, f. (7) city
urna, -ae, f. water pot
usque continually
    usque ad right up to
ūsus, -ūs, m. (53) use
ut + indic. (29) as, when
ut + subj. (34) in order to (purpose); (43) so that (consequence)
uter, utra, utrum? (29) which (of two)?
    utrum . . . an? (whether) . . . or?
uterque, utraque, utrumque each (of two)
utinam + subj. I wish that
ūtor, ūtī, ūsus sum + abl. (40) I use
ūva, -ae, f. grape
uxor, uxōris, f. (9) wife

vacuus, -a, -um (19) empty
valdē very
valeō, valēre, valuī, valitum (33) I am strong, I am well
    valēre iubeō I bid goodbye to
validus, -a, -um (49) strong

vallis, vallis, f. (41) valley
vāllum, -ī, n. (38) rampart
vānus, -a, -um vain, empty
vehemēns, vehementis (31) violent
vehō, vehere, vēxī, vectum (24) I carry
vēla, -ōrum, n. pl. sails
vendō, vendere, vendidī, venditum (18) I sell
venēnum, -ī, n. (48) poison
venia, -ae, f. (42) pardon
veniō, venīre, vēnī, ventum (4) I come
ventus, -ī, m. (11) wind
Venusīnī, m. the people of Venusia
vēr, vēris, n. (18) spring
verberō, verberāre I beat, lash
verbum, -ī, n. (10) word
verēcundus, -a, -um shy
vereor, verērī, veritus sum (36) I fear
versus, versūs, m. (20) verse
vertō, vertere, vertī, versum (8) I turn
vērus, -a, -um (17) true
    vēra dīcere (17) I speak the truth
vesper, vesperis, m. (22) evening
vestīmenta, -ōrum, n. pl. (19) clothes
vestis, vestis, f. clothes
veterānus, -ī, m. (39) veteran
vetō, vetāre, vetuī, vetitum (35) I forbid, order not to
vetus, veteris (22) old
vexō, vexāre (27) I worry, I annoy
via, -ae, f. (2) road, way
viātor, viātōris, m. (28) traveller
vīcīnus, -a, -um (46) neighboring, near
victor, victōris, m. victor
victōria, -ae, f. (24) victory
videō, vidēre, vīdī, vīsum (3) I see
videor, vidērī, vīsus sum (36) I seem
vīgintī twenty
vīlicus, -ī, m. bailiff, farm manager
villa, -ae, f. (32) villa, country house
vincō, vincere, vīcī, victum (7) I conquer
vīnum, -ī, n. (11) wine
vir, virī, m. (9) man
vīrēs, vīrium, f. pl. strength
virgō, virginis, f. (16) maiden, virgin
virīlis, virīle (25) manly, of a man
virtūs, virtūtis, f. (16) virtue, excellence, courage
vīs (acc. vim; abl. vī) f. (54) force, violence
vīsō, vīsere, vīsī, vīsum (21) I visit
vīta, -ae, f. (29) life
vītō, vītāre (41) I avoid
vīvō, vīvere, vīxī, vīctum (13) I live
vīvus, -a, -um (28) living, alive
vix (10) scarcely
vocō, vocāre (2) I call
volō, velle, voluī (15) I wish, I am willing
volō, volāre (22) I fly
voluptās, voluptātis, f. (51) pleasure
volvō, volvere, volvī, volūtum (54) I roll, turn over
vōtum, -ī, n. (46) prayer
vōx, vōcis, f. (13) voice
vulnus, vulneris, n. (17) wound
vultus, -ūs, m. (20) face, expression

Vocabulary

English – Latin

Regular verbs are given with infinitive only.

about **dē** + abl.
Academy **Acadēmīa, -ae,** *f.*
accept, I **accipiō, accipere, accēpī, acceptum**
accustomed, I am **soleō, solēre, solitus sum**
achieve, I **prōficiō, prōficere, prōfēcī, prōfectum**
advance, I **prōgredior, prōgredī, prōgressus sum**
affair **rēs, reī,** *f.*
afraid, I am **timeō, timēre, timuī; vereor, verērī, veritus sum**
again **iterum**
against **contrā** + acc.; **in** + acc.
age **aetās, aetātis,** *f.*; new age **novum saeculum**
all **omnis, omne**
allowed, I am **mihi licet, licēre, licuit**
alone **sōlus, -a, -um**
also **quoque**
always **semper**
ancient **vetus, veteris**
and **et, -que**
and so **itaque, igitur**
angry **īrātus, -a, -um**
angry, I become **īrāscor, īrāscī, īrātus sum** + dat.
announce, I **nūntiō, nūntiāre**
another **alius, alia, aliud**
answer, I **respondeō, respondēre, respondī, respōnsum**
anxious **ānxius, -a, -um**
Apollo **Apollō, Apollinis**
approach **accēdō, accēdere, accessī, accessum (ad)**
army **exercitus, -ūs,** *m.*
arrange for, I **cūrō, cūrāre**
arrive, I **adveniō, advenīre, advēnī, adventum**
ask, ask for, I **rogō, rogāre**
astonished **attonitus, -a, -um**
Athens **Athēnae, -ārum,** *f. pl.*
at once **statim**
attack, I **oppugnō, oppugnāre**
autumn **autumnus, -ī, m.**

battle **proelium, -ī,** *n.*
bear, I **ferō, ferre, tulī, lātum**
because **quod**
become, I **fīō, fierī, factus sum**
before (adverb) **anteā**
before (conjunction) **antequam**
before (preposition) **ante** + acc.
besides **praetereā**
better **melior, melius**
big **magnus, -a, -um**
bigger **maior, maius**
board (a ship), I **cōnscendō, cōnscendere, cōnscendī, cōnscēnsum**
book **liber, librī,** *m.*
born, I am **nāscor, nāscī, nātus sum**
boy **puer, puerī, m.**
bring, I = carry **ferō, ferre, tulī, lātum**
      = lead **dūcō, dūcere, dūxī, ductum**

burn, I **ardeō, ardēre, arsī, arsum**
busy **rēbus occupātus, -a, -um**
but **sed**
buy, I **emō, emere, ēmī, ēmptum**
by **ā/ab** + abl.

call, I **vocō, vocāre**
calm **tranquillus, -a, -um**
calmly **aequō animō**
camp **castra, -ōrum,** *n. pl.*
can, I **possum, posse, potuī**
captain (of ship) **magister, magistrī,** *m.*
care **cūra, -ae,** *f.*
care for, I **cūrō, cūrāre**
carry, I **portō, portāre; ferō, ferre, tulī, lātum**
celebrate, I **celebrō, celebrāre**
centurion, **centuriō, centuriōnis,** *m.*
children **puerī, -ōrum,** *c.*
chorus **chorus, -ī,** *m.*
citizen **cīvis, cīvis,** *c.*
civil **cīvīlis, cīvīle**
climb, I **ascendō, ascendere, ascendī, ascēnsum**
come, I **veniō, venīre, vēnī, ventum**
comfort, I **cōnsōlor, cōnsōlārī, cōnsōlātus sum**
companion **comes, comitis,** *c.*
compel, I **cōgō, cōgere, coēgī, coāctum**
compose, I **compōnō, compōnere, composuī, compositum**
content **contentus, -a, -um** + abl.
country (as opposed to town) **rūs, rūris,** *n.*
      native country **patria, -ae,** *f.*
courage **virtūs, virtūtis,** *f.*
cross, I **trānseō, trānsīre, trānsiī, trānsitum**
crowd **turba, -ae,** *f.*

danger **perīculum, -ī,** *n.*
dare, I **audeō, audēre, ausus sum**
day **diēs, diēī,** *m.*
      every day **cotīdiē**
dead **mortuus, -a, -um**
dear **cārus**
decide, I **cōnstituō, cōnstituere, cōnstituī, cōnstitūtum; mihi placet, placēre, placuit**
defeat, I **vincō, vincere, vīcī, victum**
defend, I **defendō, defendere, defendī, defēnsum**
delay **mora, -ae,** *f.*
delay, I **moror, morārī, morātus sum**
delight, I **dēlectō, dēlectāre**
Delphi **Delphī, Delphōrum,** *m. pl.*
deny, I **negō, negāre**
descend, I **dēscendō, dēscendere, dēscendī, dēscēnsum**
despise, I **contemnō, contemnere, contempsī, contemptum**
die, I **morior, morī, mortuus sum**
difficult **difficilis, difficile**
dine, I **cēnō, cēnāre**
dinner **cēna, -ae,** *f.*
dismiss, I **dīmittō, dīmittere, dīmīsī, dīmissum**

doctor **medicus, -ī**, *m.*
dog **canis, canis**, *c.*
don't **nōlī, nōlīte**
door **iānua, -ae**, *f.*
doubtful **dubius, -a, -um**; without doubt **sine dubiō**
drag **trahō, trahere, trāxī, tractum**
drink, I **bibō, bibere, bibī**
duty **officium, -ī**, *n.*

each (of two) **uterque, utraque, utrumque**
easily **facile**
easy **facilis, facile**
eat, I **edō, ēsse, ēdī, ēsum**
emperor **prīnceps, prīncipis**, *m.*
end, in the **tandem**
enemy **hostēs, hostium**, *m. pl.*
enjoy, I **gaudeō, gaudēre** + abl.; **fruor, fruī, frūctus sum**
 + abl.
enough **satis** + gen.
enter, I **ineō, inīre, iniī, initum; ingredior, ingredī,**
 ingressus sum
evening **vesper, vesperis**, *m.*
ever, for **semper; in perpetuum**
every day **cotīdiē**
everything = all things **omnia**
excellent **optimus, -a, -um**
excuse **excūsātiō, excūsātiōnis**, *f.*
exercise, I **exerceō, exercēre**
expression **vultus, -ūs**, *m.*

fact, in **rē vērā**
family **genus, generis**, *n.*; = household **fāmilia, -ae**, *f.*
farm **fundus, -ī**, *m.*
farm manager **vīlicus, -ī**, *m.*
farmer **colōnus, -ī**, *m.*
father **pater, patris**, *m.*
fear, I **timeō, timēre, timuī; vereor, verērī, veritus sum**
few **paucī, -ae, -a**
field **ager, agrī**, *m.*
fierce **ferōx, ferōcis**
fifty **quīnquāgintā**
fight, I **pugnō, pugnāre**
find, I **inveniō, invenīre, invēnī, inventum**
finish, I **cōnficiō, cōnficere, cōnfēcī, cōnfectum**
fire **ignis, ignis**, *m.*
flee, I **fugiō, fugere, fūgī, fugitum**
follow, I **sequor, sequī, secūtus sum**
foolish **stultus, -a, -um**
for = on behalf of **prō** + abl.
forces **cōpiae, -ārum**, *f. pl.*
forgive, I **ignōscō, ignōscere, ignōvī, ignōtum** + dat.
forum **forum, -ī**, *n.*
fountain **fōns, fontis**, *m.*
fourth **quārtus, -a, -um**
freedman **lībertus, -ī**, *m.*
freedom **lībertās, lībertātis**, *f.*
friend **amīcus, -ī**, *m.*
full (of) **plēnus, -a, -um** (+ abl.)

game **lūdus, -ī**, *m.*
garden **hortus, -ī**, *m.*
girl **puella, -ae**, *f.*

give, I **dō, dare, dedī, datum**
glory **glōria, -ae**, *f.*
go in, I **intrō, intrāre**
go out, I **exeō, exīre, exiī, exitum; ēgredior, ēgredī,**
 ēgressus sum
good **bonus, -a, -um**; very good **optimus, -a, -um**
grape **ūva, -ae**, *f.*
great **magnus, -a, -um**; so great **tantus, -a, -um**
greatest **maximus, -a, -um**
greatly **magnopere; valdē**
Greece **Graecia, -ae**, *f.*
greet, I **salūtō, salūtāre**
guard, I **custōdiō, custōdīre, custōdīvī, custōdītum**

hand **manus, -ūs**, *f.*
happy **laetus, -a, -um**
harbor **portus, -ūs**, *m.*
hard (adv.) **dīligenter**
have, I **habeō, habēre**
hear **audiō, audīre**
heart **cor, cordis**, *n.*
help **auxilium, -ī**, *n.*
help, I **adiuvō, adiuvāre, adiūvī, adiūtum**
here **hīc**; to here **hūc**
hide, I **cēlō, cēlāre**
high **altus, -a, -um**
highly (of value) **magnī**
hill **collis, collis**, *m.*
home **domus, -ūs**, *f.*; at home **domī**
honor **honor, honōris**, *m.*
hope **spēs, speī**, *f.*
hope, I **spērō, spērāre**
hour **hōra, -ae**, *f.*
house **casa, -ae**, *f*; **aedēs, aedium**, *f. pl.*
hurry, I **festīnō, festīnāre**

idle **ōtiōsus, -a, -um; ignāvus, -a, - um**
if **sī**
ill, I am **aegrōtō, aegrōtāre**
increase, I **augeō, augēre, auxī, auctum**
invite, I **invītō, invītāre**
Italy **Italia, -ae**, *f.*

join, I (battle) **proelium committō, committere, commīsī,**
 commissum
journey **iter, itineris**, *n.*

kind **benignus, -a, -um**
know, I **sciō, scīre**
know, I don't **nesciō, nescīre**

land **terra, -ae**, *f.*
last, at last **tandem**
late (adv.) **sērō**
laugh, I **rīdeō, rīdēre, rīsī, rīsum**
lead, I **dūcō, dūcere, dūxī, ductum**
leader **dux, ducis**, *c.*
leave, I = go away from **discēdō, discēdere, discessī,**
 discessum
 = leave behind **relinquō, relinquere, relīquī, relictum**
lecture **schola, -ae**, *f.*
legion **legiō, legiōnis**, *f.*
leisure **ōtium, -ī**, *n.*

lest **nē**
letter **littera, -ae**, *f.*; **epistola, -ae**, *f.*
liberty **lībertās, lībertātis**, *f.*
lie, I **iaceō, iacēre, iacuī**
life **vīta, -ae**, *f.*
light **lūx, lūcis**, *f.*
like, I **mē iuvat, iuvāre, iūvit**
listen to, I **audiō, audīre**
live, I **vīvō, vīvere, vīxī, vīctum**
= inhabit **habitō, habitāre**
long **longus, -a, -um**
for a long time **diū**; longer **diūtius**
long for, I **dēsīderō, dēsīderāre**
look! **ecce**
look after, I **cūrō, cūrāre**
look at, I **spectō, spectāre**; **īnspiciō, īnspicere, īnspexī, īnspectum**
look back, I **respiciō, respicere, respexī, respectum**
look for, I **quaerō, quaerere, quaesīvī, quaesītum**
loud (voice) **magnus, -a, -um**
love **amor, amōris**, *m.*
love, I **amō, amāre**

make, I **faciō, facere, fēcī, factum**
man **vir, virī**, *m.*
many **multī, -ae, -a**
marry, I **nūbō, nūbere, nūpsī, nūptum** + dat.
master = schoolmaster and master of a ship **magister, magistrī**, *m.*
= master of slaves **dominus, -ī**, *m.*
meet, I **occurrō, occurrere, occurrī, occursum** + dat.
messenger **nūntius, -ī**, *m.*
midday **merīdiēs, merīdiēī**, *m.*
miserable **miser, misera, miserum**
mistress **domina, -ae**, *f.*
modest **modestus, -a, -um**
money **argentum, -ī**, *n.*
month **mēnsis, mēnsis**, *m.*
more **plūs, plūris**; = more greatly **magis**
mother **māter, mātris**, *f.*
mountain **mōns, montis**, *m.*
moved **commōtus, -a, -um**
much (with comparative) **multō**
must, I **dēbeō, dēbēre**

Naples **Neāpolis**; acc. **Neāpolim**
near **prope** + acc.
need, I **opus est mihi** + abl.
neighbor **vīcīnus, -ī**, *m.*
never **numquam**
ninth **nōnus, -a, -um**
noble **nōbilis, nōbile**
nothing **nihil, nihilī**, *n.*
now **iam; nunc**

obey, I **pāreō, pārēre, pāruī, pāritum** + dat.
occupied **occupātus, -a, -um**
often **saepe**
old **vetus, veteris**
once, at once **statim**
one **ūnus, -a, -um**; one (of two) **alter, altera, alterum**
one day **diē quōdam, quondam**

open **apertus, -a, -um**
oracle **ōrāculum, -ī**, *n.*
other **alius, alia, aliud**; the other (of two) **alter, altera, alterum**; the others = the rest **cēterī, -ae, -a**
ought, I **dēbeō, dēbēre**; **mē oportet, oportēre, oportuit**
outside **extrā** + acc.
overcome, I **superō, superāre**

pardon **venia, -ae**, *f.*
parent **parēns, parentis**, *c.*
passenger **viātor, viātōris**, *m.*
peace **pāx, pācis**, *f.*
people **populus, -ī**, *m.*
persuade, I **persuādeō, persuādēre, persuāsī, persuāsum** + dat.
philosopher **philosophus, -ī**, *m.*
philosophy **philosophia, -ae**, *f.*
pick, I **carpō, carpere, carpsī, carptum**
play, I **lūdō, lūdere, lūsī, lūsum**
please, I **dēlectō, dēlectāre**; **placeō, placēre** + dat.
plow, I **arō, arāre**
poem **carmen, carminis**, *n.*; **poēma, poēmatis**, *n.*
praise, I **laudō, laudāre**
prepare, I **parō, parāre**
preserve, I **servō, servāre**; **conservō, conservāre**
proceed, I **prōcēdō, prōcēdere, prōcessī, prōcessum**
promise, I **prōmittō, prōmittere, prōmīsī, prōmissum**
punish, I **pūniō, pūnīre**
pupil **discipulus, -ī**, *m.*

quaestor **quaestor, quaestōris**, *m.*
quickly **celeriter**

race **cursus, -ūs**, *m.*
reach, I **perveniō, pervenīre, pervēnī, perventum (ad)**
read, I **legō, legere, lēgī, lēctum**
ready **parātus, -a, -um**
recall, I **revocō, revocāre**
receive, I **accipiō, accipere, accēpī, acceptum**
recite, I **recitō, recitāre**
rejoice, I **gaudeō, gaudēre, gāvīsus sum**
remove, I **removeō, removēre, remōvī, remōtum**
reply, I **respondeō, respondēre, respondī, respōnsum**
republic **rēspūblica, reīpūblicae**, *f.*
rest, I **quiēscō, quiēscere, quiēvī**
return, I = go back **redeō, redīre, rediī, reditum**
= give back **reddō, reddere, reddidī, redditum**
rouse, I **excitō, excitāre**
run, I **currō, currere, cucurrī, cursum**
run back, I **recurrō**

sad **trīstis, trīste**
sail, I **nāvigō, nāvigāre**
sailor **nauta, -ae**, *m.*
save, I **servō, servāre**
say I **dīcō, dīcere, dīxī, dictum**
he/she said **inquit**
scarcely **vix**
school **lūdus, -ī**, *m.*
sea **mare, maris**, *n.*
see, I **videō, vidēre, vīdī, vīsum**
seem, I **videor, vidērī, vīsus sum**
send, I **mittō, mittere, mīsī, missum**

send for, I **arcessō, arcessere, arcessīvī, arcessītum**
sensible **prūdēns, prūdentis**
serve (as a soldier), I **mīlitō, mīlitāre**
set out, I **proficīscor, proficīscī, profectus sum**
severe **sevērus, -a, -um**
shade **umbra, -ae,** *f.*
sheep **ovis, ovis,** *f.*
shepherd **pāstor, pāstōris,** *m.*
shield **scūtum, -ī,** *n.*
ship **nāvis, nāvis,** *f.*
shout **clāmor, clāmōris,** *m.*
shout, I **clāmō, clāmāre**
show, I (of qualities) **praebeō, praebēre, praebuī, praebitum**
shut, I **claudō, claudere, clausī, clausum**
signal **signum, -ī,** *n.*
sing, I **cantō, cantāre**
sister **soror, sorōris,** *f.*
sit, I **sedeō, sedēre, sēdī, sessum**
sleep, I **dormiō, dormīre**
slowly **lentē**
small **parvus, -a, -um;** very small **minimus, -a, -um**
so (with adj. or adv.) **tam;** (with verb) **adeō**
so great **tantus, -a, -um**
soldier **mīles, mīlitis,** *m.*
someone **aliquis**
son **fīlius, -ī,** *m.*
soon **mox;** as soon as **cum prīmum**
speak, I **loquor, loquī, locūtus sum;** for, **fārī, fātus sum**
speed **celeritās, celeritātis,** *f.*
spend, I (of time) **agō, agere, ēgī, āctum**
spring **vēr, vēris,** *n.*
stand, I **stō, stāre, stetī, statum**
stay I **maneō, manēre, mānsī, mānsum**
step **gradus, -ūs,** *m.*
still **adhūc**
stone **saxum, -ī,** *n.*
street **via, -ae,** *f.*
study **studium, -ī,** *n.*
suddenly **subitō**
summer **aestās, aestātis,** *f.*
summon, I **arcessō, arcessere, arcessīvī, arcessītum**
sure **certus, -a, -um**
sure, I am **prō certō habeō**
surely not? **num?**

talk I **loquor, loquī, locūtus sum**
tavern **taberna, -ae,** *f.*
tell, I = narrate **nārrō, nārrāre**
    = order **iubeō, iubēre, iussī, iussum; imperō,**
    imperāre + dat.
    = say **dīcō, dīcere, dīxī, dictum**
temple **templum, -ī,** *n.*
ten **decem**
terrified **territus, -a, -um**
than **quam**
their own **suus, -a, -um**
there **ibi;** to there **eō**
thing **rēs, reī,** *f.*
this **hic, haec, hoc**
three **trēs, tria**
through **per** + acc.

throw away, I **abiciō, abicere, abiēcī, abiectum**
time **tempus, temporis,** *n.;* for some time **aliquamdiū**
tired **fessus, -a, -um**
tired of, I am **mē taedet, taedēre, taeduit** + gen.
today **hodiē**
toga **toga, -ae,** *f.*
top (= highest, greatest) **summus, -a, -um**
travel, I **iter faciō**
treasury **aerārium, -ī,** *n.*
tree **arbor, arboris,** *f.*
true **vērus, -a, -um**
trust (in), I **cōnfīdō, cōnfīdere, cōnfīsus sum** + dat.
truth **vērum, -ī,** *n.* to speak the truth **vēra dīcere**
try, I **cōnor, cōnārī, cōnātus sum**
turn, I **vertō, vertere, vertī, versum**

unwilling **invītus, -a, -um**
use **ūsus, -ūs,** *m.*
use, I **ūtor, ūtī, ūsus sum** + abl.
useful, to be **ūsuī esse**

value, I **aestimō, aestimāre**
verse **versus, -ūs,** *m.*
visit, I **vīsō, vīsere, vīsī**

wait, I = stay **maneō, manēre, mānsī, mānsum**
    = wait for **exspectō, exspectāre**
wake up, I **ēvigilō, ēvigilāre** (intr.)
    excitō, excitāre (trans.)
walk, I **contendō, contendere, contendī, contentum**
want, I **cupiō, cupere, cupīvī, cupītum**
war **bellum, -ī,** *n.*
warn, I **moneō, monēre**
watch, I **spectō, spectāre**
wave **unda, -ae,** *f.*
wedding **nūptiae, -ārum,** *f. pl.*
weep, I **fleō, flēre, flēvī, flētum**
when **ubi, cum**
where? **ubi?** where to? **quō?**
whether? **num?**
whether . . . or? **utrum . . . an?**
wife **uxor, uxōris,** *f.*
without **sine** + abl.
who? **quis?**
why? **cūr?**
willing, I am **volō, velle, voluī**
wine **vīnum, -ī,** *n.*
winter **hiems, hiemis,** *f.*
wish, I **cupiō, cupere, cupīvī, cupītum**
with **cum** + abl.
wolf **lupus, -ī,** *m.*
woman **fēmina, -ae,** *f.*
wood **silva, -ae,** *f.*
wool **lāna, -ae,** *f.*
word **verbum, -ī,** *n.*
work I **labōrō, labōrāre**
worse **peior, peius**
worthy (of) **dignus, -a, -um** (+ abl.)
wound, I **vulnerō, vulnerāre**
write, I **scrībō, scrībere, scrīpsī, scrīptum**

year **annus, -ī,** *m.*
young man **iuvenis, iuvenis,** *m.*

Index of grammar

The numbers refer to chapters